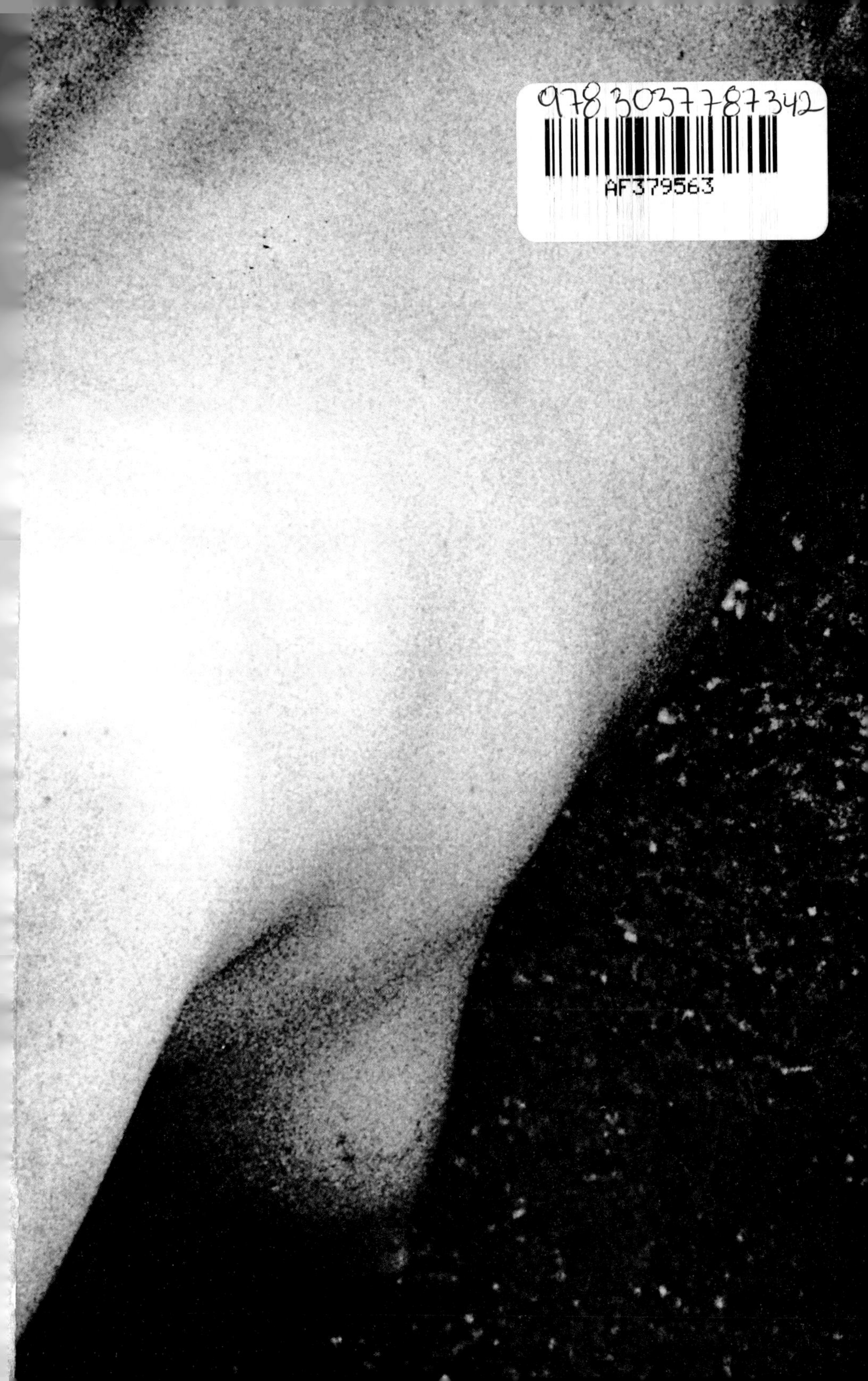

9783037787342
AF379563

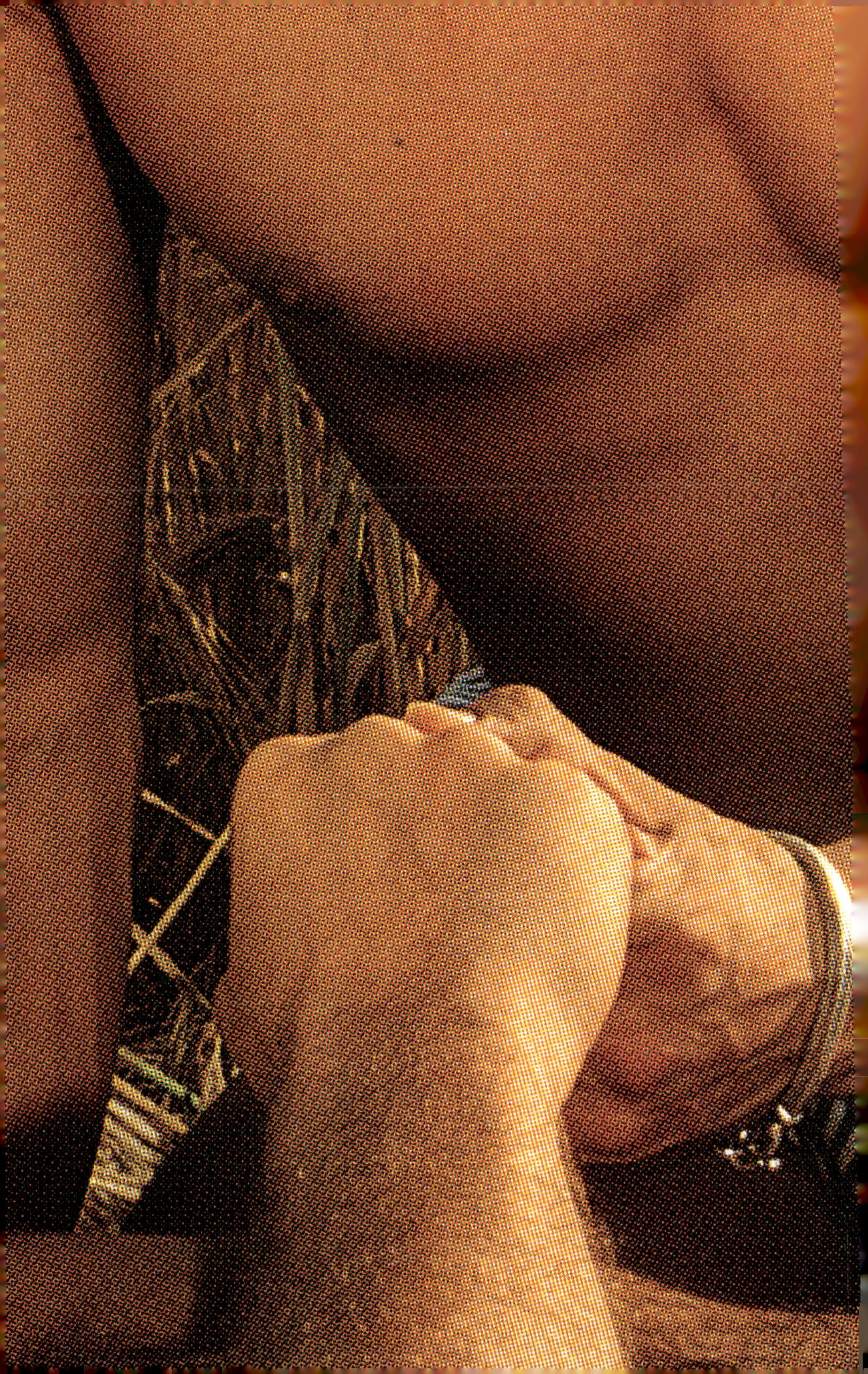

Edited by
Museum für Gestaltung Zürich
Bettina Richter

Talking Bodies

Image Power Impact

Lars Müller Publishers

Introduction

Bettina Richter

"And the acts of analysis, of deconstruction and of reading 'against the grain' offer an additional pleasure—the pleasure of resistance, of saying 'no': not to 'unsophisticated' enjoyment, by ourselves and others, of culturally dominant images, but to the structures of power which ask us to consume them uncritically and in highly circumscribed ways."[1]

Public and virtual spaces are flooded with images of bodies in the form of analog and digital posters, commercials or influencer postings; they are ubiquitous across social media and, to a large extent, a defining feature of popular culture. Produced for quick consumption and a wide audience, they are based on stereotypes and simplifications. Bodies are lumped into categories and incorporated into narratives that are invariably oriented toward a supposed norm, one that, in turn, can mostly be understood as a system of belonging or exclusion. Non-binary, queer, ill, disabled, old, and Black[2] bodies are strikingly underrepresented and only come into view when their depiction is motivated by the message. As much as typecasting is essential to quick communication, it is also dangerous. Power relations and norms regarding gendered, racialized, and non-normative bodies are continually cemented, legitimizing their marginalization and discrimination.

At the same time, today's social media landscape also provides avenues for independent content and the dissemination of new, even subversive images, for constructive debate and self-empowerment. In recent decades, technological developments have facilitated a body boom that can be traced back to the nascent stages of post-industrial, post-modern society. Gradually released from the functional

1 Annette Kuhn, *The Power of the Image: Essays on Representation and Sexuality*, London / New York 1994, p. 8 (first published in 1985).
2 Black is consistently capitalized, in keeping with the self-designation of the BIPOC community, so as to distinguish the term from the adjective black and to emphasize the construction of ethnic classifications. For similar reasons, Brown is also capitalized.

contexts of physical labor in the Global North, the body has increasingly turned into an individual identity project and the symbol of a pluralistic society—yet it is still subject to political and social control.[3] Opportunities for self-realization such as nutrition, sports, cosmetics, and plastic surgery remain bound by commercial constraints as well as societal norms and value systems. Consequently, the incessant interplay of conformity, subjective hedonism, emancipatory aspirations and rebellion has given rise to a prolific production of body images, particularly in virtual spaces, which, in the case of resistant body practices, mostly manifests itself on non-profit and cooperative platforms. Here, contradictions and ambivalences must be endured and re-negotiated time and again, because that is precisely the way established hierarchies and criteria of order can be challenged and critically interrogated.

The body as a subject in art has been widely discussed and, especially in recent years, has also become a topic of debate with regard to its gender-specific and ethnic positings. Yet when it comes to mass media representations of the body, these aspects have only been studied to a very limited extent. For a long time, sociology did not give significant attention to the body either. It was only in the wake of the social and political upheavals of 1968 that a more thorough examination of the body as a product and producer of society ensued.[4] Published in 1979, Erving Goffman's study in visual sociology, which has since become a classic, was the first to take an in-depth look at the body in advertising communication. Applying comparative image analyses to the representation of men and women, he was able to show how advertising constructs reality and thus strongly shapes our self-images and views of the world.[5] Some two decades later, Judith Butler radicalized Goffman's approach. Challenging any essentialist understanding of biological sex, she demonstrated how it, too, only emerges through interplay with a social and historical construction of gender.[6] Sociologist Pierre Bourdieu focused, above all, on the habitus, which is to say, the behavior that shapes people within their social conditions, and brought the concept of "body capital" into play.[7] The body can be used to achieve both social recognition and material success, and—always depending on social class and economic means—becomes a manipulatable project in which investments can be made in a targeted manner. If we apply Bourdieu's concept to advertising images, the vast majority of them can be read as illustrations of high body capital.

3   Foucault made this subject a key focus of his work and provided the basis for further research. Cf. Michel Foucault, *Discipline and Punish: The Birth of the Prison*, New York 1977 (first published under the original title *Surveiller et punir: Naissance de la prison*, Paris 1975). In her book, *Beyond the Periphery of the Skin: Rethinking, Remaking, and Reclaiming the Body in Contemporary Capitalism,* Oakland 2020, Silvia Federici also explores strategies of resisting the political, social, and economic appropriation of bodies. This aspect is also explored by Jule Govrin: *Politische Körper: Von Sorge und Solidarität*, Berlin 2022.

4   Cf. Robert Gugutzer, *Soziologie des Körpers*, 5th ed., Bielefeld 2015 (first edition Bielefeld 2004).

5   Erving Goffman, *Gender Advertisements*, London 1979.

6   Judith Butler, *Gender Trouble: Feminism and the Subversion of Identity*, London 1990.

7   Pierre Bourdieu, *Distinction: A Social Critique of the Judgement of Taste*, Cambridge, MA 1984 (first published under the original title *La Distinction. Critique sociale du jugement*, Paris 1979).

The beautiful, healthy, young, and high-performing body is the guarantor of and basic prerequisite for success in life and, as such, itself becomes a product.

Stuart Hall highlighted the brutal consequences of stereotypes, which are particularly apparent in mass media and pop culture images of the body: "Stereotyping *reduces, essentializes, naturalizes* and *fixes* 'difference' … Stereotyping, in other words, is part of the maintenance of social and symbolic order. It sets up a symbolic frontier between the 'normal' and the 'deviant,' the 'normal' and the 'pathological,' the 'acceptable' and the 'unacceptable,' what 'belongs' and what does not or is 'Other,' between 'insiders' and 'outsiders,' Us and Them."[8]

To this day, old, ill and impaired bodies are not so much stereotyped as they are scandalized or deemed outright taboo. By focusing her research on body narratives in art and popular culture, cultural studies scholar Rosemarie Garland-Thomson made an important and innovative contribution towards the establishment of disability studies and feminist disability research on an international level.[9] Just as the so-called "human zoos" or "ethnographic exhibitions" of the nineteenth century put people from non-European countries on public display, so-called "freak shows" presented "extraordinary" bodies to their audiences. Supposedly scientific knowledge and popular culture thus backed each other in communicating normative notions of the body.[10] Journalist, comedian, and disability activist Stella Young coined the now well-established term "inspiration porn." It is illuminating with regard to the representation and intended reception of people with disabilities in social posters, pointing to their misuse as mere "objects of inspiration," which reduces them to their disability.[11]

This publication accompanies the *Talking Bodies—Body Images in the Poster* exhibition shown at Museum für Gestaltung Zürich, which brings together international posters from across all thematic categories, revealing continuities as well as changes and deviations in their rendering of the human body. The publication continues its exploration of various mechanisms of representation of the body in media cultures and places them in a historical, cultural and sociological context. The first in a series of essays discusses the manner in which mass media are oriented towards images that have inscribed themselves in our collective memory through masterpieces of art history. The following contributions examine the continuity and disruption of gender

8   Stuart Hall, "The Spectacle of the 'Other,'" in: *Representation: Cultural Representations and Signifying Practices*, ed. Stuart Hall, London 1997, p. 258.

9   Rosemarie Garland-Thomson, *Extraordinary Bodies: Figuring Physical Disability in American Culture and Literature*, New York 1997.

10   Tragically, the pathologization and public display of queer bodies is also part of this history.

11   See Stella Young's talk on "Inspiration Porn and the Objectification of Disability" at the 2014 TEDxSydney conference: www.youtube.com/watch?v=SxrS7-I_sMQ.

stereotypes as well as the persistence of the regime of the white[12] gaze in the depiction of Black bodies. A critical light is shed on depictions of disabled and non-normative bodies, self-dramatization and body optimization on social media, along with all its implications, and the potentials and limits of concepts of diversity.

The illustrations show a selection of the posters on display at the exhibition. Their focus goes back to the Swiss collection from which they originate. For the most part, these consumer posters are the product of Western media culture and thus reflect a Western perspective. Particularly in the case of posters showing Black bodies, which includes so-called commodity racism posters, it is therefore the white gaze, and more specifically the white gaze from Switzerland, that is manifested in them. This also exemplifies the country's involvement in colonial history and enslavement. Due to their different outer appearance, the bodies of Black people have always been at the center of what was perceived, and marked, as the Other and, by the same token, became the preferred vehicles for advertising in a certain period of time.

The arrangement of the posters is not motivated by thematic considerations, but by a purely associative approach. With sometimes irritating, perhaps even provocative compositions, our goal is to encourage viewers to discover new visual dialogues, from which further inquiry and lines of thought can ensue. We are aware of the problems associated with the reproduction of sensitive imagery and concepts. Our approach is based on the assumption that a historical reappraisal and critical insight is only possible if they are renegotiated and viewed in the respective context of their time. In the spirit of the opening quote by Annette Kuhn, we therefore hope to contribute to a new, unbiased and critical view of media images of the body.

12   "white" is consistently lowercase. In this context, it does not denote an adjective of color but marks a privileged social, cultural, and political position. Capitalizing it, however, risks following the lead of white supremacists.

Templates—Body Narratives in Art

Bettina Richter

It is impossible to imagine the visual arts without the human body as a subject. Its depiction varies between academic representation, expressive study, and symbolic exaltation; the body is the arena of sociopolitical negotiation or existential urgency. Selected works of art and artistic positions from various eras reveal how the body images of a primarily Western, but internationally prevalent art history continue to hold sway in the form of dominant body narratives and shape our gaze to this day. The echoes of these templates are palpable throughout mass media and popular culture, thus informing our view of the world, especially with regard to notions of gender or ethnic codification.

Art and Mass Culture
In the early 1970s, John Berger described publicity as the "culture of the consumer society" and pointed to the ways in which the rhetorics of art and advertising are closely intertwined.[1] When the focus is placed on bodies, these parallels are immediately apparent. Mass media depictions of male, female, or even racialized bodies directly draw on Christian culture and a Eurocentric historiography of art whose images are deeply inscribed in our collective memory. Their powerful impact is evident precisely in the fact that they have remained unquestioned and unchallenged for so long. Only belatedly were feminist and anti-racist approaches introduced into art history. Art-immanent, formal-stylistic and iconographic perspectives and methods still dominate art history today, while new approaches are enriching the field.[2] Early on, art historian Daniela Hammer-Tugendhat approached art history from a cultural

1   John Berger, *Ways of Seeing*, London 1972.
2   Starting in the 1980s, art scholars increasingly addressed the question as to the percentage of women artists in the production of art and their contribution to art history. For a long time, however, biographical aspects were still in the foreground, along with the issues of the "specifically feminine" or the image of women in male artistic creation. Ellen Spickernagel was the first to publish a German-language introduction to a feminist approach to art history in 1985: "Geschichte und Geschlecht: Der feministische Ansatz," in: Hans Belting et. al. (eds.), *Kunstgeschichte: Eine Einführung*, Berlin 1985, pp. 264–282. This marked the beginning of a gradual paradigm shift that illuminated the art historical canon, among other things, in terms of incorporated relations of power and domination. However, so far a feminist outlook is only marginally represented in university art history teaching. The influence of critical whiteness studies in art history is an even more recent development. In 2020, six art historians at the University of Zurich joined forces to form the collective CARAH (Collective for Anti-Racist Art History) to raise awareness of racist stereotypes and structures in art and art history: www.khist.uzh.ch/de/research/projects/carah.html.

studies perspective and thereby sought to bring about a change of outlook.[3] She was able to show how body images construct differences between genders and ethnicities and naturalize them.

Unambiguously readable body images, which still define advertising stereotypes today, are based on endlessly repeated dichotomies rooted in traditional image templates and stories handed down through the ages. Aside from the binary gender model, this includes, above all, the contrast between white and Black bodies.[4] Dichotomies are also conveyed by omission, in that certain bodies are not, or hardly ever, brought into the picture: old or sick bodies, or ones that are considered less attractive. This is a testament to the fact that images of the body are never just external images, but that they are always charged with essentialist notions and cultural positing.[5]

Visual Constructions of Gender

Already the sculptures of classical antiquity attest to an effort at constructing gender through representations of the body and asserting a naturally given gender difference. In this early period, the male figures were depicted in the nude, while women were wrapped in robes. It is the athletic male nude that was exalted as the ideal human image per se, that epitomized the true, the beautiful and the good as well as the unity of body and mind. The classical contrapposto of this hero, as exemplified by Greek sculptor Polykleitos (fifth century B.C.), signaled both poise and movement, a balanced virile sovereignty. In antiquity, only the goddess of love was already carved in stone in the nude. With his *Aphrodite of Knidos*, Praxiteles introduced the type of Venus

3   Significant inspiration for this essay is owed to Daniela Hammer-Tugendhat's lecture series *Kunstgeschichte als Kulturwissenschaft* (Art History as Cultural Studies): https://www.youtube.com/playlist?list=PLjR8HTOEMQuf_tkFoVsadjWa5Ofqk_Y4e.
4   Black is consistently capitalized, in keeping with the self-designation of the BIPOC community, so as to distinguish the term from the adjective black and to emphasize the construction of ethnic classifications.
5   In 1949, Simone de Beauvoir penned her famous sentence "One is not born, but rather becomes a woman." See Simone de Beauvoir, *The Second Sex,* London 1953, p. 273 (originally published under the title *Le Deuxième Sexe. Les faits et les mythes,* Paris 1949).

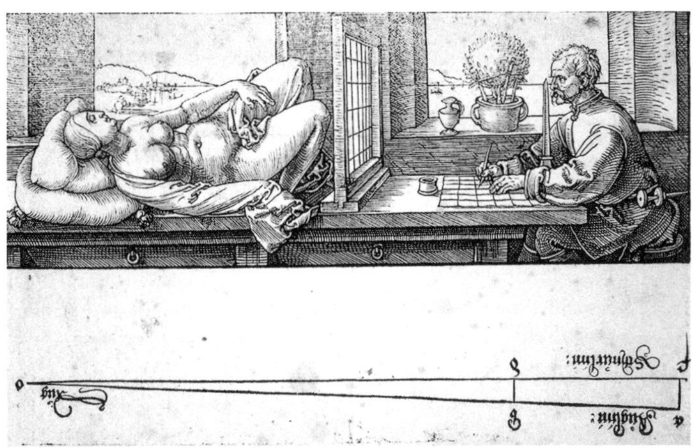

pudica (350–340 B.C.) whose right hand shields her pubic area. Later depictions often show her also covering her breast with her other hand, for instance in Sandro Botticelli's popular painting *The Birth of Venus* (ca. 1485/86), a work frequently cited in posters [(p. 159)]. The male nude of ancient Greece is self-confident and self-sufficient, while the female nude, through her gestures, reacts to the voyeuristic gaze from the outside and has thus been sexualized since her first appearance in the arts.[6]

Apart from scenes of Christ's birth and the crucifixion, images of the body largely disappeared from the art of the Middle Ages,[7] before Renaissance artists succeeded in reviving the ancient patterns. Albrecht Dürer's passion for science and anatomically accurate renderings of the human body cannot belie the fact that his representation of the sexes drew on a long established relationship of power and violence. His woodcut *Draughtsman Making a Perspective Drawing of a Reclining Woman* (1512–1525) illustrates this in an exemplary manner. The male figure's supposedly inquiring and, at once, voyeuristic gaze is fixed on the nude female sitter reclining directly in front of him, while separated from him by the precision tool of the lattice grid. The woman is rendered as a supposedly scientific and, at the same time, sexualized object. Pictures of the first human couple Adam and Eve served as the biblical pretext for the study of the body under the new realism. It heralded the normativization of the body and gender hierarchies whose ideological significance persists to this day. Prominent examples of this include Jan van Eyck's figures of Adam and Eve on the *Ghent Altarpiece* from 1432 and Albrecht Dürer's copperplate engraving *Adam and Eve* from 1504.

6   See Berger, *Ways of Seeing* (note 1), p. 44: "*Men act* and *women appear*. Men look at women. Women watch themselves being looked at. This determines not only most relations between men and women but also the relation of women to themselves. The surveyor of woman in herself is male: the surveyed female. Thus she turns herself into an object— and most particularly an object of vision: a sight."
7   Cf. Hans Belting, *Menschenbild und Körperbild*, Münster 2000, p. 15.

The comparison proposed by Hammer-Tugendhat between Michelangelo's statue of *David* (1501–1504) and Giorgione's famous *Sleeping Venus* (around 1508/10) is illuminating with regard to the continued marking of gender difference during the Renaissance.[8] The body ideal represented by *David*—a muscular upper body, broad shoulders, narrow hips—has persisted to this day as the male ideal of beauty and is echoed in mass media [(p. 174, p. 177)]. David, however, is not just a beautiful body but, by the same token, embodies the masculine principle of power and victory per se. By comparison, Giorgione's slumbering Venus is embedded in a natural setting and, vulnerable and unguarded, surrenders herself to the observer's gaze. In this direct juxtaposition, the gender dichotomy between subject and object, culture and nature, active and passive, mind and body as well as public and private radically comes to a head. Hammer-Tugendhat has called for a conscious reading of representations of men and women as relational so as to see through these attributions.

The consistency of the male ideal of beauty over the centuries is testimony to the equally invariable notion that here, physiognomy is a reflection of character. Concepts of female beauty, of course, which are almost exclusively about the young female body, changed continuously over the ages and were essentially defined by men. Lucas Cranach the Elder's painting *The Fountain of Youth* (1546) shows only old women dragging themselves, or being led, to the basin to undergo miraculous rejuvenation. Realistic portrayals of old age, physical frailty and physical decay are rare in the arts until well into the twentieth century. The few that do exist are usually expressions of misogyny or disdain for the lower social classes.[9] By contrast, ancient gods, philosophers and statesmen, as well as the prophets and saints of Christian art, were often endowed with an exalted or spiritual facial expression and the idealized figure of an old man, so as to convey wisdom and experience.[10]

Nude and Clothed Bodies as a Mirror of Power Relations

The female nude as an independent pictorial motif has been an integral part of art history since the Renaissance. The nude male body, however, was mostly treated solely as an academic subject or incorporated into large painting compositions. Depictions of men's bodies from the perspective of female artists only emerged in the

8   See Hammer-Tugendhat, *Kunstgeschichte als Kulturwissenschaft: Körper- und Geschlechterkonstruktionen*, 37:19 ff.: https://www.youtube.com/watch?v=f5vdRrH_mQA&list=PLjR8HTOEMQuf_tkFoVsadjWa5Ofqk_Y4e&index=5&t=2277s.

9   This also applies to two impressive late nineteenth century sculptures: *Celle qui fut la belle Heaulmière (She Who Was the Helmet Maker's Once-Beautiful Wife)* by Auguste Rodin and *Clotho* by Camille Claudel, both of which were modeled on the same elderly female sitter. The very title of Rodin's work makes it clear that realistic depictions of old age were created to epitomize ugliness and misery.

10   On the depiction of the aged body in art see Bettina Ullrich, *Das Alter in der Kunst: Die Darstellung des alten Menschen in der bildenden Kunst des 20. Jahrhunderts*, Oberhausen 1999.

Male dominance and female submissiveness
in Corinth's self-portraits with his wife:
Lovis Corinth, *Self-Portrait with Charlotte
Berend and a Glass of Champagne*, 1902

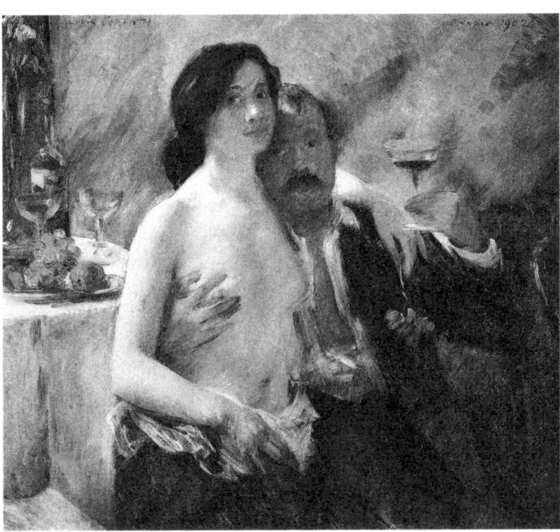

11 Already at the time of its creation, the Baroque sculpture *Ecstasy of Saint Teresa* by Giovanni Lorenzo Bernini was read, among other things, as sexual ecstasy.
12 Roland Krischel and Anja K. Sevcik, *Susanna: Bilder einer Frau vom Mittelalter bis MeToo*, exh. cat. Wallraf-Richartz-Museum Köln, Petersberg 2022.
13 Cf. Pierre Bourdieu, *Masculine Domination*, Redwood City, CA, 2001 (originally published under the title *La Domination masculine*, Paris 1998).

twentieth century. Yet male artists used mythological and religious narratives as a welcome legitimation to refashion their staging of the nude female body over and over: the birth of Venus, the judgment of Paris, Susanna in the bath, among many others.[11] Endless variations were produced especially on the theme of the bathing Susanna being watched by two lecherous old men. For a long time, the fact that the story it tells is one of attempted rape was hardly an issue, even though the voyeuristic male gaze is itself part of the picture content.[12]

The female nude *in* paintings generally suggests the clothed male viewer *in front of* the paintings. Images of the artist and his model, or his muse, have made the nude female body alongside the clothed male body a topos that has continued well into our own times. Its legitimacy is derived from the subject itself, even if gender roles are clearly assigned. Still, in Édouard Manet's famous picnic scene *Le Déjeuner sur l'herbe* (1863) there is no content-related reason why the woman in the foreground is sitting naked next to the elegantly dressed men—especially since even the woman bathing in the background is clad in a light dress. The repeat self-portraits of Lovis Corinth with his nude wife unabashedly reveal that this is always also about the hierarchical relationship of male dominance and female submissiveness, which continues to be conveyed throughout popular culture and mass media (p. 174).[13]

Manet's *Olympia* (1863) marks a break in the history of the regime of the patriarchal gaze, as she confidently looks back at her spectators and thus reclaims some of her autonomy. However, if current advertising images are taken into consideration, we may wonder, again, whether the empowerment gained through a reversal of the gaze really suffices to negate the status of the object—or whether its status is even emphasized as a result [(p. 123)].

The Regime of the white Gaze

In addition to the dichotomy of male and female bodies, that of white and Black bodies is, likewise, a constant in Western art history. While Manet's *Olympia* challenges the male gaze, the painting does not break with the depiction of Black people in the role of servants, which had been a common theme since the late Renaissance. Above all, they valorize the main protagonists. The nude white body of the model, Victorine Meurent, in the image foreground, obscures the portrait of the Black model, Laure, which is only visible on second glance, her face barely standing out against the dark background. Laure's last name is unknown and only very limited biographical data has been preserved. It is only thanks to efforts in cultural studies in recent years that the mystery of her identity has been unlocked at all, restoring individual histories to some of the nameless Black sitters and leading to the renaming of artworks.[14]

In the art of the Middle Ages, Black people appeared in only a few fixed roles, such as that of Saint Maurice or King Balthazar.[15] Dürer was among the first to create portraits that included openly racist aspects in their depiction of the portrayed. Colonialism and enslavement brought more Black people to Europe, but works of art continued to present them as marginal characters within a tightly defined repertoire of figures. Anonymized and stereotyped, their inclusion was primarily owed to compositional, formal or stylistic interests. In the pictorial and literary works of the late stages of colonialism in the nineteenth century, Black people remained fictions and constructions of white fantasies: They were exoticized, sexualized, allegorized, ideologized, and, as a direct consequence of their one-sided representation, always marginalized and exploited.[16]

In the same period, drawings were circulated of naked, tormented Black bodies alongside white slaveholders—bodies that were consistently depicted in crowds and de-individualized. This illustrates a dangerous paradox: while they certainly called for the abolition of enslavement, on a visual level, they invariably solidified a supposed white supremacy.[17] On the pictorial level, skin color remained the

14 Annie Dufour (ed.), *Le Modèle noir: De Géricault à Matisse*, exh. cat. Musée d'Orsay, Paris 2019.

15 Cf. Olivette Otele, *African Europeans: An Untold History*, London 2020.

16 The paintings by Swiss painter Frank Buchser that have recently become the subject of heated debate in Switzerland are characteristic of purely exoticizing, objectifying representations of Black women as slaves in the nineteenth century.

17 For more on this topic, see also Elyse Nelson and Wendy S. Walters, *Fictions of Emancipation: Carpeaux's* Why Born Enslaved! *Reconsidered*, exh. cat. Metropolitan Museum of Art, New York 2022.

Black wet nurses breastfeeding the white children of the slave masters: Anonymous, *Slave Nursing White Baby*, 1861–1865

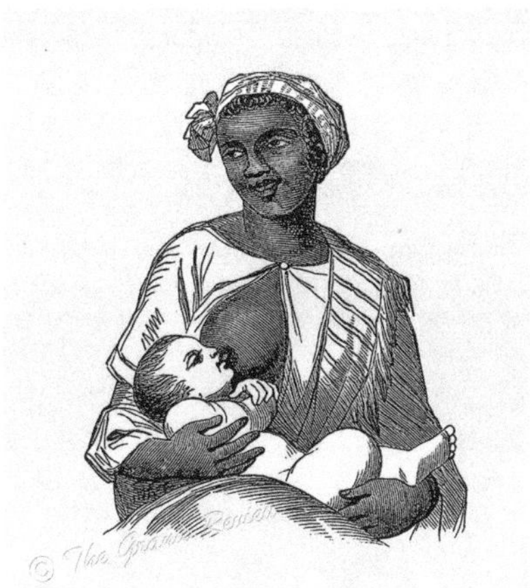

18 Achille Mbembe, *Critique of Black Reason*, trans. Laurent Dubois, Durham, NC 2017, p. 38 (originally published under the title *Critique de la raison nègre*, Paris 2013).
19 Recent exhibitions and publications have critically examined the worldview of the Brücke artists and the ways in which it was rooted in their own time: Brücke-Museum (ed.), *Kirchner und Nolde: Expressionismus. Kolonialismus*, exh. cat. Brücke-Museum Berlin, Munich 2021; Natasha A. Kelly, *Millis Erwachen—Milli's Awakening: Schwarze Frauen, Kunst und Widerstand—Black Women, Art and Resistance,* Berlin 2018.

most obvious approach for the process of Othering, which always linked external appearance with inferiority and dehumanization. Historian and political scholar Achille Mbembe discusses the long historical process that facilitated the fabrication of a "racial subject," in which images played, and still play, an essential role. "'Africa' and 'Blackness': these two notions took shape together … But if Africa has a body, and if it is a body, a *thing*, it gets it from the Black Man—no matter where he finds himself in the world."[18]

In view of the continuing impact of the colonial gaze, campaigns such as those launched by Benetton in the 1990s must be critically challenged, once again, for using skin colors primarily as a contrast intended to refract clichés in a playful and humorous way [(p. 144)]. Its reach also extends to contemporary art where it is evident, for instance, in the works of Expressionists who projected their own yearning into distant worlds. The Black bodies they depicted only served to imbue their pictorial worlds with the aura of the "foreign," the Other.[19]

New Beginnings and Setbacks
And yet, at the beginning of the twentieth century, body images temporarily diversified. A new sense of beauty and image-worthiness emerged, gender stereotypes were interrogated and challenged as a result of fierce struggles for equal rights. Avant-garde artists broke with conventional notions of art and found innovative forms of visual expression. Hannah Höch collaged radically new notions of femininity. With his series on the dying and death of his partner Valentine Godé-Dare, Ferdinand Hodler created

Monumental group of bronze figures at the entrance of the German pavilion at the Paris World's Fair: Josef Thorak, *Kameradschaft* (Comradeship), 1937 (current whereabouts unknown)

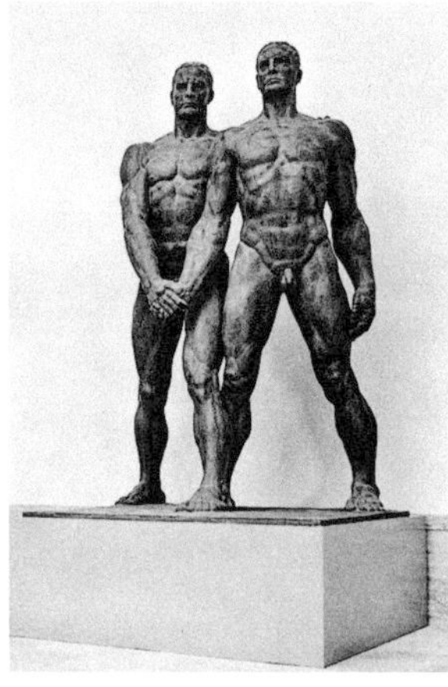

a monument to the ailing, suffering body.[20] Egon Schiele portrayed his body in fragile poses. Artists championing socially engaged realism showed elderly people and bodies that did not conform to common standards of beauty. Otto Dix, Käthe Kollwitz and other contemporaries focused on damaged, injured, and abused bodies as a scathing indictment of war, and in doing so deconstructed male hero myths.

World War II and fascism dealt an extremely brutal setback to this nascent development and made it disappear from view for years to come. The normative body politics of National Socialism took the stereotype of masculine virility and white hegemony to new heights of devastating dominance and established it as a symbol of national renewal while dissociating it from so-called antitypes. Arno Breker or Josef Thorak paid homage to this new and old hero with monumental statues. The worker-soldier, already invoked after the Russian Revolution, adhered to the same aesthetic principles, albeit with different political connotations. He appeared in paintings as well as propaganda posters, which were widely distributed in "realsocialist" countries [(p. 128)].[21]

Contemporary Counter-Concepts

Body art conquered the stage in the 1960s, concurrent with the social and political upheavals of that era. Turning their own bodies into the medium and object of their art and conceiving of them as an emancipative project, artists resisted old narratives and challenged cultural assumptions. They questioned the male view of women's bodies and, on a general level, entrenched gender and ethnic categories.[22]

20 Erica Pedretti's 1984 novel *Valerie oder Das unerzogene Auge,* which won her the Ingeborg Bachmann Prize, raises the question of the extent to which an artistic recording of another person's death is morally justified, even when it is created as a means of coping with a personal crisis, and to what degree the traditional role patterns of painter and model are, once again, manifest in this process.
21 Cf. George L. Mosse, *Das Bild des Mannes*, Frankfurt a. M., 1997, and Klaus Theweleit, *Male Fantasies*, Cambridge, UK 1987.
22 Cf. Gabriele Schor (ed.), *Feministische Avantgarde: Kunst der 1970er-Jahre aus der Sammlung Verbund, Wien*, Munich 2015.

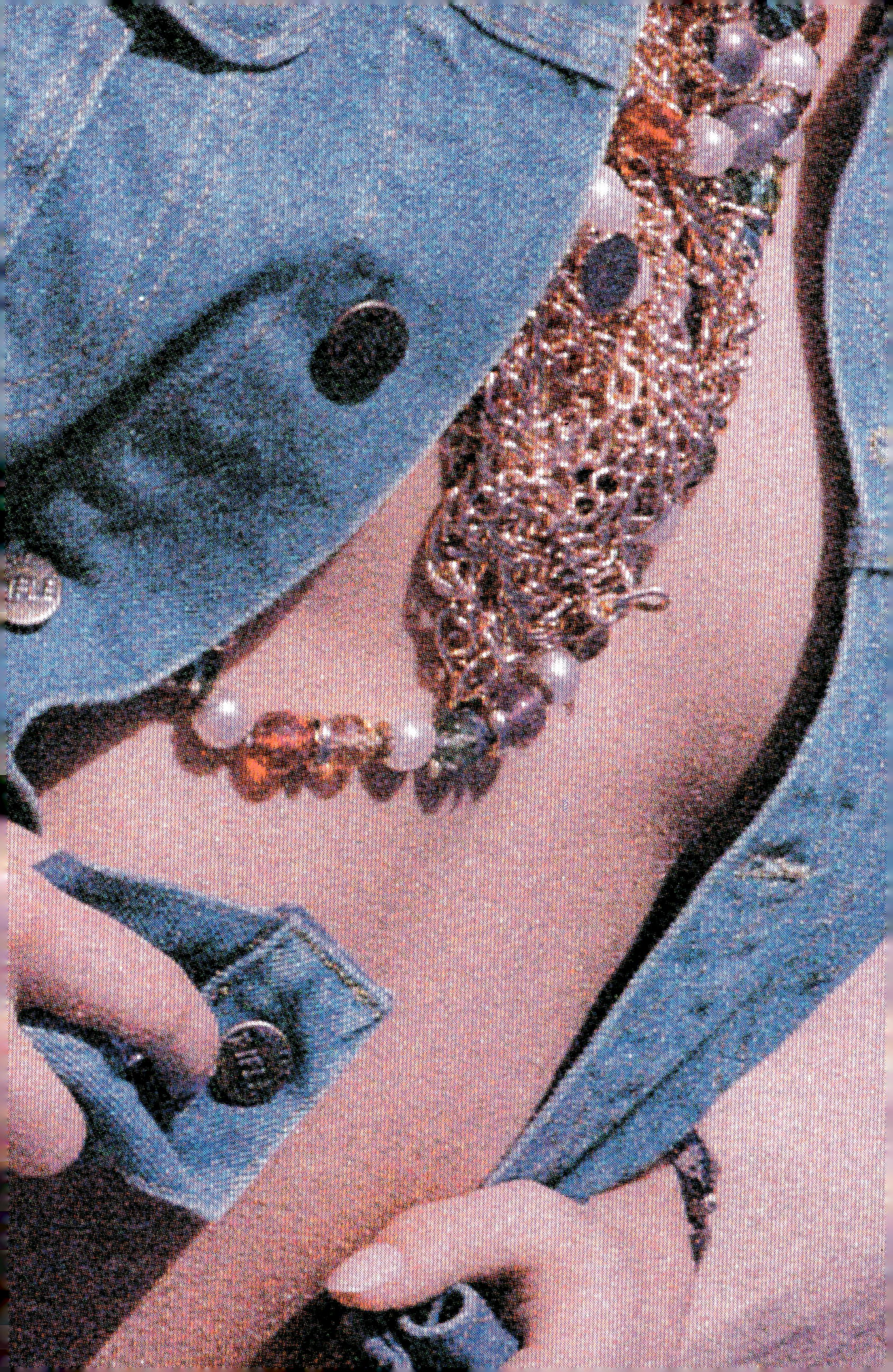

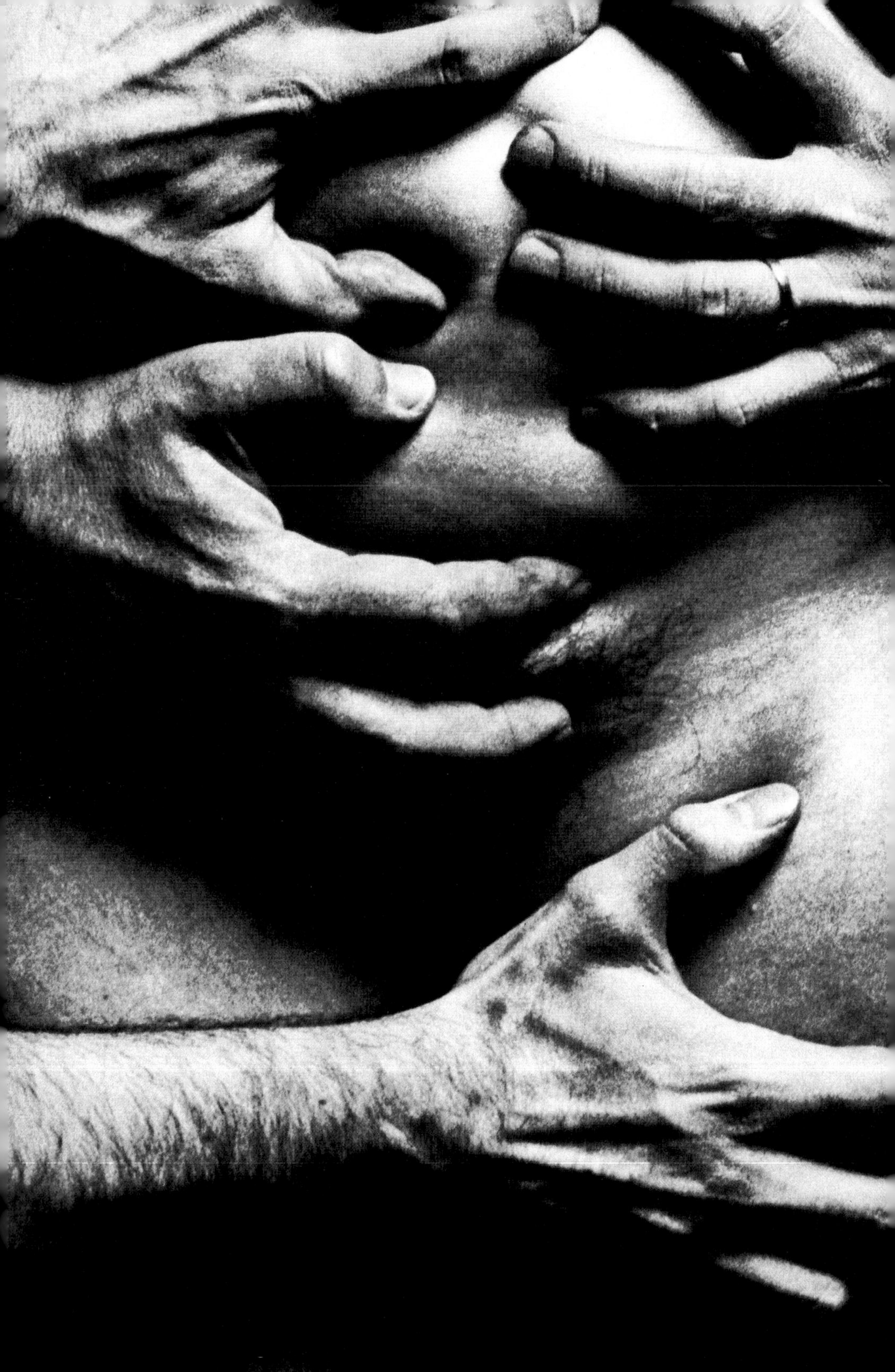

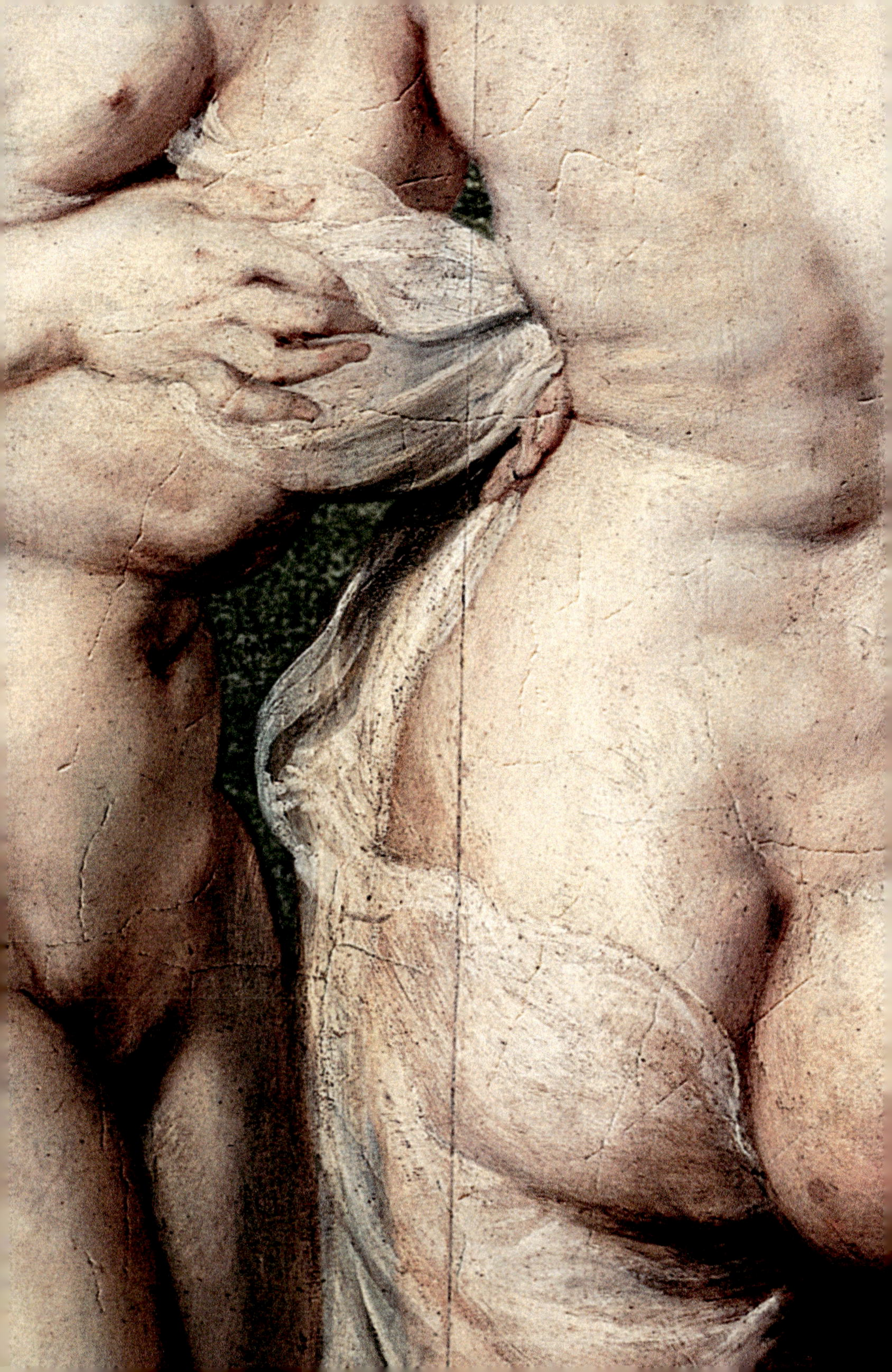

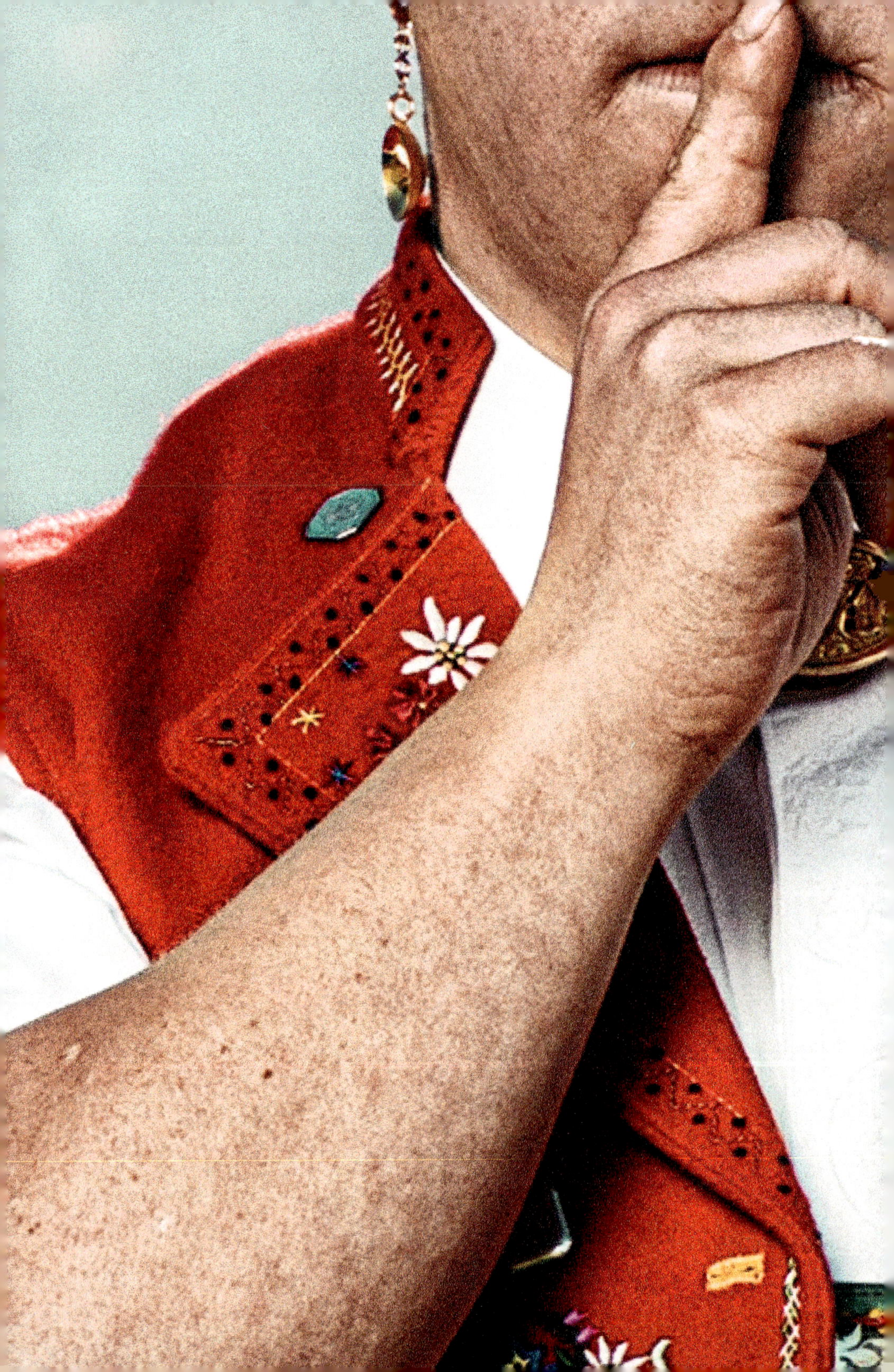

23   Markus Brunner, "'Körper im Schmerz'—Zur Körperpolitik der Performancekunst von Stelarc und Valie Export," in: Paula-Irene Villa (ed.), *Schön normal: Manipulationen am Körper als Technologien des Selbst*, Bielefeld 2008, pp. 21–40; here p. 32.
24   In the Baroque era, which, once again, celebrated the body, non-normative bodies were deliberately painted, too, but always as part of a sensationalist presentation of the Other. Diego Velázquez and his contemporaries portrayed people of small stature in their function as court jesters and in other servant roles. Jusepe de Ribera painted a breast-feeding bearded woman in 1631.
25   Cf., for instance, Florian Steininger and Ekow Eshun (eds.), *The New African Portraiture. Shariat Collections*, Cologne 2022.

Most notably, Valie Export pioneered this art movement, conceiving of her body as a site of political struggle and exploring this theme in her radical performances: "Valie Export's performances should thus be read as an endeavor towards deconstructing both the body and the gaze perceiving it, to expose the body as one described and inscribed by society, to irritate the male gaze directed at it and thus to render it visible in the first place."[23] Hannah Wilke was one of the first proponents of body art as well. Her body remained the subject of her art when she fell ill with cancer and she documented its transformation in unvarnished, painful pictures—autonomous, self-determined counter-images to Hodler's series of paintings.

At the same time, the photographic self-stagings created by artists such as Urs Lüthi and Jürgen Klauke illustrated a longing for body images that reached beyond normative attributions and binary gender models. Artists from homosexual subcultures depicted men as erotic, emotional subjects and introduced a new version of the male nude into art. Men make similar appearances in the, often monumental, paintings of Lucian Freud, who radically opened the gaze to queer bodies and bodies beyond stereotypical definitions of beauty in the 1990s and early 2000s.

The existential dimension of the body takes on a different sense of urgency when it is negotiated as an injured, vulnerable, or impaired body. With her frequently allegorical self-portraits, Frida Kahlo popularized this theme and introduced it to art history in the mid-twentieth century. In the 1980s, Swiss painter Hans Witschi likewise challenged socially defined norms of beauty and perfection with his expressive self-portraits and paintings of bodies.[24] This was also the point of departure for Irish artist Mary Duffy, who posed as an armless nude in a 1995 performance, thus inserting her body into the long tradition of torsos in art history, while at the same time directing the medical and societal gaze to her "flawed" body. By the same token, Berlinde De Bruyckere's maltreated, tortured bodies reference art historical precedents. With their dramatic exaggeration of physical pain, they create awareness of the fact that vulnerability is a basic constant of human life.

Currently, figurative art by Black artists is the subject of considerable attention on the art market and feted with exhibitions and publications.[25] The portraiture dominating here is a testament to the long period during which the white gaze was only focused on the collective

Artistic exploration of the sexualization
and exploitation of the Black female body:
Frida Orupabo, *Leda and the Swan*, 2021

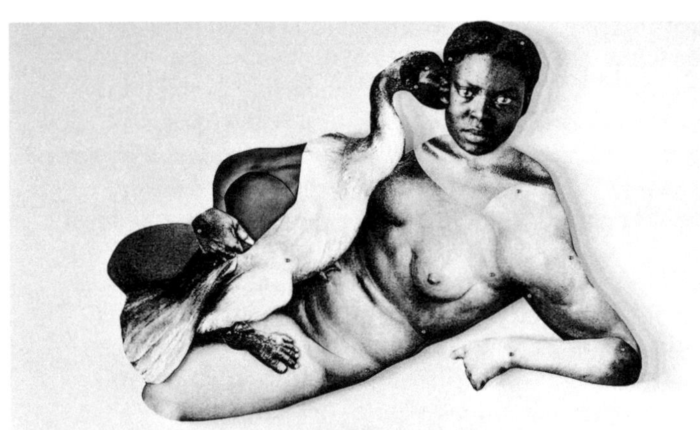

Black body and individual portraits by Black artists hardly ever found their way into art history. Thus, ways of looking at the Black body that previously had not been taken into consideration in the Global North have now gained in presence, which can be seen as the most recent chapter in a new diversity of bodies. Of course, the danger of appropriation remains, as illustrated by the rapid rise to fame of artists such as Amoako Boafo and Maxwell Alexandre, whose works now command high prices on the art market, partly as an outgrowth of the Black Lives Matter movement. More unwieldy works such as those by Kara Walker or Frida Orupabo defy this process. In different ways, these artists invariably reference colonial power structures and the lasting impact of the binary structures of Black and white, rendering a superficial consumption of their works impossible.[26]

While contemporary art increasingly liberates body images from their normative confinement, taking up and accompanying sociopolitical discourses along the way, body images in advertising and popular culture prove to be astonishingly resistant to any form of transformation. Particularly in times of political unrest and the rise of a new brand of authoritarianism, heroic white male figures and stereotypical images of white femininity are making a comeback and asserting themselves as a source of reassurance. This renders all the more important the contributions of artists who continue to query, challenge and resist any power of definition over bodies through their designs and are thereby gradually breaking open the encrusted representations perpetuated by the mass media.

26 Walker summed up the problem with a provocative rhetorical question: "Is race less fluid than gender? Like viscous dehydrated semen? Caked upon your face?" Quoted after: Kunstmuseum Basel (ed.), *Kara Walker: A Black Hole Is Everything a Star Longs to Be*, exhibition booklet, Basel 2022.

What Do Bodies Say?
Interpretations of the Female*
Body in Media Culture

Paula-Irene Villa

Images of popular culture have a paradoxical effect: they show something, make something visible. What is shown often appears clear and evident in everyday life. However, these images are far from being unequivocal in what they "say." Not just upon closer examination, such as in an academic context, but also and particularly in their mundane everyday nature, images are ambiguous, that is, polysemous. "A picture is worth (more than) a thousand words," as the saying goes, once again seemingly clear and evident in its statement. Pictures say a lot, and they do so ambiguously. In this regard, images and words are more similar than the proverb suggests. Words, too, are always highly ambiguous. The understanding of the polysemy of signs, whether textual or visual, can be gleaned from relevant intellectual and academic discussions. The arguments and analyses from feminist and queer studies on media, art, and images, cultural and pop studies, media, cultural and art sociology, as well as historical perspectives on media, images, and art, demonstrate that images are anything but simple representations of an extra-pictorial reality.[1] Neither allegedly purely documentary photographs nor visibly (re)constructed images are mere reflections of a given reality; rather, images constitute a reality of their own.

[1] For example, in the works of Susan Sontag, Stuart Hall, Judith Butler, John Berger, Teresa de Lauretis, Antke Engel, Linda Hentschel, bell hooks, Sigrid Schade, Silke Wenk, and many others.

Intersectional Contexts, Precarious Meaning: the Obstinacy of Images

One characteristic of images, including those on posters, is that they are static and captured within a format, such as a picture frame, while extra-pictorial reality can never remain still in any respect. Since each image embodies the difference between itself and the surrounding world, images are notoriously precarious. They make visible things, dimensions, and dynamics that undoubtedly exist "otherwise," while simultaneously abstracting and fixing this "otherwise." In comparison to the abundance, diversity, and transience of reality, an image is always a spatial-temporal abstraction because it shows only a portion of that reality. However, showing and speaking about images depends on and is conditioned by their reference to the extra-pictorial reality. No image, poster or photo, no painting or social media post is intelligible without reference to the world outside the image. This also applies to abstract or challenging images, such as those from avant-garde art movements, and even more so to images created for commercial purposes or for popular cultural circulation, such as in advertising. Images, including those on posters, are meaningless without social and historical context. Only what can be socially seen, is seen. Therefore, as much as images abstract the world they speak of and partially describe, images are also inherently and necessarily constitutively related to and dependent upon the world surrounding them: images are only conditionally autonomous, they do follow their own logic, albeit only partially.

The focus of this text—the question of what images and the bodies depicted in those images say—is thus not easy to answer and certainly never conclusive. Therefore, interpretations of historical images are always subject to reinterpretation; when we see or read a poster, we perceive the image differently from the generations before us. While context is essential, it is not individually accessible. Our eye, our "ear," is socially influenced, and the extent of that influence is not entirely within our individual control. However, context alone does not determine our understanding. Contexts are far too diverse, complex, and internally contradictory. Contexts also vary depending on location and time—whether the poster is displayed on a billboard in a European metropolis in the 1920s, in a feminist bar in a provincial town in the 1980s, or in a museum. They also vary depending on the environment and the individual.[2] This variation due to intersectional context specificity applies everywhere and in all instances. This means that the necessarily complex social positioning of images, the perceiving individuals, and the contexts along relevant social differences such as gender, environment, class / social background, formal education, age, desire, ethnicization / racialization, physical condition, and so

2   As a white, queer, Jewish sociology professor living in Germany, I may perceive a poster differently here and now than my 80 plus-year-old mother, who hails from Buenos Aires and who is a retired chemistry professor and a proud grandmother; and she, in turn, may see it differently than my teenage daughter, who, in turn, sees it differently than my colleague, or her friend at the gym.

on, shape and condition what images say, but they do not determine it definitively.

Female* Bodies:
Conventional Perspectives

If we accept all of this, and if the body in posters and other mass media can be read as a visual, social, political, and cultural sign, as the exhibition *Talking Bodies* aims to demonstrate, what does this mean for the representation of the female* body?[3] If what images say is always conditioned by context and simultaneously ambiguous, always new, always different, what does this imply for interpreting images of women's bodies? Can body images then not be attributed to societal norms or traditions and understood through them? I believe they can, but—and hence the expansive framing—the connection between societal norms and specific images is loose, complex, dynamic, and indeed contradictory. There is no single femininity or gender norm, no single tradition, no single form for female* bodies. And there is not a single interpretation of what is being shown. Female* bodies also convey more than is commonly assumed. This means that what is often held as overly evident and clear from a critical, even feminist perspective may not be as clear-cut as it seems. Common interpretations, even those that consider themselves critical, tend at times to assume familiarity with an image in those instances where the image mirrors gender-related norms in a societal situation: i.e., that the gendered nature of the image would automatically and clearly emerge from gender relations. However, this understanding is too simplistic. Because there is neither "the" norm of gender, something that is inherently feminine in a singular, unavoidable imprint, nor is there, as stated, "the" image. Images tell stories of gender norms and relations, but they do so in a stubborn and ambiguous manner, never randomly.

There are indeed identifiable hegemonic norms of gender in modernity, especially since the early twentieth century. There are normative hegemonies, notably regarding image conventions and media forms when it comes to body images of femininity*. The "naturalization" of gender difference, particularly femininity*, as a dimension constitutive of "naturalizing" other groups in modern society, is central and highly effective. Modern societies are founded on the promise and assertion of equality and universality of human rights. However, throughout their existence, modern societies also structurally break this

3   I use an asterisk here to indicate that what constitutes a female body can by no means be considered pre-established nor precisely pre-defined. The asterisk represents the diverse variations and options of bodies perceived, felt, understood, and portrayed as female*. The asterisk refers not only to explicitly queer femininities, although it certainly includes them, but also encompasses those female bodies that appear perplexing, subversive, ambiguous, etc., as "female"—even, and perhaps especially, when this may not be intended.

promise. "Naturalization" is crucial for this. Women who are objectified, who become sex objects for heterosexual men, are perhaps the predominant image of female* sexuality in modernity [p. 123]. This is accompanied and intensified by actual legal norms in Europe that until very recently provided women with a legal status derived from their husband, father, or son. Women are considered the "fair sex" insofar as they actually (have to) circulate in marriage and kinship markets in order to acquire rights, to become "significant subjects." [4] Their status, in a way, as trophies of men—to whom autonomy, success, status, education, and income are legitimately granted in modernity—is not merely a discursive construct but materializes through corresponding economic and legal structures. These structures relegate women to the realm of dependent, protected, infantile, nature-like beings who men circulate among themselves.

John Berger summarized the hegemonic cis-heteronormative image convention as follows: *"Men act* and *women appear*. Men look at women. Women watch themselves being looked at. This determines not only most relations between men and women but also the relation of women to themselves. The surveyor of woman in herself is male: the surveyed is female. Thus, she turns herself into an object of vision: a sight." [5] Such gender norms are inscribed in numerous images: The "fair sex" is portrayed as either foolishly childlike or as a hypersexual adornment to status symbols by which masculinity is measured: cars, watches, glamorous vacation spots or tailored suits [p. 126]. This may seem funny and transparent, but it also points to serious, highly discriminatory empirical realities for women.

Body Politics:
Visibility as a Political Issue

However, hegemonic norms and forms are always precarious. They imply at least two essential dynamics that relativize themselves: firstly, norms are by definition phantasmatic; [6] they are not—or only extremely rarely—really and concretely applicable, let alone livable. Norms are idealized fantasies, not actual empirical practices. They should be understood more as guidelines, both guiding and enabling practice, as well as limiting and preventing it. In this sense, images can indeed represent norms so long as they are recognizable as images, but not as nonpictorial, lived practice. *Cosmopolitan* fashion spreads should not be confused with everyday reality. The distance between

4   Alluding here to Judith Butler's *Bodies That Matter: On the Discursive Limits of Sex,* New York 1995.
5   John Berger, *Ways of Seeing,* London 2008 (first published in 1972), p. 47.
6   Judith Butler, "Imitation and Gender Insubordination" in: Henry Abelove, Michèle Aina Barale, David M. Halperin (eds.), *The Lesbian and Gay Studies Reader,* New York / London 1993, pp. 307–320, here p. 313.

real-life and the image also generates the pleasure and fun in the image; it allows for irony and subversion as well as violence and contempt. This distance is also evident in numerous poster images of female* bodies when they become, for example, fruit [p. 135] or landscapes [p. 127]. The fact that these images make sense, especially in their humor or in their bizarre-grotesque forms, is precisely because they refer to norms, i.e., normative contexts that give meaning—but these images also constantly go beyond that meaning. Nevertheless, there are always alternatives: there is criticism, questioning, alternative approaches, and protest against hegemonic norms [p. 134] materializing in images; and these images also form contexts for what all body images convey.

In these complex dynamics of signification, political relationships are also realized. Visibility itself is a central element of political participation and recognition; visibility is also an element of critique and political protest. Especially in feminist movements and struggles, visibility and the fight over images have been and still are central. This struggle is crystallized in the modern era, not least and particularly in relation to the body. Body politics is a central theme, perhaps even *the* central theme of second-wave feminism, i.e., the women's movement of the 1970s and 1980s. This is also evident in many posters in the context or aftermath of the second wave. For example, when female* bodies are staged as strong and self-determined, as belonging to themselves, knowing what they are doing, or when nudity is presented not for the sexual disposition of male viewers but instead as a woman's self-determination. However, even these images cannot escape ambiguity. A naked female* body, presented as "beautiful" according to prevailing conventions, does not quite escape heteronormative objectification, no matter how "feminist" the intent may be. Conversely, the supposedly most stereotypical image of hypersexualized women can also be interpreted as drag, as a queer implosion.

Body politics was also a topic in the first wave of feminism, particularly regarding the criticism of constricting, restrictive, and paralyzing norms of clothing and movement in the literal sense. The protest against the corset, the development of reform clothing, and the appropriation of modes of movement in public spaces that were considered bourgeois, masculine, and consequently unfeminine (such as cycling) were essential practices of feminist and emancipatory body politics around the turn of the century. This first wave of feminism already included different,

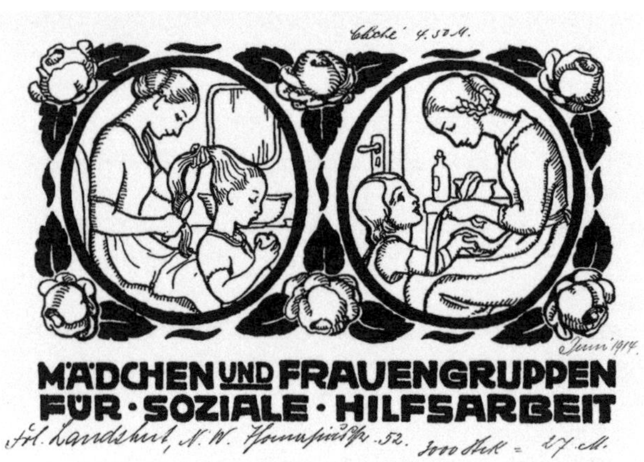

Staging of femininity as care, devotion, and relationship: Advertising postcard of the "Mädchen- und Frauengruppen für soziale Hilfsarbeit" (Girls' and Women's Groups for Social Aid), ca. 1914

and occasionally conflicting, currents. In no way did the engaged women (and sometimes men) always agree on everything; in fact, they rarely did. From what did which women need to be liberated, and why? Which norms were criticized while at the same time being reproduced and consolidated? Normative notions of the emancipated woman in the German-speaking bourgeois women's movement strongly aligned with the implicit ideal of white, heterosexual, naturally virtuous and motherly femininity, which demanded higher education, access to certain professions and occupations, as well as specific protective and political rights (such as suffrage). Women* were portrayed as virtuous individuals naturally capable of empathy, motherhood, and devotion which the card "Girls' and Women's Groups for Social Aid" illustrates perfectly.

The physically laboring yet determined and combative strong proletarian female body or a sensous, sexually active, extravagant, and adventurous embodiment of femininity were not visible as negative foils or forms of differentiation but were excluded from the image—and thus contained within this omission. Those nurturing bodies that correspond to the specifically modern convention of femininity are characterized by a focus directed inward to the private and the family realm, portraying women as mothers and caregivers, turned away from the world, devoted to inner values, and immersed in immanence: femininity as care, devotion, and relationship. The text-image coupling reinforces this message: women—and girls—destined for social interaction and needing help. The flowers that surround and frame the image emphasize and specify this presumed destiny as a natural fate.

Naturalness as Ideology

Nature as authenticity, materializing and manifesting itself in and through the body, is the central, if not decisive, element of modern body language, especially femininity*. In the modern era, the body is argued to be the material expression of its inner truth, not just philosophically and politically, but also (natural) scientifically. Normatively, it is expected that the body eloquently displays this truth, so to speak, in its gestures and forms. It is presumed to be a truth that exists as a natural fact, unchangeable, beyond human control, ahistorical, and beyond the realm of society. Legions of natural scientists and scholars, particularly from the mid-nineteenth century onwards and continuing to this day, have emphatically stated that femininity is inherently motherhood or caretaking: "[I]n general, it cannot be emphasized enough that nature has assigned to women their calling as mothers and housewives, and that the laws of nature can under no circumstances be ignored without causing severe damage, particularly to the succeeding generation."[7] And more succinctly: "… everything that we admire and venerate in the true woman is merely a dependency of the ovaries."[8]

However, in the latter quote by Rudolf Virchow, the inherent ambiguity is evident, not only in the body images but also in the language itself. While this formulation appears to be sober and medical, and was perhaps intended to be so, it is also simultaneously adorned with a pathetically normative flourish. Femininity is revered and admired in its physiological essence, which resides in the reproductive organs. The combination of an internal organ and moral exaltation creates a restless tension. It is within this dynamic that images of female bodies oscillate between the animalistic-natural, beyond social constructs and beyond human control on the one hand, and morally exalted, embodying earthly virtue and a specific social norm on the other. The liminality, that is, the borderland between nature and culture embedded in this dynamic, is of concern in modern societies and also renders body images precarious, challenging the overt definiteness of the female* body in the image.

This is evident in numerous images that portray female bodies as objects, as raw materials, as nature to be conquered, dominated, exploited, and appropriated. However, at the same time, these images are anything but "natural"—untouched by practice, society, and norms—but rather highly artificial. Naturalness is staged, arranged, and

7   Max Planck, 1897, cited in Arthur Kirchhoff (ed.), *Die akademische Frau: Gutachten hervorragender Universitätsprofessoren, Frauenlehrer und Schriftsteller über die Befähigung der Frau zum wissenschaftlichen Studium und Berufe*, Berlin 1897, p. 255; full text: www.archive.org/details/dieakademischef02kircgoog.
8   Rudolf Virchow, 1865, cited in Ulrike Klöppel, *XXOXY ungelöst: Hermaphroditismus, Sex und Gender in der deutschen Medizin: Eine historische Studie zur Intersexualität*, Bielefeld 2010, p. 257.

choreographed. The card "Girls' and Women's Groups for Social Aid" perfectly illustrates this again: clothing, hairstyles, tools, interior spaces, furniture—all products and expressions of human practice, craftsmanship. Even the flowers are cultivated, fabricated, readable as an expression of a modern obsession with order in the sense described by Zygmunt Bauman,[9] with society acting as a gardener, working against any disorder and "weedy growth."

Just as in everyday "doing gender" in modern societies, images of gendered bodies also speak a paradoxical language: they embody an allegedly pre-existing body nature through performative practices and elaborate mise en scène, a nature that supposedly exists on its own, beyond practice. The norm of depicting gender difference follows this pattern in various contexts, including images. At the same time, this practice carries its own inherent failure within itself—the elaborate practices would not be necessary if "nature" simply realized itself as it allegedly does.

White, Proletarian, Powerful, Jewish …
Who Sees What?

Despite the suggestion of objectivity and the fiction of clarity ("the virtuous bourgeois German woman") in the image, it should not be forgotten that the postcard—for me, from a present-day perspective, but possibly already at the time it was created—appears not only exaggerated but downright caricatured. Moreover, it is imbued with such "blonde whiteness" that it evokes racism and an "ethnic" ideology. This is especially true considering that in the first decades of the twentieth century, there also existed an effective and prevalent colonial-racist visual language. This language was evident, particularly in posters advertising violent "ethnographic exhibitions" or "human zoos" or colonial goods such as chocolate, sugar, and coffee, often featuring sexualized and brutally racialized female bodies: female bodies as available resources, akin to animals or commodities, certainly not viewed as human beings on equal footing.

It is interesting to note that this postcard is now housed in the archive of the Alice Salomon University of Applied Sciences in Berlin. Alice Salomon (1872–1948) was a liberal social reformer in the context of the first women's movement in Germany, a pioneer in professionalizing social work, and actively engaged in the fight for women's access to higher education. A liberal German Jew, she converted

9   Zygmunt Bauman, *Modernity and Ambivalence,* Cambridge, UK, 1991. For a more detailed discussion, see Paula-Irene Villa, "Zygmunt Bauman und die Geschlechterforschung. Eine viel versprechende Liaison?" in *Österreichische Zeitschrift für Soziologie*, vol. 33 (2008), no. 4, pp. 45–61.

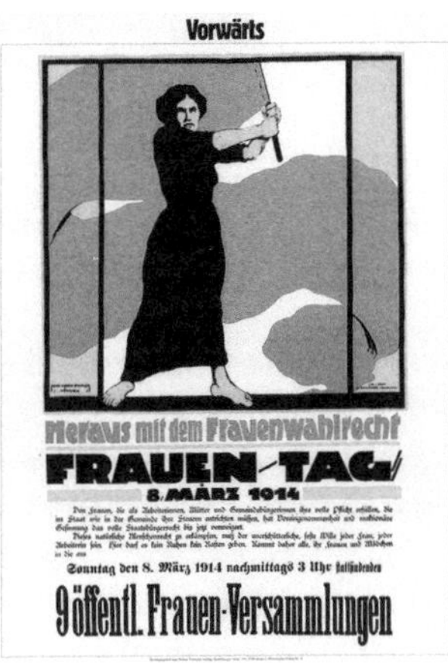

to Protestantism in 1914 but was forced out of all positions by the Nazi regime in the 1930s. To put this a different way, this image contains traces of the aforementioned intersectional femininities* and their internal differences: the female* body as (simultaneously) white, bourgeois, virtuous, German, Jewish, natural, civilized …?

Juxtaposed with this image, the visualization of the female* body in posters within the context of the proletarian women's movement also expresses physical strength and determination, anger and resistance. Here, neither kindness, patience, nor other moral virtues are staged, nor is there any hint of eroticized nudity or aestheticized opulence, as seen, for example, in the poster for the automobile exhibition in Geneva from the same era (p. 140). This body resists, gazes out into the world, and is firmly grounded in reality. It does not conform, refusing to be objectified or succumb to shame in the awareness of being looked at.

And finally, another essential element of the visual language of female* bodies, beginning in the late ninteenth century and continuing into the present, is the presence of disparaging sexist caricatures in posters. Particularly in the political sphere, but also in advertising and popular culture, numerous depictions of the "unfeminine woman" circulate. What is suggested in these depictions is that politically active women are unfeminine, insofar as they are unnatural (p. 150). They are caricatured as monstrous figures who exist outside the realm of normality, outside of what is deemed "essential."

So, what becomes visible in posters and how? Building on what has already been described, posters, and especially the representation of female* bodies, attract particular attention through the skillful play of (paradoxical?) simultaneity between conventionality and unconventionality. These depictions are, on the one hand, conditioned by and understandable only within the context of gender conventions, such as those of natural and essential femininity*—as motherhood, as "animalistic" sexuality, as conquerable decorum—but on the other hand, posters always play with these conventions, exaggerating them, taking them literally, being radically consistent, or critically engaging with them politically. This may not always be intentional. Rather, posters inherently carry their own ambiguity and uncertainty, which may be more or less visible. It is always important to ask who sees these images and how, and in what context they are viewed. Ultimately, what they convey is subject to interpretation and the perspectives of the viewers.

When Is a Man a Man?
A Brief Cultural History of Masculine Representations of the Body as Reflected in the Media

Florian Diener

In Thomas Mann's novel *The Magic Mountain*, set in the early twentieth century, the protagonist Hans Castorp hails from a well-to-do background and has just graduated from university. He travels from Hamburg to Davos to visit his cousin, who was staying at a sanatorium hotel, for a period of three weeks. Without being ill himself, Castorp enjoys his idle life in Davos. He ends up being so enthusiastic about it that, instead of taking up a confirmed job offer, he goes on to reside at a luxury sanatorium for seven years, indulging in philosophical conversations about the meaning of life with numerous health resort patrons. At one point, he reflects on his role as a man: "I am not at all masculine in the sense that I see in another man only a rival male and nothing more. Perhaps I am not masculine at all—certainly I am not in the sense which I tend to call 'social,' I don't exactly know why."[1]

On the one hand, Hans Castorp's remark shows him firmly dissociating himself from the middle-class ideals of masculinity that prevailed at the dawn of the twentieth century. On the other hand, it points to the protagonist's insecurities in dealing with his own—biologically based—gender role and the social implications that come with it. The gender trouble Castorp refers to, which is rooted in the challenges posed by a discursively generated attribution of gender first described by Judith Butler,[2] is by no means new. Uncertainties and reflections about what constitutes women and men or what distinguishes them from one another have been part of the standard repertoire of scholarly discussions and popular cultural discourses since antiquity. His 1984 song *Männer* (Men) with its mythically sounding question "When is a man a man?" made singer Herbert

1 Thomas Mann, *The Magic Mountain*, New York 1965, p. 585.
2 Judith Butler, *Gender Trouble*, New York / London 1990.

Grönemeyer a household name in the German-speaking world—perhaps precisely because, following up on this refrain, the lyrics promptly provide numerous answers to the question.

Scholarly analysis of the structural category of gender is, of course, faced with an infinitely more complex subject-matter, because gender is not a static construct, but a dynamic one that is informed by cultural, geographical and historical factors and is subject to constant change.[3] In this context, contemporary notions of masculinity can be gleaned by examining the media as a mirror of their respective times. Of course, the media play a dual role here. On the one hand, they serve as a resonance chamber for societal notions of gender; on the other hand, they actively contribute to the discursive production of "bodies, gender identities and sexualities,"[4] as well.

The Invention of Masculinity in the Nineteenth Century

The beginning of the Enlightenment period lends itself as a particularly useful point of departure for our current understanding of masculinity, because it categorized humans within the framework of modern knowledge systems (such as medicine, biology and psychology) and provided standardized determinants for human life.[5] Thus, in the early nineteenth century, a patriarchally dominated scientific discourse laid the foundation for clearly defined gender roles that were organized in a decidedly binary fashion and would become further entrenched in the course of industrialization. In this context, the feminine became a special case, a pathological one that needed to be explained, while the masculine, as a normative concept, "merged into the general category of human nature and vanished."[6] According to Ute Frevert, an analysis of encyclopedia entries for "woman" yields numerous articles on women's history, biological specifics, women's work and so forth.[7] The entry for "man" in the 1851 edition of *Das grosse Conversations-Lexicon für die gebildeten Stände* (Great Encyclopaedia for the Educated Classes) simply states: "See especially Human being."[8]

It is beyond dispute that the radical transformation of nearly all aspects of life due to industrialization also resulted in a reinterpretation of masculine identities, which subsequently manifested themselves through demarcation from the feminine and the creation of gender-connoted functional spheres:[9] "To the man the state, to the woman

3 Raewyn Connell, *Gender*, 2nd ed., Cambridge, UK 2020, p. 89.

4 Tanja Maier, "Feminismus, Gender und Queer," in: Andreas Hepp, Friedrich Krotz, Swantje Lingenberg, and Jeffrey Wimmer (ed.), *Handbuch Cultural Studies und Medienanalyse*, Wiesbaden 2015, pp. 53–54.

5 Cf. Michel Foucault, *Discipline and Punish: The Birth of the Prison*, New York 1977.

6 Ute Frevert, "Soldaten, Staatsbürger: Überlegungen zur historischen Konstruktion von Männlichkeit," in: Thomas Kühne (ed.), *Männergeschichte, Geschlechtergeschichte: Männlichkeit im Wandel der Moderne*, Frankfurt a. M. / New York 1996, p. 71.

7 Ute Frevert, *"Mann und Weib, und Weib und Mann": Geschlechter-Differenzen in der Moderne*, Munich 1995, p. 51.

8 "Mann," in: Joseph Meyer (ed.), *Das grosse Conversations-Lexicon für die gebildeten Stände*, vol. 20, Hildburghausen 1851, p. 523.

9 Cf. Elizabeth Prommer, "Der kühne Abenteurer, der fleissige Forscher und der geniale Denker: Das Männerbild in der Gartenlaube," in: Christiane Hackl, Elizabeth Prommer, and Brigitte Scherer (eds.), *Models und Machos? Frauen- und Männerbilder in den Medien*, Konstanz 1996, pp. 13–50.

the family!"[10] This quote from the 1894 edition of *Meyers Konversations-Lexikon* sums up with unrivalled succinctness the demand for bipolar gender roles. This imperative not only speaks to the gender model of the time, which was based on binarity and difference, but also points to the consequences of a patriarchally dominated discourse on gender roles whose effects continue to be felt to this day and are manifested, for example, in the increased sexualization of the female body in the media, the gender pay gap, the glass-ceiling effect, and the double socialization—in other words, the double burden on women who, far more often than men, are required to provide both care work and take up gainful employment.

The manner in which masculinity was described in contemporary nineteenth century media is illustrated by Elizabeth Prommer's analysis of the *Gartenlaube*, the most popular German-language illustrated magazine of the time: The ideal man was supposed to be, among other things, heroic, courageous, brave, strong-willed, and eager to work.[11] Against this background, it would seem rather obvious that Hans Castorp, the long-term vacationer mentioned at the outset, was unable to properly identify with the masculine ideal of the time.

Proletarian, Soldier, Citizen and Fine Gentleman— the Male Body Before 1945

In the proletarian environment, a man appeared, among other things, as a factory worker, a machinist, a farm laborer, or a gymnast. Posters often show idealized depictions of well-trained and young male bodies, which were patterned on ancient ideals or mythical heroic figures [(p. 133)]. However, the staging of muscular male bodies was not so much inspired by an aesthetic end in itself. The emphasis was rather on the display of male performance. The proletarian body was thus mostly embedded in a utilitarian, functional context, and a well-trained body was the logical outcome of hard work.

Besides industrialization, the nineteenth century was also characterized in many countries by increasing militarization, which went hand in hand with the establishment and sedimentation of military norms and values in society.[12] As is still the case today in some countries, doing military service was considered a "male initiation ritual."[13] It was only the army, it was claimed, that could "mold the recruited youth into a man."[14] The question "Where did you serve?"

10 "Politische Gleichstellung," in: Joseph Meyer (ed.), *Meyers Konversations-Lexikon: Ein Nachschlagewerk des allgemeinen Wissens*, 5th ed., vol. 6, Leipzig 1894, p. 822.
11 Prommer, "Der kühne Abenteurer" (note 9), p. 34.
12 Thomas Kühne, "Staatspolitik, Frauenpolitik, Männerpolitik: Politikgeschichte als Geschlechtergeschichte," in: Hans Medick and Anne-Charlott Trepp (eds.), *Geschlechtergeschichte und Allgemeine Geschichte: Herausforderungen und Perspektiven*, Göttingen 1998, pp. 175–176.
13 Florian Diener, *Stereotype Darstellungen von Alter und Geschlecht in der Werbung: Eine quantitative Bildinhaltsanalyse ausgewählter Zeitschriftenanzeigen der Jahre 2000 und 2020*, dissertation, Friedrich-Alexander-Universität Erlangen 2023, p. 65.
14 Frevert, "Soldaten, Staatsbürger" (note 6), p. 82.

is not just a common line in Carl Zuckmayer's drama *The Captain of Köpenick*, but was ubiquitous throughout the German Empire. And, undergoing sanatorium treatments, together with Castorp, his cousin, Joachim Ziemßen, repeatedly excuses the interruption of his military service by citing the medical orders he was given, to his own regret, due to his fragile health. Ziemßen, of course, translates the strict military discipline he has internalized into the rigid observance of the rules and procedures patrons at the Hotel Berghof are asked to follow. In keeping with this zeitgeist, the depiction of the male body of the soldier was also reflected in pictorial posters until the end of the World War II. Consistent with Prommer's findings on ideal-typical masculinities, the poster of that era staged the soldierly male body as strong, firm, and combat-ready. Often, the single individual took a back seat and merged into an army of homogeneous and battle-ready bodies [p. 125].

From the second half of the nineteenth century, a loose-fitting suit inspired by the military uniform became the definitive garment for male members of the bourgeoisie and remained so for over a century. The suit provided the wearer with freedom of movement, concealed the outlines of the body under several layers of fabric and thus made it invisible to the viewer. In contrast to women's fashion, this "civilian uniform" functioned as a sign of "masculinity elevated to universal humanity"[15] and resulted in the desexualization of the masculine body.

In the picture poster of the late nineteenth and early twentieth century, attributions of stereotypical masculinity were expressed by means of various typologies of representation. In early commercial advertising on the threshold of the twentieth century, male bodies underwent a social differentiation along the lines of economic status. In the process, the fine gentleman visually distinguished himself from the common man. In poster advertising, he was portrayed as an upper-class urban dandy, slim, wearing a tightly fitting tailcoat and a top hat, embodying the financial profiteer of industrialization and promoting high-priced status symbols (such as the automobile).

However, depictions of men in billboard advertising were by no means limited to the display of young, powerful and muscular bodies; on the contrary, the diversity of masculine bodies seems to have been taken into account in advertising to a greater extent than it is today. In the same matter-of-fact manner that idealized male bodies were depicted, men with overweight bodies, at an advanced age,

15   Sabina Brändli, " '… die Männer sollten schöner geputzt sein als die Weiber.' Zur Konstruktion bürgerlicher Männlichkeit im 19. Jahrhundert," in: Kühne, *Männergeschichte* (note 6), p. 114.

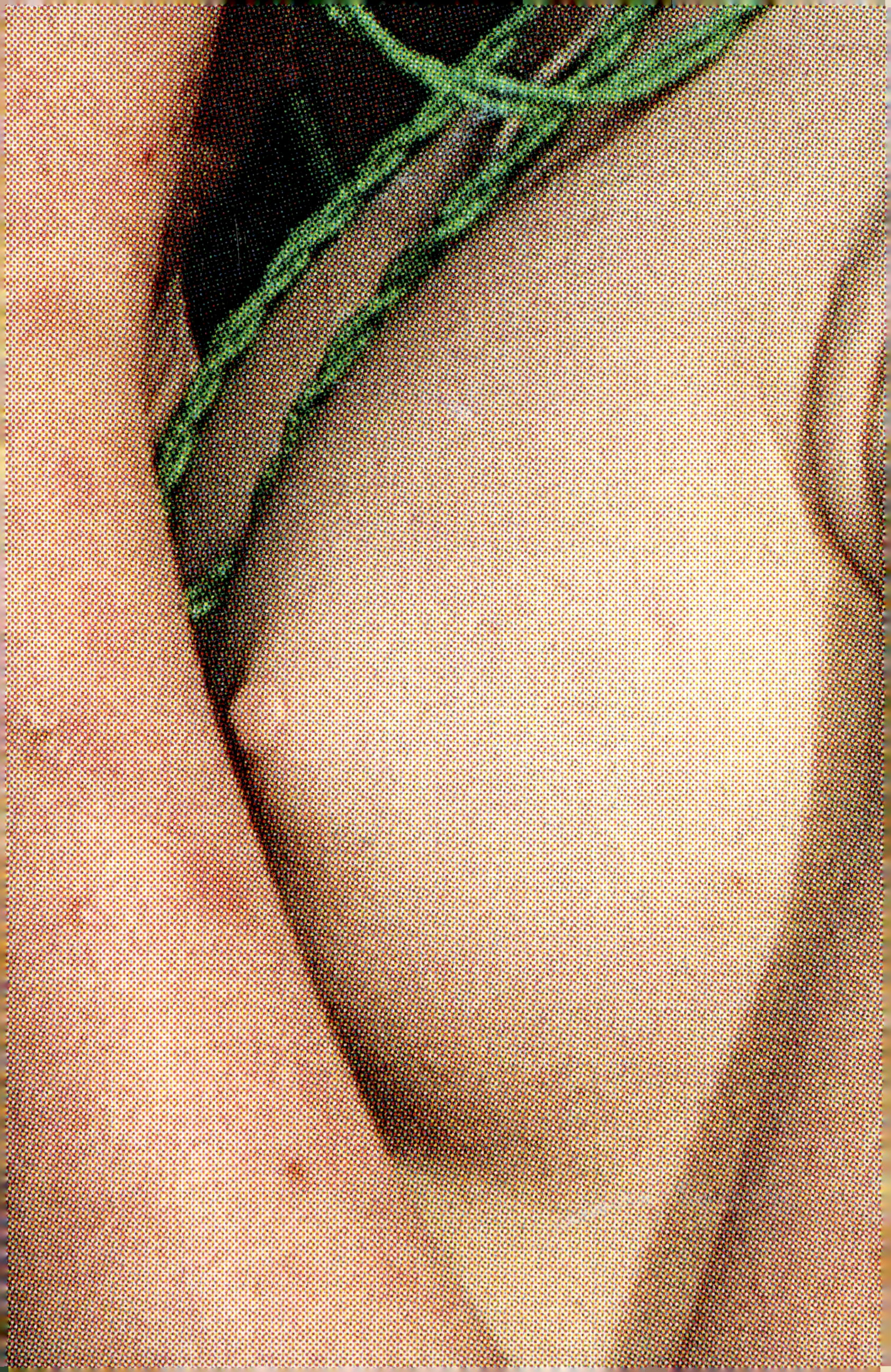

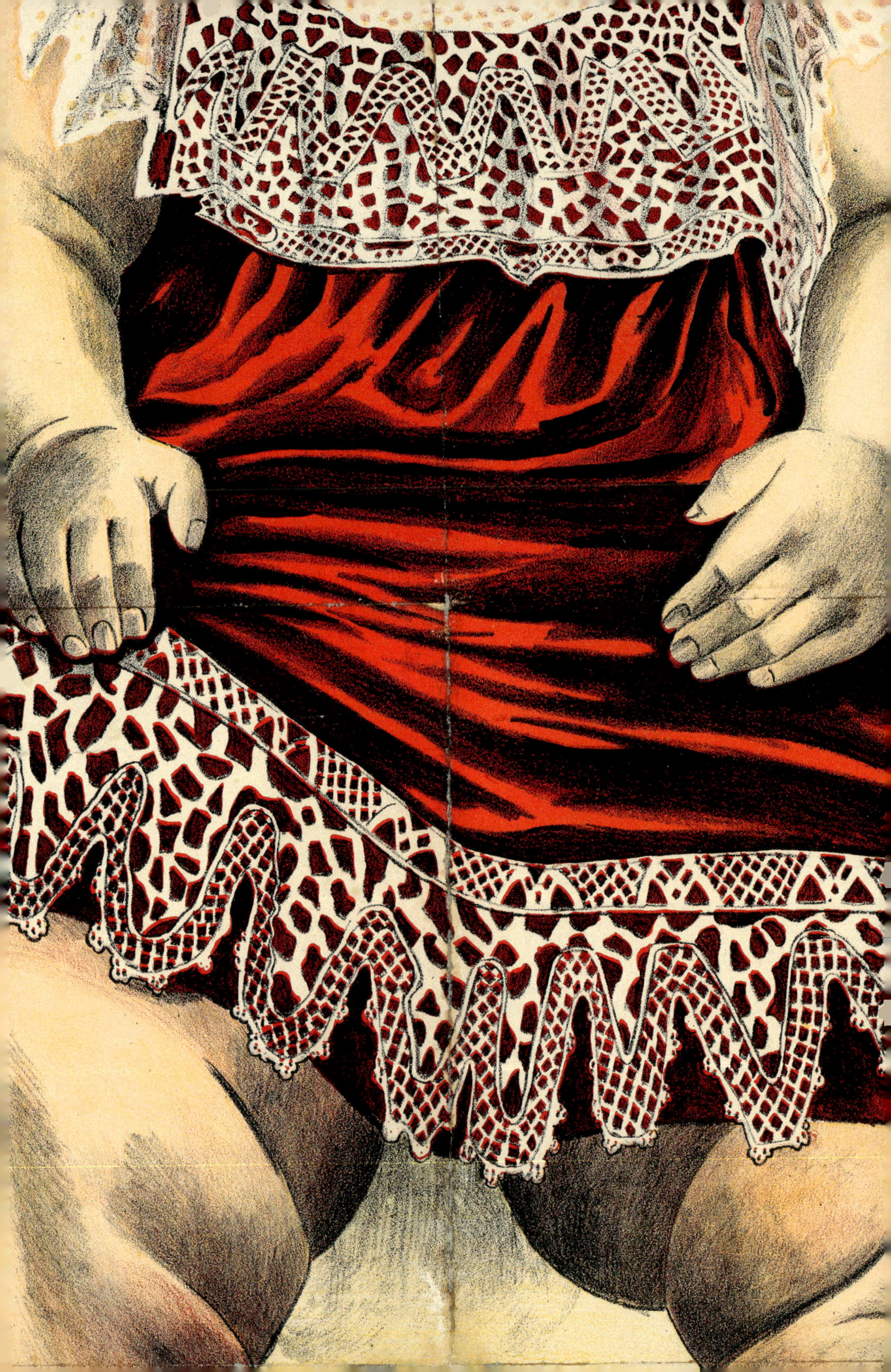

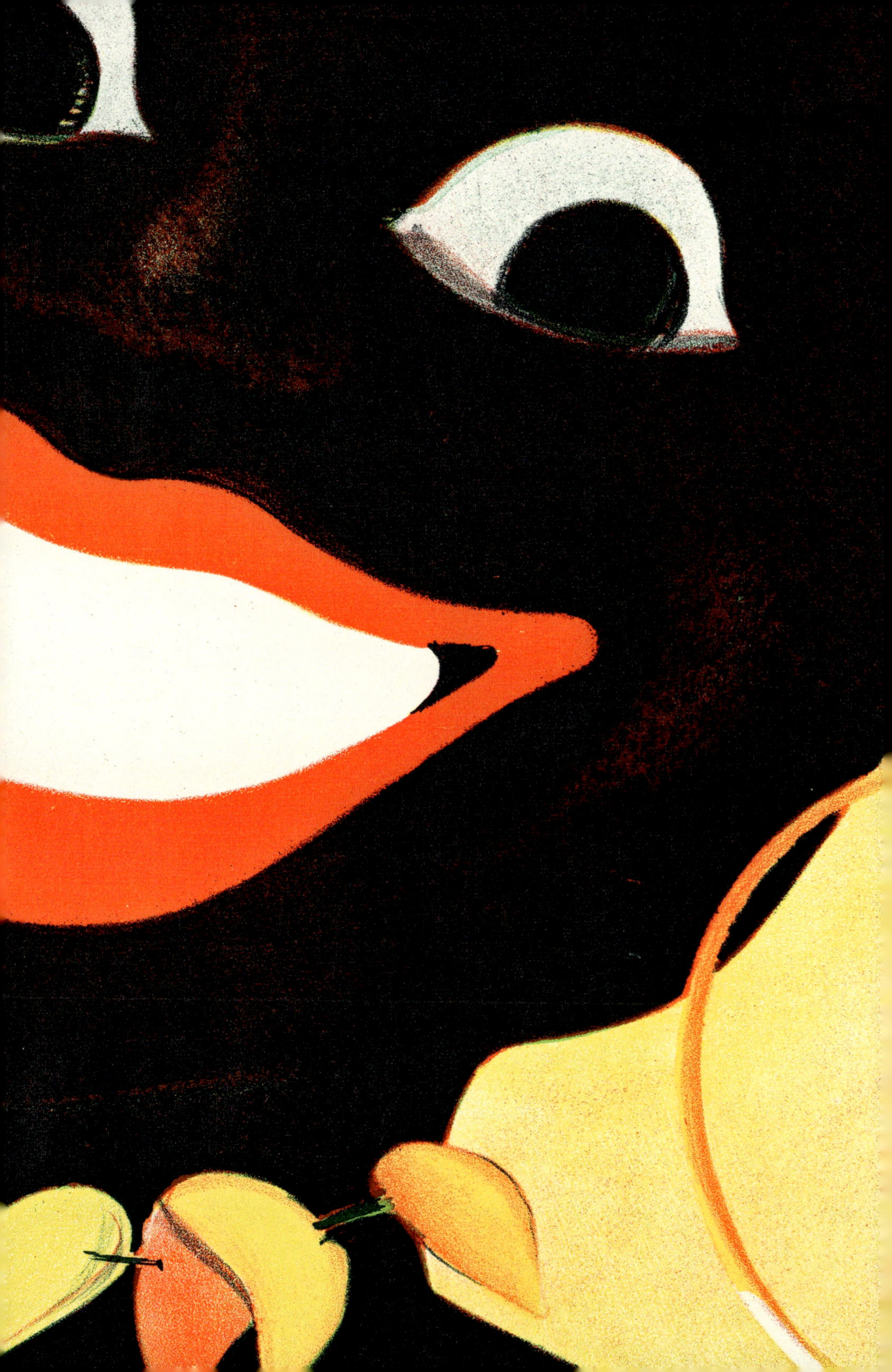

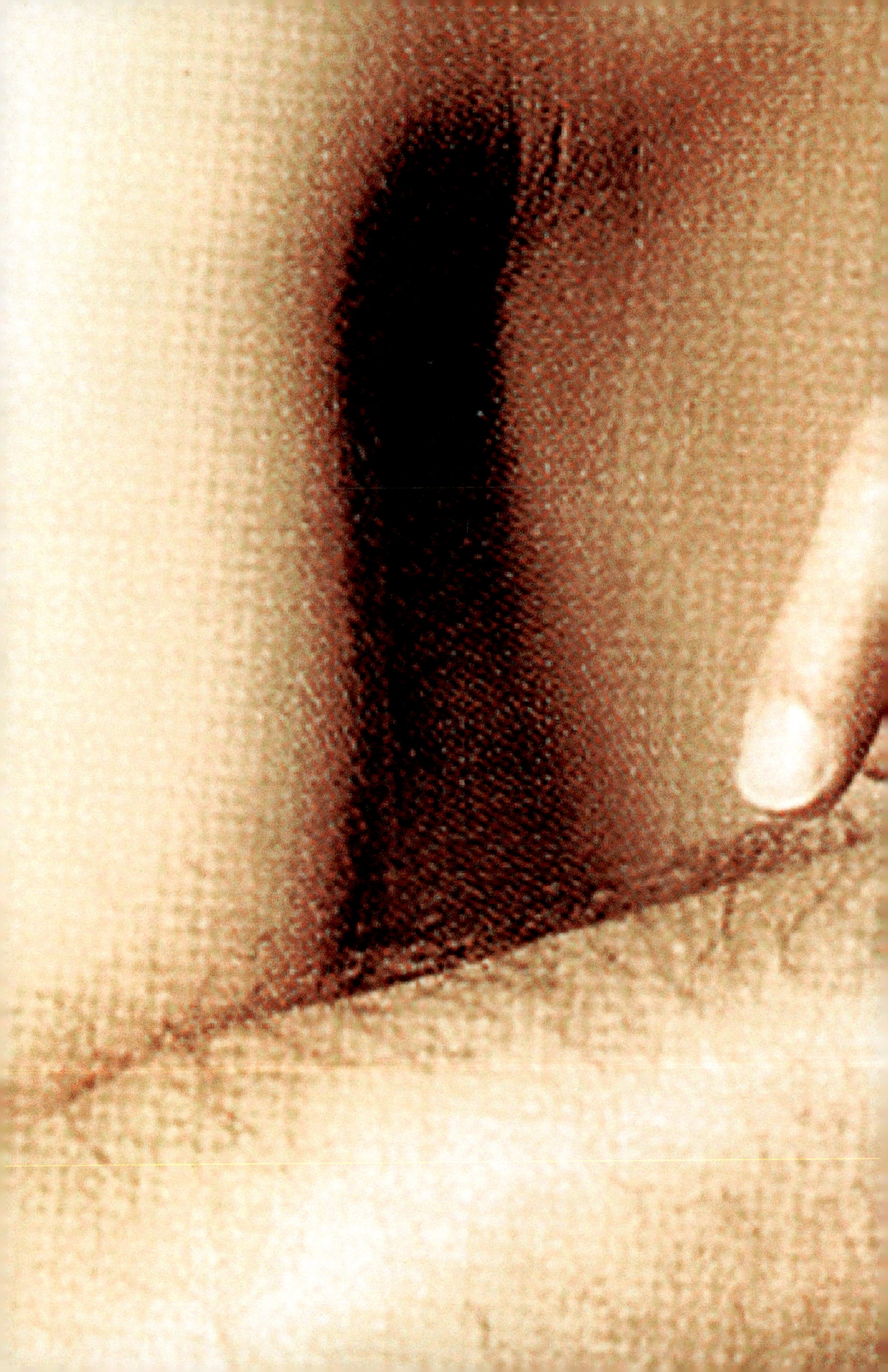

A representational type in advertising with a 120-year tradition: the male expert. Advertisement for Persil, ca. 1900

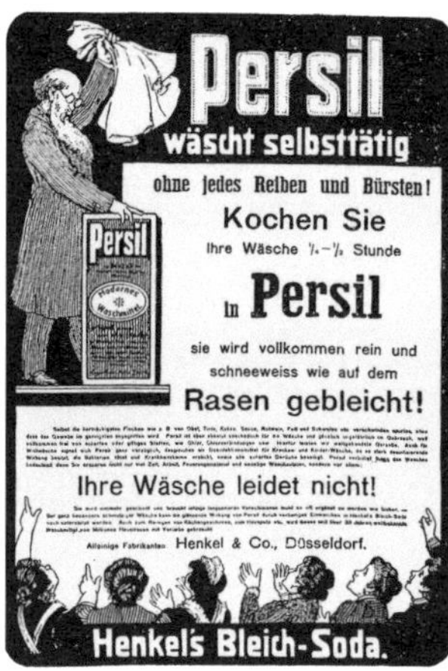

In early pictorial posters, the male beer drinker rarely lived up to normative beauty ideals. Advertisement for Hamburger Bürger Bräu, ca. 1905

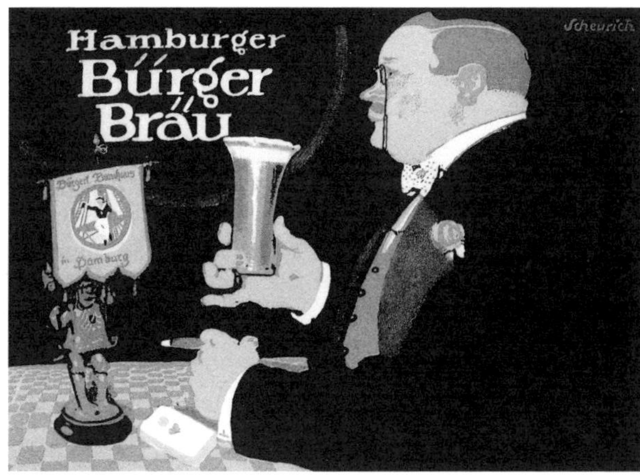

or with "beauty flaws" also appeared in the advertising posters of the time.

One example is the representational type of the expert, which has been a constant presence since the dawn of commercial advertising. Since, according to the reasoning of a patriarchally dominated scientific discourse, rationality was a natural characteristic of men, the expert of that time was exclusively male. The expert is distinguished, among other things, by the long-cut white coat, which later reappears in the context of baby food (Hipp) or toothpaste (Dr. Best) and is designed to vouch for his competence, which is founded on the achievements of scientific research. Additionally, the expert's advanced age conveys the experience and wisdom it takes to produce quality products.

Another representational type that deviated from the normative body ideals of the time was the beer-drinking man. While today's male beer lovers generally live up to normative ideals of beauty, in the first half of the twentieth century they appeared as good-natured pub patrons and mostly overweight senior connoisseurs who often indulged in their penchant for the juice of the barley alone. This representational type dominated beer advertising until the 1960s; in the years that followed, younger, slimmer men as well as women were successively featured in beer advertising as well.[16]

Rock 'n' Roll, Hippies and New Fathers— the Post-War Decades

In the years following World War II, societal notions of masculinity were undergoing radical changes in many Western and Central European countries. Particularly in the newly

16 Heinrich Tappe, "Der Genuss, die Wirkung und ihr Bild: Werte, Konventionen and Motive gesellschaftlichen Alkoholgebrauchs im Spiegel der Werbung," in: Peter Borscheid and Clemens Wischermann (eds.), *Bilderwelt des Alltags: Studien zur Geschichte des Alltags*, Stuttgart 1995, pp. 230–232.

The elegant affluent type of the late 1950s
in an advertisement for Mercedes-Benz, 1958

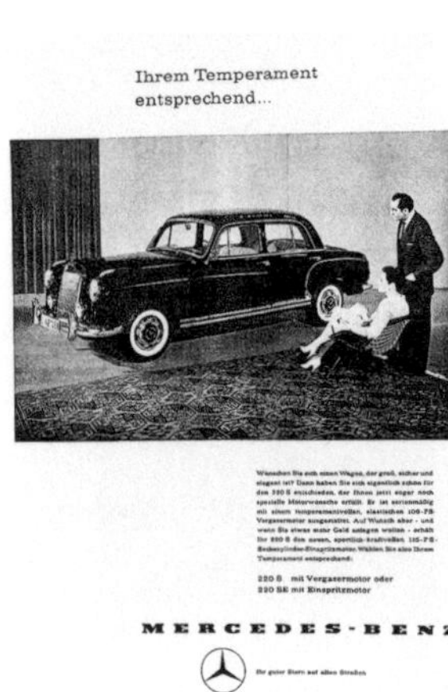

founded Federal Republic of Germany, the image of men that had been propagated by Nazi ideology, which was defined by strength, discipline and militarization, had to be reinvented. The returning soldiers, many of them physically disabled and mentally broken, had adhered to an inhuman ideology and could neither serve as identification figures in advertising nor as positive role models for the new youth culture of the post-war period. On top of that, the American occupation forces countered the image of the snappy Nazi soldier, which still stuck in people's minds, with their markedly cool and relaxed demeanor.

In the 1950s, U.S. pop culture began its triumphant sweep through many European countries. Jazz and rock 'n' roll music as well as role models such as James Dean or Elvis Presley introduced an American way of life to European audiences, which the young avant-garde enthusiastically sought to emulate.[17] Instead of uniforms or suits, jeans along with leather and college jackets came into fashion. Hats disappeared, revealing pompadour hairstyles, which were brought into shape with pomade. Advertisements of the time portrayed this "new type of man" as an often casual go-getter with sunglasses and showed him promoting, for example, fancy cars or fashionable clothes. In the world of advertising imagery, he complemented the more prevalent "affluent type"—a middle-aged or elderly man who, after years of privation during the war, had profited from the overall growth of the economy and now enjoyed the pleasant aspects of life.[18] Not much was felt of these developments on the other side of the Iron Curtain. Under the control of the communist propaganda apparatus, bronze casts, mosaics, murals, and advertising posters

17   Kaspar Maase, "Entblösste Brust und schwingende Hüfte: Momentaufnahmen von der Jugend der fünfziger Jahre," in: Kühne, *Männergeschichte* (note 6), pp. 194–200.
18   Raphaela Dreßler, "Vom Patriarchat zum androgynen Lustobjekt – 50 Jahre Männer im *stern*," in: Christina Holtz-Bacha (ed.), *Stereotype? Frauen und Männer in der Werbung*, 2nd ed., Wiesbaden 2011, pp. 145–147.

Florian Diener

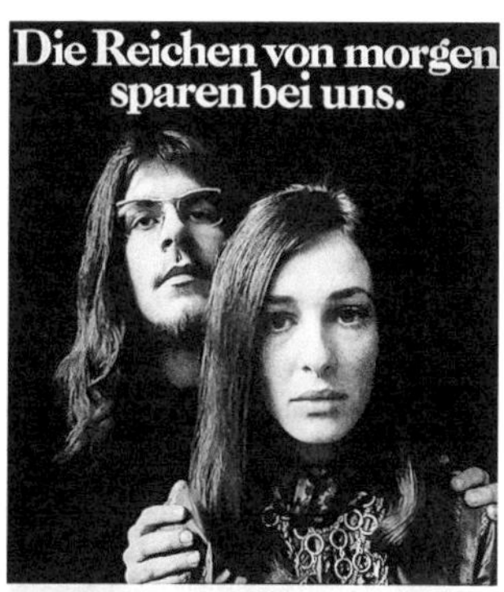

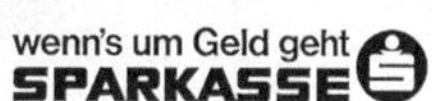

continued to depict male bodies as soldiers ready for battle, heroic cosmonauts or vigorous proletarians and peasants [(p. 129)].

The period of the late 1960s and 1970s was marked by powerful social upheaval, which also resulted in a redefinition of the male gender role identity. The confluence of 1968, Woodstock, the women's movement and the worldwide protests against the Vietnam War gave rise to the hippie movement and, with it, to an increasing aversion among young people towards traditional hegemonic models of masculinity, which were still largely dominated by militarism.[19] Inspired by feminist calls for more equality, progressive concepts of masculinity began to emerge, which stood in stark contrast to those of the "Golden Age of Marriage" of the 1950s and 1960s. At the same time, the imagery and metaphors associated with the male hippy body, such as long hair, colorful clothing, and an often unkempt appearance, decidedly set them apart from the establishment. Singers like Jimmy Hendrix and Bob Dylan, as well as bands like The Who and The Beatles, served as a blueprint for a lifestyle defined by "love, peace and happiness." In many places, differing views regarding the "revolutionaries" and "radicals" created divisions in society and raised concerns about the decline of conventional mores, traditional role models and sexual morals.[20]

The image of men in consumer advertising also changed. While it predominately showed dapper men with well-fitting suits and coiffed hair in the 1960s, it suddenly featured long-haired rebels in jeans in the early 1970s. The German Sparkasse savings bank ad that read "Die Reichen von morgen sparen bei uns" (The Rich of Tomorrow Save with Us)

19　Wolfgang Schmale, *Geschichte der Männlichkeit in Europa (1450–2000)*, Vienna 2003, pp. 246–249.
20　Julia Paulus, Eva-Maria Silies, and Kerstin Wolff, "Die Bundesrepublik aus geschlechterhistorischer Perspektive," in: idem (eds.), *Zeitgeschichte als Geschlechtergeschichte. Neue Perspektiven auf die Bundesrepublik*, Frankfurt a. M. / New York 2012, p. 24.

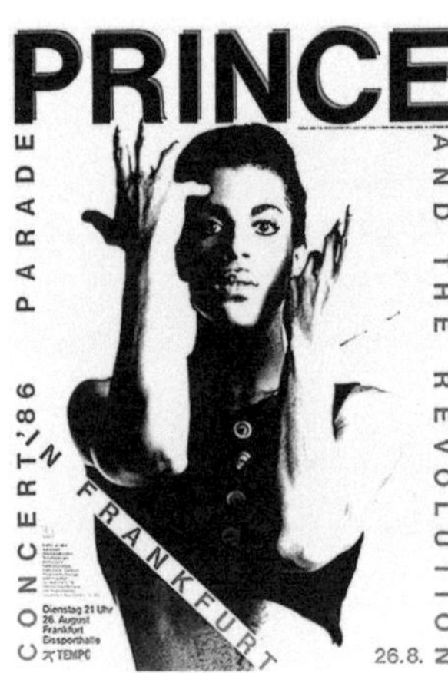

illustrated and captured the intergenerational conflict
as well as the newfound self-assurance of a rebellious
youth that resisted the established order.[21] The protest
movements of 1968 spawned not only new bodily identities, but brought about a realignment of the gender
roles promoted in ads and commercials, as well. Thus,
starting in the 1970s, men began to appear in advertisements (at first in homeopathic doses) who were actively
involved in raising children or doing household chores.

Modern Masculinities

In the 1980s, the further differentiation of male gender roles
that had been set in motion continued to progress. On
movie screens, in pop music and in commercial publicity,
a diverse range of masculine identities replaced the previous repertoire of one-dimensional gender roles. On the
one hand, movie theater fans celebrated toxic masculinities, which were characterized, among other things, by
high-risk, aggressive behavior, the chauvinistic denigration
of women and LGBTQIA* members, but also by a willful
display of a lack of empathy and emotion. Arnold Schwar-
zenegger playing the Terminator, for example, or Sylvester
Stallone in the role of John J. Rambo [(p. 124)] were stylized
as heroes on account of their violent and assertive habitus,
and their muscular bodybuilding looks became emblematic of this notion of masculinity. By contrast, androgynous
antiheroes like Michael Jackson and Prince danced their
way into the hearts of millions of fans and scaled the
Olympus of pop culture on the strength of their talent and
their alternative ideas of masculinity, which defied traditional expectations. From the mid-1980s onwards, media

21   Peter Borscheid,
"Sparsamkeit und Sicher-
heit. Werbung für Banken,
Sparkassen und Versi-
cherungen," in: Borscheid /
Wischermann, *Bilder-
welt des Alltags* (note 16),
p. 337.

representations of androgyny and homosexuality carefully began to question the concept of heteronormativity as an integral part of masculinity. Even if male homosexuality became visible in 1990s advertising, which played a significant role in the construction and mass media dissemination of stereotypical body images of homosexual men, in quantitative terms, these representations were and are absolutely exceptional phenomena [(p. 129)].[22]

Since the mid-1980s, the differentiation of masculinities has also been accompanied by increased sexualization and aestheticization of the male body in the media. Male bodies are supposed to be muscular, well-groomed, and strong. The fitness trend that had commenced (and continues to this day) has ensured that the general population was able to strive for those physical ideals.[23] The aesthetic target values of modern masculinity have been defined, among others, by *People Magazine*, which has awarded the title "Sexiest Man Alive" annually since 1985. As Raphaela Dreßler notes, it was not only in movies and TV series, but also in advertising that golden boys and sex symbols were increasingly featured.[24] The media representation of a muscular appearance was no longer an expression of proletarian manpower, but rather served an aesthetic end in itself and the display of the male body [(p. 128)]. Such ideal-typical masculinities were not only well-trained and good-looking; they also countered the "bad boy image" of the 1980s by offering insights into their own emotional world, by appearing empathetic and friendly. Especially in the melodrama of the 1990s, emotional masculinities conquered the screen.

Ever since the turn of the millennium, opportunities for masculine identification and thus the socially accepted range of male role repertoires have expanded significantly. Thus, cliché-laden notions of masculinity that applaud toxic behavior, professional success or technical savvy exist, in equal measure, alongside men who work in jobs primarily attributed to women, live in queer relationships, or raise children on their own. Since 2010, social media influencers have increasingly joined the ranks of those exploring the conventionalized boundaries of masculine body identities and role repertoires. Against this background, we are witnessing a trend towards gender assimilation of aesthetic bodies in media representations. In the 1980s, Christiane Schmerl observed, and criticized, that women in advertising found themselves in a "cosmetic straitjacket," which afforded them significantly less latitude for physical

22 Diener, *Stereotype Darstellungen* (note 13), pp. 316–317.
23 Klaus R. Schroeter, "Altersbilder als Körperbilder: Doing Age by Bodyfication," in: Frank Berner, Judith Rossow, and Klaus-Peter Schwitzer (eds.), *Individuelle und kulturelle Altersbilder: Expertisen zum Sechsten Altenbericht der Bundesregierung*, Wiesbaden 2012, pp. 172–175.
24 Dreßler, "50 Jahre Männer im *stern*" (note 18), p. 151.

representation than men.[25] However, studies show that men featured in advertising have likewise become increasingly handsome since 1950,[26] and that they have ever more frequently become subject to normative beauty standards since the beginning of 2000. In 2020, men were far more likely to be attractive, wealthy, kempt, and athletic in advertisements than they were in 2000.[27]

"When is a man a man?" We find far more answers to this question in the media today than in the early days of the picture poster. Still, there is reason to doubt that Hans Castorp would have come to terms more easily with his role as a man in the 2020s; but he surely would have appreciated some of the facets of modern masculinity.

25　Christiane Schmerl, "Kosmetische Zwangs-jacken," in: idem (ed.), *Frauenfeindliche Werbung: Sexismus als heimlicher Lehrplan*, Reinbek bei Hamburg 1983, pp. 41–47.
26　Guido Zurstiege, *Mannsbilder—Männlichkeit in der Werbung: Zur Darstellung von Männern in der Anzeigenwerbung der 50er, 70er und 90er Jahre*, Opladen 1998, p. 190.
27　Diener, *Stereotype Darstellungen* (note 13), p. 406.

Black Bodyship Entangled: Between Essentialism and Constructivism

Marilyn Umurungi

"I am an invisible man … I am a man of substance, flesh and bone, fiber and liquids—and I might even be said to possess a mind. I am invisible, understand, simply because people refuse to see me … When they approach me they see only my surroundings, themselves, or figments of their imagination—indeed, everything and anything except me."[1]

When, in 1909, photographer Robert Lohmeyer arrived in former German Southwest Africa, now Namibia, aboard the steam lighter Martha, one of the coastal fleet of the Deutsche Ost-Afrika-Linie (German East Africa Line), he had hardly slept a wink all night. He had a hard time keeping his curiosity in check, because for months the news of fabulous diamond finds in the African colony had triggered something of a gold rush fever across the German Empire. Twenty-five years earlier, Bremen merchant Franz Adolf Eduard Lüderitz had succeeded in convincing local tribal leaders to sell large parts of their territory. Subsequently, the country from the Orange River to the Kunene River was first declared the so-called "protectorate" of German Southwest Africa and later a German colony. In a bay in the ǁKharas region of southern Namibia, blue shimmering "Klippekies" (cliff pebbles), as the Germans called the diamonds, could be picked up from the sand on the beach and in the dunes of the desert hinterland. Lohmeyer, who was thirty at the time and later went down in history as a pioneer of color photography, had been commissioned by the Internationaler Weltverlag publishing house in Berlin to take color photographs around the four German colonies (Togo, Cameroon, German East Africa and German

1 Ralph Ellison, *Invisible Man*, New York 1952, p. 7.

Southwest Africa) following Adolf Miethe's system, so as to spark enthusiasm among the German population for the colonies and colonization.

German Southwest Africa was not Lohmeyer's first stop—he had previously been assigned to travel to Togo—but it was probably the one that was most disappointing, as he later wrote to people back home in Germany.[2] The coast was bleak and not a sight that would allow the public to appreciate the beauty of the colonies, because it consisted only of desert and sand. Lohmeyer had been tasked with taking pictures of "types" among the population: The images were supposed to show the indigenous peoples of Africa, classified by ethnic groups and tribes, and ostensibly illustrate that they differed in character, appearance, and degree of civilization. At that point, Lohmeyer presumably did not anticipate the significance his pictures would later acquire. What he certainly did know at the time was that he would return home with the very first color photographs ever taken of the inhabitants of this continent. The empire was eagerly awaiting Lohmeyer's pictures of Africa. When he finally sent the first prints, they caused a huge stir, far beyond the borders of the German Empire.[3]

The German Empire did not only need "pictures of types" because it wanted to show what the populations of its colonies looked like. Two stereotypical images of African people prevailed since eighteenth century Europe: that of the "savages" who, according to Geneva-born Jean-Jacques Rousseau, were closer to the "pure" natural state of man than Europeans, by virtue of their simplicity, and that of the "uncivilized" strangers. Rousseau believed that advances in knowledge and technology contributed to human misery by causing us to develop desires and passions that primitive peoples supposedly did not know.[4] Thus the image of the "noble savage" became established in the wider culture as a projection of the notion of a lost, peaceful, more natural world (as yet) untouched by civilization and progress.[5] This supposedly positive and, as was later often argued, "valorizing representation" of primitive peoples was paralleled by tendencies towards presenting African people as backward, impure, and uncivilized in a negative sense. Photography was the best tool for this purpose, as these "pictures of types" were intended to reflect precisely this view by focusing on (external) differences between Germans and Africans, thus confirming the biologistic theories of racial doctrine. More specifically,

2   Lohmeyer was portrayed in the documentary *Die Erfindung des Rassismus in Farbe*. Directed by Michael Mueller, Germany 2021.
3   Ibid.
4   Jean-Jacques Rousseau, *Discours sur l'origine et les fondements de l'inégalité parmi les hommes*, Amsterdam 1755.
5   Cf. Achille Mbembe, *Critique of Black Reason,* trans. Laurent Dubois, Durham, NC 2017.

the images were designed to show that the European race was superior to all other races in appearance, degree of civilization, and ultimately in character.[6] Photography thus became the most important accomplice of racist colonial policy.

The Body at the Focus of the Gaze
The invention of (color) photography, the colonial expansion of Europe as well as the development and popularization of ethnology and ethnography were contemporaneous and mutually conditioned phenomena that supported each other. According to social anthropologist Hartmut Krech, anthropology as the scientific study of human self-knowledge and self-encounter emerged in the wake of the introduction of printmaking. The term "anthropology" first appeared in the magnum opus of German philosopher Magnus Hundt (1449–1519).[7] Presenting diagrams he called "situs figures," Hundt sought to enlighten readers about the position and function of the organs in the human body. As knowledge of the human body progressed, interest increased not only in somatology, but also in the study of human behavior and environmental influences on genetic predisposition and evolution. In his *Anthropographia*, French physician Jean Riolan (1580–1657) celebrated insights into the workings of the human body as the "true philosophy," even examining social conditions in the context of anatomy.[8]

Nevertheless, Riolan and his colleagues attached greater importance to physiological observation, which distinguished people according to their outer appearance, skin color and facial shape than to knowledge about organic functions in the human body or its sociality. As the Nigerian Associate Professor of Sociology Oyèrónkẹ̀ Oyěwùmí noted in *The Invention of Women*, this entails the idea that a society is primarily made up of bodies—male bodies, female bodies, Jewish bodies, Aryan bodies, Black bodies, white bodies, rich bodies, poor bodies.[9] Oyěwùmí speaks of bodies in two ways: on the one hand as a metonymy for biology, and on the other hand in the sense of the essentialization of corporeality, which, in her view, determines the being in Western culture.

In Oyěwùmí's view, the body acquires its own logic in Western ontology. Under this logic, the visualization and gendering of the body becomes the object of negotiation and the norming of embodied subjects. In other words, the body becomes the central site of the construction of

6   Note: This essay includes content with, in part, racist, sexist and discriminatory terms that may be offensive or distressing to some readers.
7   See Hartmut Krech, "Lichtbilder vom Menschen: Vom Typenbild zur anthropologischen Fotografie," in: *Fotogeschichte: Beiträge zur Geschichte und Ästhetik der Fotografie*, vol. 4 (1984), no. 14, pp. 3–15.
8   Ibid., p. 15.
9   Oyèrónkẹ́ Oyěwùmí, *The Invention of Women: Making an African Sense of Western Gender Discourses*, London 1997.

legitimacy in a society.[10] The question as to the legitimacy and disciplining of bodies was explored by French philosopher Michel Foucault in the 1970s. In his lectures on *The Birth of Biopolitics*, Foucault explained how, under the logic of biopolitics, the body becomes a text, a system of signs that can be decoded, read and read into.[11] Consequently, the body becomes the foundation on which the social order is based and which legitimizes it.

Oyĕwùmí's reflections are particularly valuable because they put into stark relief how, in this Western logic of the body, the body is always in view and always the focus of the gaze. In historical terms, the most enduring gaze is that of differentiation, the one that racializes and is gender specific. Oyĕwùmí highlights how prioritizing the gaze in Western anthropology facilitated the regime of a racializing and gendering gaze that became the instrument through which European knowledge about other cultures was produced.

The Concept of Visual Representation and Its Relationship to Hegemonic Discourses

In order for the geographical classification of humanity according to races to take shape, several events had to coincide, which included, in addition to colonial expansion, Orientalism in literature and painting as well as the invention and proliferation of photography. Of course, photography would later become the subject of criticism for its reductionist character. Half a century after the inflationary dissemination of anthropological photographs of non-European[12] people, writer and cultural theorist Susan Sontag took a critical stance on this matter: "The photograph is a thin slice of space as well as time … Through photographs, the world becomes a series of unrelated, free-standing particles."[13] Photography thus allows for a re-arrangement that is far removed from the original primary experience and, consequently, facilitates altogether different associations.

If we follow Sontag's interpretations, images can also be understood as a mere construction. Foucault defined them as *discursive* constructions. This is based on the notion that images invariably function as representations that are instrumental in the production of meaning and reality. This discursive-constructivist approach developed by Foucault has proven to be particularly plausible for visual representations, as it is a historically situated approach. Visual representations can thus never be considered in

10   Cf. Elke Grittmann et al. (eds.), *Körperbilder—Körperpraktiken: Visualisierung und Vergeschlechtlichung von Körpern in Medienkulturen*, Cologne 2018.
11   Michel Foucault, *The Birth of Biopolitics: Lectures at the Collège de France, 1978–1979*. ed. Michel Senellart, trans. Graham Burchell, New York 2008.
12   I use this term with caution here, as *non-white* and *non-European* can also be taken to mean that whiteness and Europeanness represent the norm and all other people a deviation, mutation, or variation of white people and the characteristics associated with whiteness.
13   Susan Sontag, *On Photography*, New York 1977, p. 20.

14 Cf. Anika-Brigitte Kollarz, *Aus dem Rahmen—Ein weisses Gedicht auf 'nem schwarzen Gesicht? Visuelle Repräsentationen Schwarzer Frauen zwischen der deutschen Kolonialzeit und der Weimarer Republik,* dissertation Technical University of Darmstadt, 2012.

15 Here, Black and white do not denote skin colors, but social and political constructions in a global power structure. Black spelled with a capital "B" is a political self-designation intended to emphasize that it refers to the collective experience of people of African and Afro-diasporic descent. White carries a different set of meanings; capitalizing the word in this context risks following the lead of white supremacists. The term "white" refers to the sociopolitical position of those so designated: belonging to the majority within the framework of racializing ideas, exercising power, setting norms. When used to indicate one's own membership in a privileged group, it also serves as a self-designation.

16 I have intentionally refrained from reproducing racist and discriminatory terms in the selected source citations. Where they are necessary for our understanding, only the first letter is shown and the remaining letters are replaced by asterisks.

17 Cf. Terri J. Gordon, "A 'Saxophone in the Movement': Josephine Baker and the Music of Dance," in: *Nottingham French Studies,* vol. 43 (2004), no. 1, pp. 39–52.

isolation from social and cultural processes and are always part of the discourses of the societies in which they are created.[14] Foucault's investigations have contributed to our understanding of discourse as a system of representations. In the Foucauldian sense, discourses are conceived as practices that systematically form the objects of which they speak. The knowledge that is produced in and through discourses is always linked to power (and bodies) as well. One highly accessible aspect of Foucault's theory about the relation between body, knowledge and power is the following observation: When discourses materialize in bodies and attributions are thereby normalized and naturalized, they always result in a shift in power. Within the discourse on (the perception of) bodies, three strategies of representation have decisively influenced the history of the representation of Black bodies: individualization, typification or stereotyping and fetishization.

Wild, Erotic and Exotic— Black Female Bodies as Entertainment for white High Societies[15]

In 1810, Saartjie (Sarah) Baartman was taken to London and publicly exhibited there because of her "exotic" physical features. When she performed as the "Hottentot Venus" for the amusement of upper-class London audiences, this arguably marked the beginning of the development of a highly specific genre in the European entertainment industry, which I am cautiously naming the "Dancing Black Venus." Over a century later, French revue critic André Levinson referred to Josephine Baker, the Black American dancer, as the "Black Venus" when she appeared at the Théâtre des Champs-Élysées in 1925 and wowed Paris audiences with her performance of the Charleston (p. 134). The French had never seen this exuberant dance before. After seeing Baker in the premiere of *La Revue N****,*[16] Levinson wrote that Josephine Baker's poses had the power of "the finest examples of n**** sculpture." She was, he noted, no longer a "grotesque Black dancing girl" but the "Black Venus" that had haunted the poet Baudelaire in his dreams. This colonial and racist interpretation of her performance made Josephine Baker an overnight sensation. Two years later, she made her first movie appearance in the feature film *La Sirène des Tropiques* and earned more money than any other entertainer in Europe.[17] At that time, people were put on public display in so-called "human zoos" in various major European cities. The main attraction that drew the public to these events was the display of foreign, non-white bodies in the nude. The fact that the individualized nudity exhibited was often elaborately staged, was irrelevant to the voyeuristic spectators.

As with Baartman, Baker's particular appeal to Europeans—both men and women—was based on her Black body, to which all manner of qualities were attributed, including "wild," "erotic," "exotic," "raw," and "natural." All these attributes were designed to stress the ways in which she was different in contrast to white bodies. While Baartman decided not to return to South Africa when an attempt was made to force her into doing so in 1815, Baker returned to the United States, only to realize, once there, that she had become the target of sexist and racist defamation by the American public. The *New York Times* and other newspapers referred to her as "n**** whore,"[18] and many hotels and restaurants refused to welcome her. The hypersexualization of her body in Europe earned Baker hate and rejection in her homeland. She therefore moved back to Paris where she passed away in 1975.

Baartman also died in Paris. In his notes about her body, French anatomist Henri-Marie Ducrotay de Blainville wrote that her shoulders were "graceful," her arms "slender," her hands and feet equally "charming" and "pretty." He went on to say that she could dance according to the traditions of her country. However, as he was fully invested in his theories on racial evolution, he did not forget to mention that Baartman also possessed ape-like traits.[19]

Helpless, Poor and Grateful—
Black Bodies and white Altruism

The notion of the "type," or of "pictures of types," is intrinsically based on the ambiguity of norm and deviation. In most cases, a representation of a "type" is understood to denote a certain group of people (individuals) characterized by unique features and, above all, by their Otherness. In this sense, "the concept of the type distinguishes both standardization according to a uniform scheme and deviation from the norm, so that the contrasts that also come into play between the type, in the sense of group or class, and type, in the sense of an odd character, are mutually dependent. This binarity culminates in stereotyping."[20]

The three fundamental effects of stereotyping are naturalization, essentialization and reduction. The essentialization and reduction to—often arbitrary—characteristics

18   Ibid., p. 41.
19   Clifton Crais and Pamela Scully, *Sara Baartman and the Hottentot Venus: A Ghost Story and a Biography*, Princeton, NJ 2009.
20   Cf. Kollarz, "Aus dem Rahmen," in: Bernd Stiegler (ed.), *Texte zur Theorie der Fotografie*, Stuttgart 2010, p. 35.

facilitates the fixation of binary opposites (Black–white, woman–man, et cetera). British sociologist Stuart Hall considered the separation of norm and difference an essential component of hegemonic power. According to Hall, stereotypes are used to establish, legitimize and exercise power.[21] Under colonialism, hegemony was forged largely through the development of specific racialized types (and, at the same time, stereotypes) and racialized discourses. In colonial societies, the level of stereotyping of the colonized continued to escalate over time. In this context, it is important to note that stereotypes refer both to imaginary ideas and to what is perceived as real. Hall understood fantasy and projection as fundamental to the development of stereotypes.[22]

With the advent of "development aid" in the 1960s and the era in which many African states successively gained their independence, a highly specific stereotype of Black bodies was widely propagated: the image of poor bodies in need of help [(p. 143)]. The notion of the "white man's burden," which Rudyard Kipling had coined and which had already served to legitimize Christian missionary work, now lived on in a variety of approaches to "development aid" while also finding its way into the imagery of international aid organizations. Emaciated children with bloated bellies and big wide eyes or helpless parents unable to provide for their offspring were at the core of the visual narrative of frequently paternalistic "development aid" from the 1960s to the 1980s. However, this form of aid hardly differed from colonial practices in terms of its power dynamics. Today, there is much discussion in international "development aid" circles about the "decolonization" of their visual language and a more critical approach to the power relations involved in working together. In international cooperation, the image of the malnourished, powerless African has become less common and collaboration, rather than paternalism, is the order of the day. But the old ideas of poor, needy Black people have not faded all that much, neither in the archives nor in the minds of Europeans.

Cool, Strong and Invincible— the Unscathed Black Male Body in white Fantasies

There is hardly another Black body that has sparked as much fabulous storytelling as Muhammad Ali's. For almost thirty years, Ali held the Guinness record as the person

21 Cf. Stuart Hall, *Rassismus und kulturelle Identität*, Hamburg 2021.
22 Ibid.

Muhammad Ali defeating Sonny Liston on May 25, 1965, in Lewiston, Maine. Ali knocked out Liston with a blow that went down in history as the "phantom punch." Photo: Neil Leifer

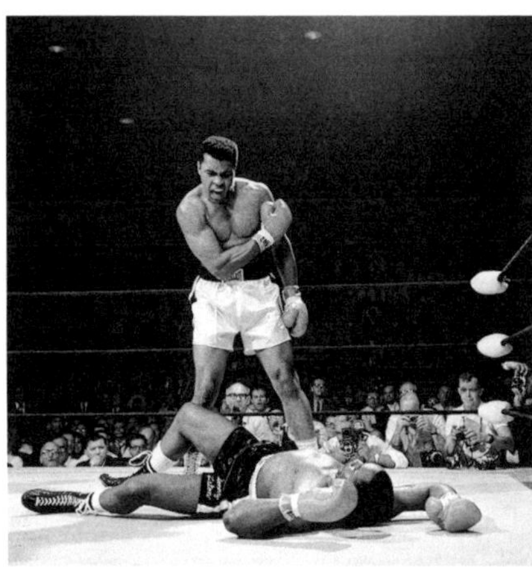

most written about in history. Without a doubt, "The Greatest" ranks as one of the most influential and famous athletes in competitive sports in the twentieth century. His body was the focal point of this fascination, which reached its peak in the 1980s. For decades, Ali was portrayed by the popular media as the fastest and most agile boxer in the world, whom nothing and no one could touch. Ali himself also turned the fetishization of his body into a practice of self-empowerment and self-determination. Before his 1964 fight with then world heavyweight champion Sonny Liston, he was asked how he was planning to get the win. Ali answered with his famous phrase: "Float like a butterfly, sting like a bee."[23]

Basketball player Michael Jordan [(p. 160)] similarly tapped into the narrative of the cool, strong, invincible Black man when his popularity soared in the 1990s and he was lauded with similar titles as Ali: "The Greatest of All Time." The fact that these two men achieved cult status at a time when Black men in the United States (and beyond) were repeatedly portrayed as aggressive, hypersexual and violent is by no means a contradiction. Both Ali and Jordan are good examples of the various facets of racialized fetishization, which is essentially characterized by differentiation, naturalization and the reduction of a person to his or her body. The immense strength and invulnerability of Black men that (colonial) fantasies associated with the Black body had both a fascinating and threatening effect on white society—which created the need for it to identify these differences. It was, of course, not only the fetishization of their bodies that earned Ali and Jordan their iconic status, but also their passion for sports and tenacity in their

23   "Float like a butterfly, sting like a bee," in: Anthony O. Edmonds, *Muhammad Ali: A Biography*, Westport, CT 2005.

disciplines. However, the repeat reactivation of the inscription of their bodies in the discourse of supposed invulnerability greatly contributed to the fact that they are remembered today as the "strongest" and "greatest" of their time.

Forgotten and/or Hypervisible— the Negotiation of Black Bodies in white Discourses

In a groundbreaking exhibition at the Musée d'Orsay in Paris in the spring of 2019, which focused on the "forgotten" Black sitters of French avant-garde artists, Black identities moved into the spotlight of the international art world. It was supposed to be the first exhibition that focused on Black bodies in European painting. But why exactly? And why just then? In Switzerland, Black models are increasingly seen in advertising, too—staged as main figures, and not just as a counterpoint to white models or background characters. Reactions among the Swiss population are varied: Some complain about the overrepresentation of minority groups, others are glad they are "included" in the marketing plans of diversity-minded companies. Still others remain skeptical and are convinced that the increasing trend towards "non-white" models is simply an ethno-marketing tactic designed to increase consumer acceptance among marginalized groups. This, they maintain, has nothing to do with their representation and recognition in society.

The fact that "being non-white" can have a high marketing value, especially in an advertising context, is something that Christine Bischoff already addressed in her essay "Kommt die nächste Miss Schweiz aus dem Kongo?" (Will the Next Miss Switzerland Come from Congo?). Here, Bischoff explained how major advertising campaigns have frequently shown that not only is the "staging of the opposites 'Black' and 'white'" used as a media marketing strategy, but so is "the performative play with an ethnicizing color palette."[24] In the 1990s, the Benetton company pretentiously played with the strategy of the Black-white opposition as a constructive marker, declaring this kind of juxtaposition, in Bischoff's words, to be a "plea for cross-boundary friendship, harmonious international understanding, and the encounter of world cultures."[25]

But how did this increased focus on Black bodies come about? Certainly, international solidarity with the Black Lives Matter (BLM) movement has had its influence on the current hypervisibility of Black identities. But George Floyd died in 2020 and the exhibition at the Orsay opened one

24   Christine Bischoff, "Kommt die nächste Miss Schweiz aus dem Kongo? Postkoloniale Blickregimes in den Medien," in: Patricia Purtschert, Barbara Lüthi, and Francesca Falk (eds.), *Postkoloniale Schweiz: Formen und Folgen eines Kolonialismus ohne Kolonien*, Bielefeld 2012, pp. 65–88, here p. 70.
25   Ibid.

year earlier. One possible explanation could be that the need for the representation of a pluralistic society has grown and demands for it have become more explicit. As far as I can tell, attributing the hypervisibility of Black identities solely to the BLM movement misses the big picture. For several years now, voices in art and academia have been pointing out that it is imperative to continually challenge one-dimensional perspectives and bipolarity. A multilateral understanding of research that deconstructs ethnocentric, androcentric and Eurocentric gaze regimes has led to a new awareness of race and gender, and ultimately to greater courage in dissolving dichotomous constructs in the visual representation of racialized and gendered bodies.

Black Pain and New Forms of Representation

There is, of course, a direct connection between the international BLM movement and the discourse on visual representation of (racist) violence against Black bodies, which is becoming more and more vocal and perceptible. Movements critical of police power call for stronger surveillance and accountability of state power. A growing number of voices are also calling for a more sensitive approach to the circulation of images depicting violence perpetrated against Black bodies (*Black bodies in pain*). Debra Walker King has suggested that the visual instrumentalization of (racialized) violence on Black bodies can have two entirely different outcomes: On the one hand, it reactivates racial stereotypes; on the other, such images can also foster social engagement. Even though *Black pain* can be read as a sign of resistance against racism, it repeats and perpetuates hegemonic political and social effects of a racist system.[26]

With his 1983 painting *The Death of Michael Stewart*, also known as *Defacement*, Jean-Michel Basquiat memorialized the fate of the young Black artist Michael Stewart who died at the hands of the New York Transit Police after allegedly tagging a wall in an East Village subway station. Basquiat's picture, originally painted on the wall of Keith Haring's studio within a week of Stewart's death, was a deeply personal lamentation; in his work, Basquiat used Black pain as a means of resistance against racism.

Today, we are seeing artists such as photographer Kenny Dunkan, video artist Arthur Jafa and painter Kara Walker redefine and, in some cases, challenge the representation

26 Debra Walker King, *African Americans and the Culture of Pain*, Charlottesville/London 2008.

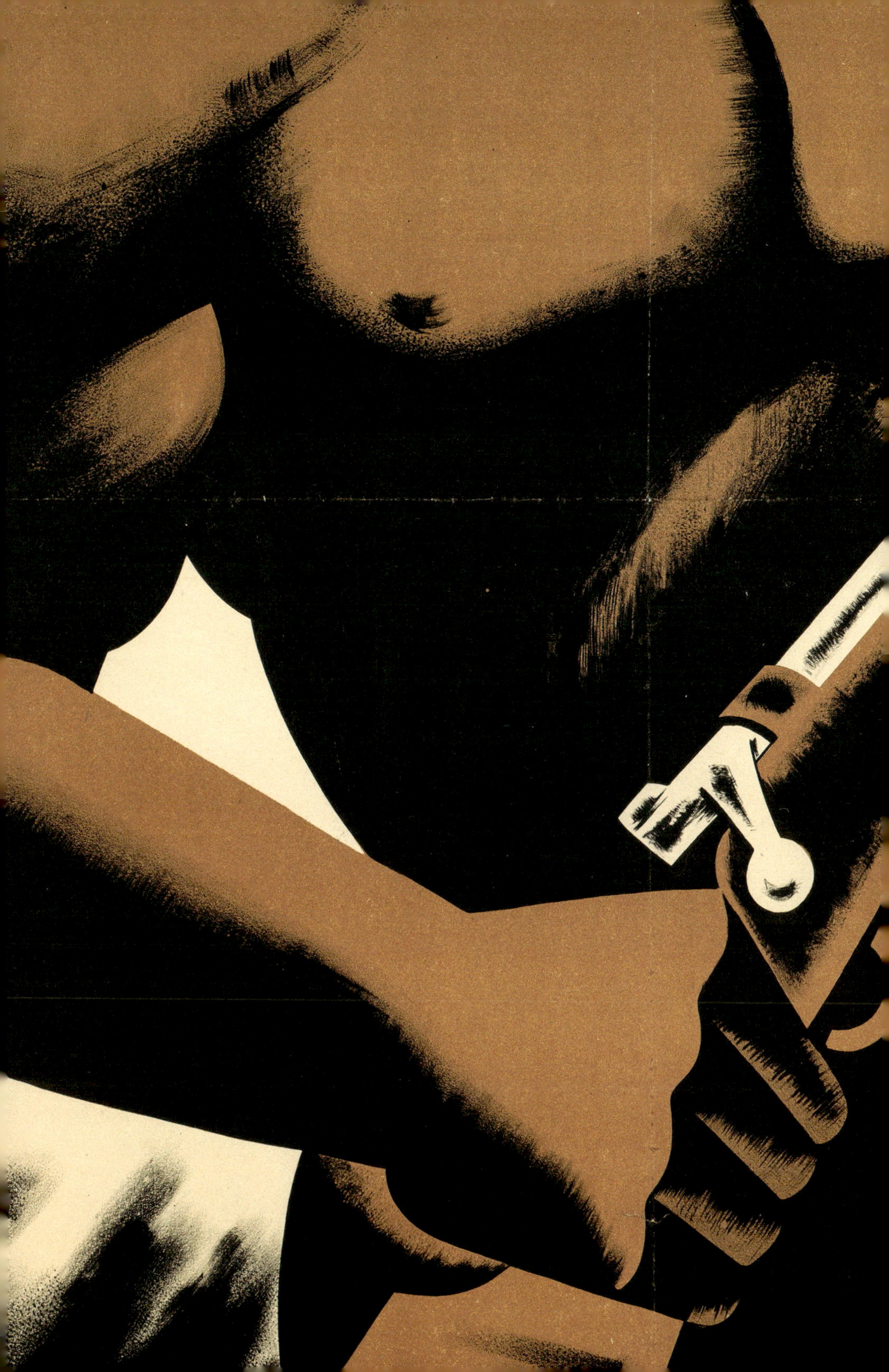

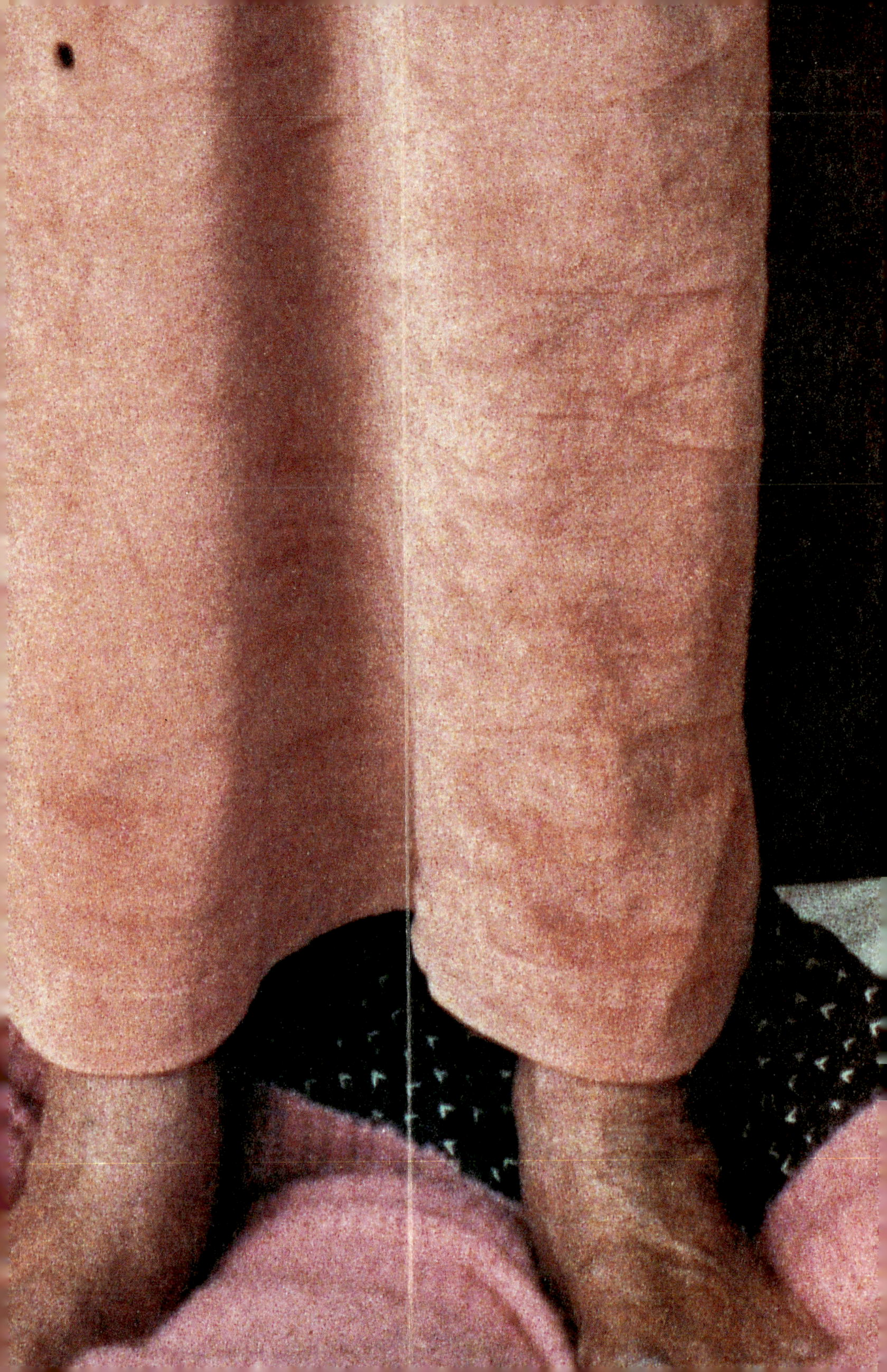

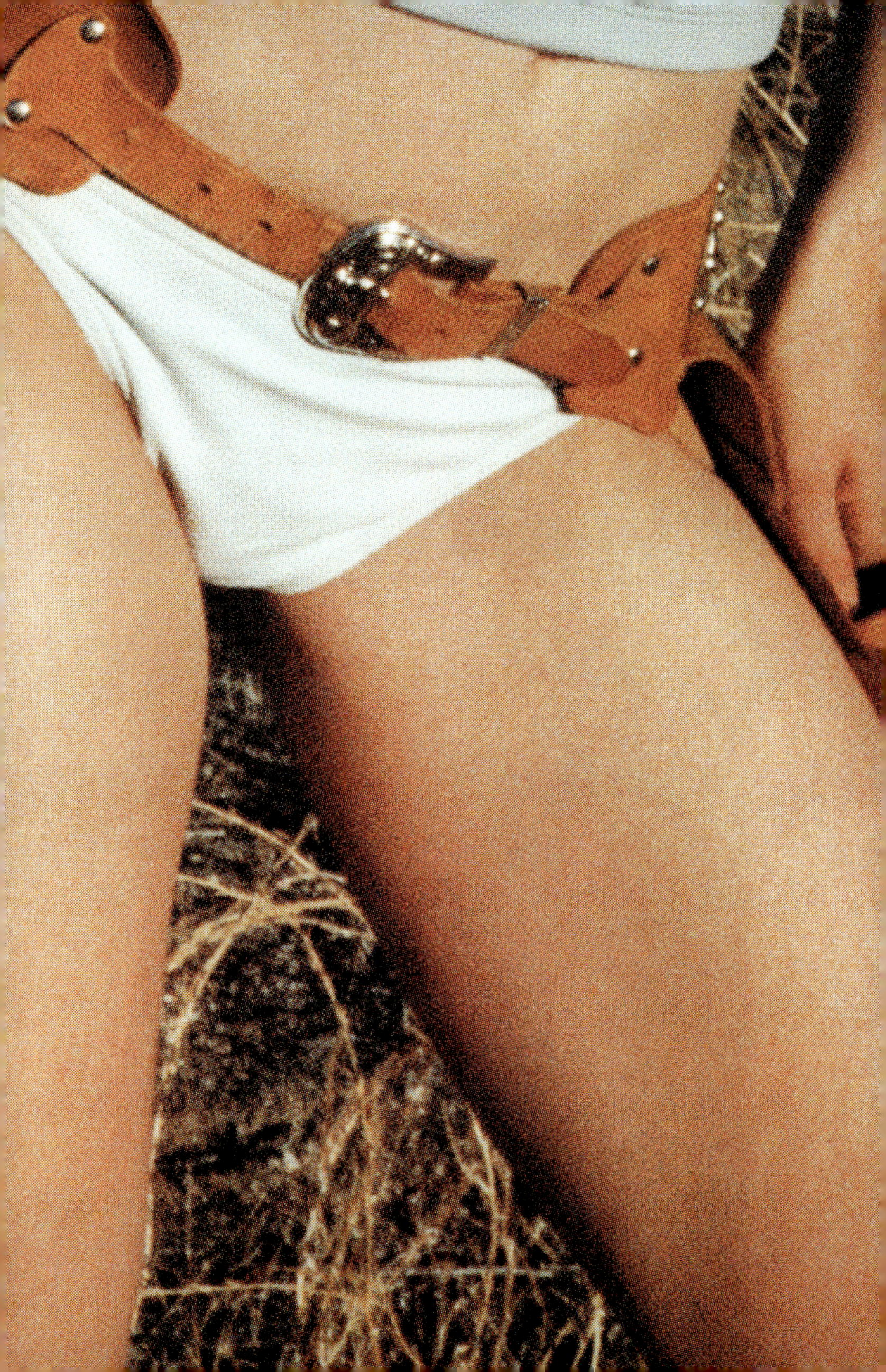

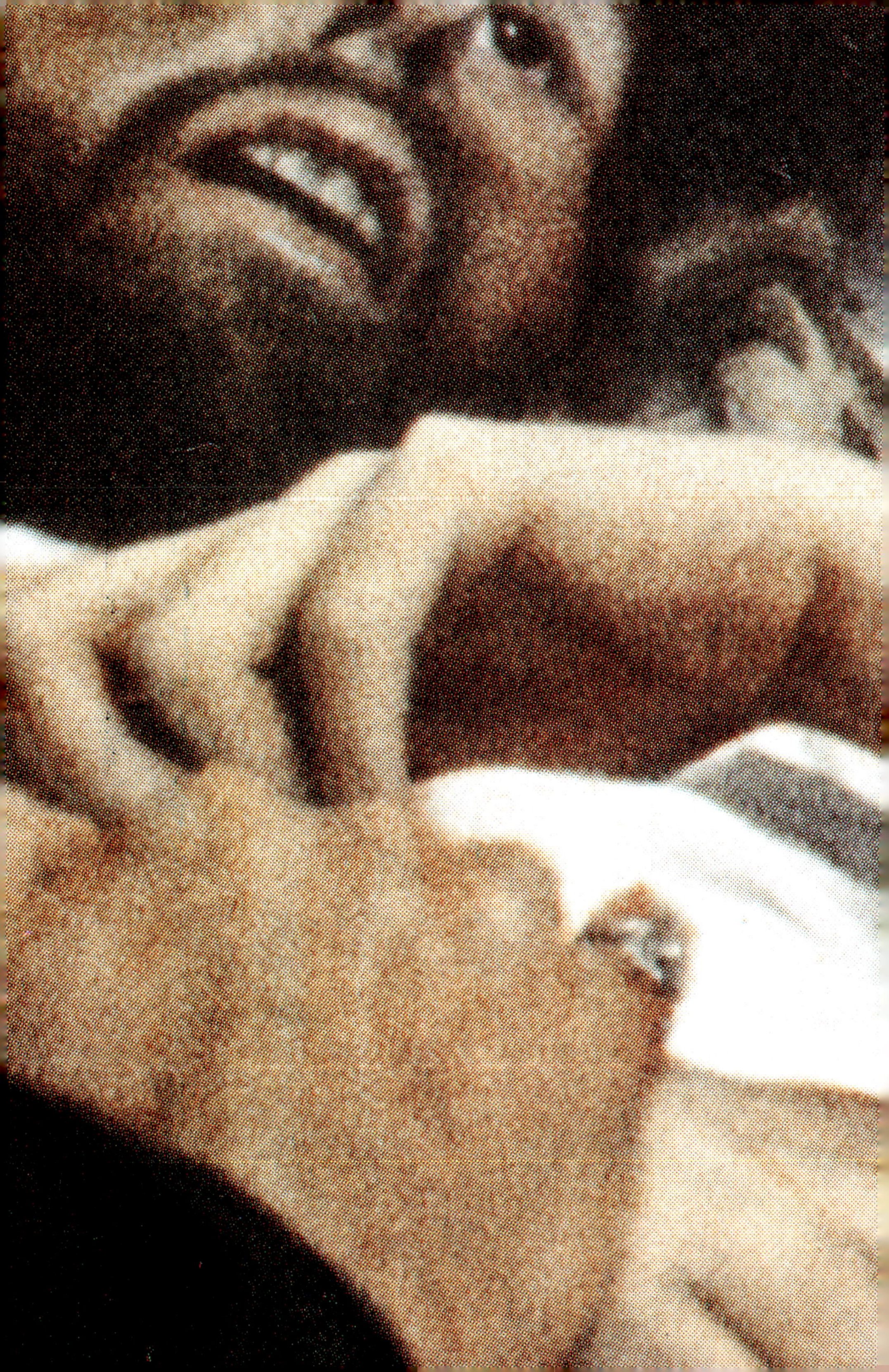

of Black bodies through their work. They are calling for
the dissolution of old binary constructions and the development of new forms of representation that incorporate
inherent differences, ambivalences and contradictions, so
as to prevent the hierarchization of original and likeness.
Within the cracks that have opened in the dominant discourses on the (in)visibility of Black bodies, it is, above all,
art that is able to initiate negotiations as well as interro-
gations in which representations of Black bodies can take
on entirely new forms.

Message to Max on the State of Colonial Matters and Other News

Hans Fässler

"Once again, dear Max, a year has passed, as you have probably noticed." So begins the book *Mitteilungen an Max* (Messages to Max),[1] in which Wolfgang Hildesheimer addressed his fellow writer Max Frisch in 1982. Dear Max, I don't know if you will ever read these words from me, which are directed to you. I certainly hope so.

At around this same time, a time when you proudly held up three fingers when asked your age, I was asked to write a contribution for the catalog accompanying a poster exhibition at the Museum für Gestaltung Zürich.[2] Can you still remember what posters are? Those large screens with advertising images[3] actually existed in paper form back then! The exhibition and the book aimed to show how human bodies are depicted in posters, photographs, and other everyday objects. Part of the exhibition was dedicated to the Black or non-white body and was titled *Black Bodies Matter*. And that's where the two of us come into play.

You were born in 2019 as my grandchild of color, the child of the white Swiss son from my white Swiss wife's first marriage to a white Swiss man and a Black woman from Sri Lanka. This

1 Wolfgang Hildesheimer, *Mitteilungen an Max über den Stand der Dinge und anderes,* Frankfurt a. M. 1982. The book, created to commemorate the arrival of a new year, is simultaneously sad and funny, containing various reflections based on proverbs, idioms, and famous poems.

2 *Talking Bodies—Body Images in the Poster*, November 3, 2023 to February 25, 2024, Museum für Gestaltung Zürich.
3 By 2018, the Zürcher Kantonalbank had already installed so-called "intelligent screens" that identified viewers through facial recognition and thus were able to personalize advertising messages.

is a strange sentence, isn't it?[4] I have pondered for a long time whether, when, and how I should address skin color or pigmentation. After you were born, we used to take care of you for one day a week, along with Emil, the white Swiss-German child of my white son from my first marriage to a white Swiss woman. Sometimes, when I saw both of you side by side, I would think, "Emil is quite pale, maybe he's sick?"

I imagine you reading this text at the age of twenty, around the year 2040. I assume that your skin color and background will have been discussed several times by then. Or rather, "skin color." Or *skin color*?

My dream, of course, is that this will not have been the case at all for you.[5] That you will be able to grow up just the way we activists and historians of colonialism hope, in a society where skin color isn't any more important than tooth alignment.[6] I hope you'll never become conscious of your "different" appearance because of some dumb remark or silly question. I hope you belong to the first generation that can unlearn or throw away all those skin color labels and their "correct" usages, and also that those "skin color crayons for everyone"[7] with which I (unsuccessfully) tried to artistically grasp your skin color, can be donated to the archive of the Museum für Gestaltung Zürich.

But I've spent enough time studying racism, colonial history, and slavery to be realistic. The moment *will* come, and for your sister, it already has— when you were still too young to notice. She once said that she and her father are white, and only her mother is Black, hinting at what has happened countless times throughout history: the construction of skin color identity

4   At the time of writing this text, recommendations (e.g., in the *New York Times*) argued that the adjective Black should be capitalized to highlight its political self-designation and shared experiences of racism among people of African descent. For similar reasons, the adjective Brown should also be capitalized. There is no single consensus in the English-speaking realm on the topic, but this publication has made the effort to reflect the current discourse.
5   Martin Luther King Jr., speaking at the Lincoln Memorial (1963): "I have a dream that my four little children will one day live in a nation where they will not be judged by the color of their skin but by the content of their character."
6   Loosely based on the so-called "War Speech" delivered 60 years ago, on October 4, 1963, by Ethiopian Emperor Haile Selassie I before the United Nations General Assembly: "… until the color of a man's skin is of no more significance than the color of his eyes …"
7   A set of 12 colored pencils available from www.hautfarben-bunt stifte.de, Berlin: "With our 12 skin-tone colored pencils, children can finally draw themselves and their friends as they truly look."

to create divisions. But I'm also an optimist. I believe there's hope that in Switzerland, this increasingly colorful and diverse country, you'll belong to the *last* generation that has to deal with such categorizations, these products born from centuries of ideologically constructed perspectives.

Okay, that might have sounded a bit complicated. My plan was to make this text as accessible as possible.[8] So, let me try my best to explain to you what your Nonno[9] was passionate about long before you came into this world. Maybe then you'll understand why, during your visits to me in the nursing home, I will still remember all those plantations in Suriname, Guyana, Haiti, and Brazil, but won't be able to recall what I had for lunch. And if you really want to dive into the nitty-gritty and if this topic grabs your attention (or you grab it by the collar), you can also check out the footnotes.[10]

Do you remember that drawing of the playground in the picture book by Rotraut Susanne Berner? We must have looked at her *Wimmelbücher* of all seasons dozens of times, and in those illustrations, filled with so many people going about their business, there were also Black people and people of color.[11] While I was looking at those illustrations with you and telling you the stories, I often felt like an overly trained athlete who can't see a track without immediately thinking about interval training. But you, I assume, just saw kids playing, a truck, a slide, and maybe that cheeky fox. Meanwhile, my mind was filled with thoughts of slave plantations and heated debates on racism. It gave me a sense of satisfaction, though, to realize that in a book from 2004, there was a Black mom with her Black child.

8   Christiane Taubira, who in 2001 made the French Parliament recognize slavery and the slave trade as crimes against humanity, has made an attempt at transgenerational education: Christiane Taubira, *L'Esclavage raconté à ma fille*, Paris 2016. Preceding her work were Tahar Ben Jelloun's *Le Racisme expliqué à ma fille*, Paris 1998, and Ta-Nehisi Coates' *Between the World and Me*, New York 2015. Additionally, the aforementioned Max Frisch explored a dialogue between a grandfather and his grandson in a different highly political topic: *Schweiz ohne Armee? Ein Palaver*, Zurich 1989.

9   When a child is born, one must come to terms with the terminology used for two grandfathers (grandfather, grandpa, gramps, granddad, etc.) This becomes even more relevant in patchwork families. Thus, our preference for the Italian language and culture made us choose "Nonno."

10   Footnotes, as I have realized while working with books, can be quite substantial. On occasion, they contain information that is even more important than the main text itself. However, they can also be off-putting or simply "showing off."

11   For instance, Rotraut Susanne Berner, *Frühlings-Wimmelbuch*, Hildesheim 2004.

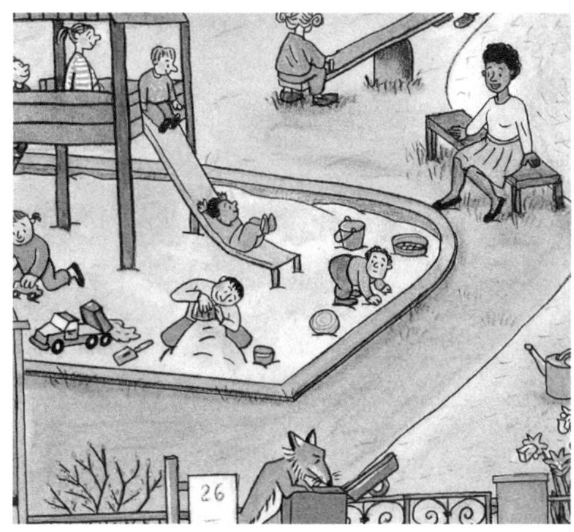

Did you indeed look at these pictures (color-)blindly at that time?[12]

Actually, dear Max, among historians, I consider myself more of a practitioner and craftsman. Theories often tire me out, or I simply don't understand them. Maybe I'm just lazy. Back then, when we were looking at those illustrated books together, I had already spent more than twenty years studying Switzerland's connections to slavery and anti-Black racism. This entanglement—or rather, complicity—began as early as 1528 when a merchant from St. Gallen signed a slave trade agreement with the Spanish king, allowing the Augsburg trading house of the Welser family to colonize distant Venezuela.[13]

The first Swiss or rather "Eidgenosse"[14] to comment on Black bodies in this colonial context was probably Samuel Brun, a surgeon from Basel. In 1611, in the service of the Dutch colonial power, he traveled along the West African coast from Sierra Leone to the mouth of the Congo River. At a slave market in Benin, he described the people there as "a dark brown people, but beautifully shaped" and bought "four exceptionally beautiful young boys"[15] for his ship's

12   On www.mirsindvoda.ch, I came across the statement: "Racism is an acquired behavior, and children begin to recognize, among other things, different skin tones as early as a few months old." I had my doubts about this and initiated a correspondence with members of the Vo da. collective, as well as conducting my own research. Other sources were somewhat more cautious, such as www.lovevery.eu: "Studies have shown that your two-year-old child may already notice different skin tones."

13   Hieronymus Sailer, together with Heinrich Ehinger of Constance, finalized the "Asiento de negros" [contract for the trade of African slaves]. See S. Conradin Bonorand, "Hieronymus Sailer aus St. Gallen, Schwiegersohn des Augsburger Grosskaufherrn Bartholomäus Welser, und seine Tätigkeit im Lichte seines Briefwechsels mit Vadian," in: *Zwingliana*, vol. 20, 1993, pp. 103–125.

14   I use the term "Eidgenosse" (citizen of the Swiss confederation) rather than Swiss because Switzerland as a nation state did not exist in the seventeenth century. It only began with the establishment of the federal state in 1848.

15   Samuel Brun, *Samuel Brun, des Wundartzet und Burgers zu Basel, Schiffarten: welche er in etliche newe Länder und Insulen, zu fünff underschiedlichen Malen, mit Gottes Hülff, gethan: an jetzo aber, auff Begeren vieler ehrlicher Leuthen, selbs beschrieben: und menniglichen, mit Kurtzweil und Nutz zu läsen, in Truck kommen lassen,* Basel 1624, p. 39.

captain. Did you notice the word "but" in his description?

Half a century later, Bernese Albrecht Herport visited the Cape of Good Hope during his journey to Java, Formosa, British India, and Ceylon (the "homeland" of half of your ancestors). He made sketches of the local population, whom we now refer to as Khoikhoi (or Nama, Koranna, and Griqua). In his travel report from 1669, he writes: "The inhabitants, who are an ugly nation of people, are called Hottentots. They are black in body, their hair is like wool, similar to the Angolan inhabitants. In their lives, they are like wild people with little reason."[16]

Thus, in the seventeenth century, attributions were already established with which European people encountered those who looked "different:" from "exceptionally beautiful" to "ugly," along with the devaluation of character through terms like "wild" and "little reason." Even 200 years later, the *Schweizerische Kirchenzeitung* still used the term "Hottentot" to mock efforts for Jewish emancipation in Switzerland and the abolition of slavery in the United States.[17] In anti-Semitic caricatures of the nineteenth century, Jews were intentionally depicted as ugly and dehumanized, with hunchbacks, warts, hooked noses, and an animal-like nature.[18] This underscores the connection between perception and devaluation, which led to racism, exclusion, discrimination, and exploitation from the sixteenth century onwards, and in the twentieth century, to genocide and annihilation.[19]

From the sixteenth to the nineteenth century, an estimated twelve million men, women, and children were abducted from Africa, transported across the Atlantic in ships, and forced to work

16 Albrecht Herport, *Eine kurtze Ost-Indianische Reiss-Beschreibung,* Bern 1669, p. 13.
17 Josef Lang, *Demokratie in der Schweiz. Geschichte und Gegenwart,* Baden 2020, p. 33.
18 Cf. Eduard Fuchs, *Die Juden in der Karikatur. Ein Beitrag zur Kulturgeschichte,* Munich 1921, and Sarah Holzinger, *Die Darstellung von Juden und Jüdinnen im humoristischen Volksblatt Kikeriki,* Master's thesis, Karl-Franzens-Universität Graz, 2015.
19 George M. Fredrickson, *Rassismus,* Stuttgart 2011, especially the chapter "Die Entstehung des modernen Rassismus," pp. 70–72.

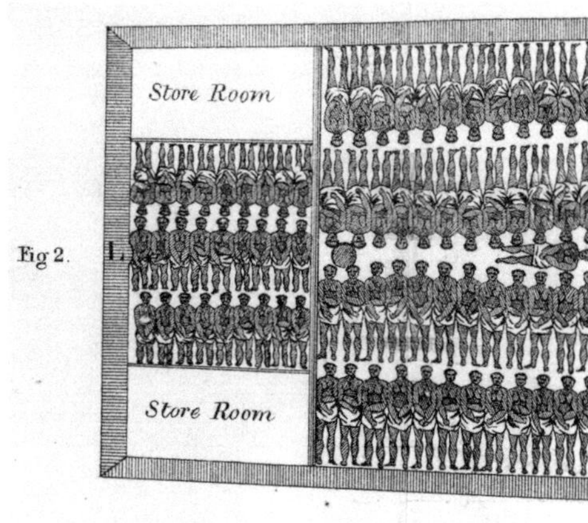

Black bodies on a slave ship: adults on the right, children on the left. Detail from a diagram of the British slave ship Brookes, 1789

in the mines, households, and plantations of the American colonies. Initially, skin color played a minor role, but by the eighteenth century, an almost inseparable connection had formed between "Black" and "slave." Swiss individuals ("Eidgenossen" and "Eidgenossinnen")[20] were also involved in this transatlantic business model, or rather this crime against humanity,[21] which enriched Europe and essentially gave rise to capitalism. When I was fifty years old and you were not yet born, awareness of Swiss participation in slavery was all still relatively new. By the time you were three, word of it had gone round.

What did this involvement entail? To begin with, more than 170,000 enslaved individuals were shipped with Swiss financing, and Basel around 1800 was more or less the slave trade capital of Switzerland. In total, 16,000 enslaved people departed from the West African coast with Basel investments (money and goods), while 14,000 arrived in the so-called "New World."[22] Secondly, there were more than 100 slave plantations under Swiss ownership or administration in Brazil, Cuba, Berbice (now Guyana), Suriname,

20   For about a year I have been using a gender distinction because I have come across women who owned or managed plantations in colonies of the Americas, due to inheritance or the death of their husbands: A part of the La Liberté plantation in Suriname was owned for a time by Salomé Rietmann (1763–1750) from St. Gallen. Elisabeth Roux-Dandiran (1751–1800), from a Geneva family, owned or co-owned several plantations in Suriname. Celeste Rose Peschier (1755–1817) inherited Paradise Estate plantation in Trinidad upon the death of her husband Henry Peschier (1741–1791) from Geneva. Margarethe Maria Faesch (1763–1827), from Basel, received a plantation in Suriname as a dowry from her parents upon her marriage in 1782.

21   In 2001, the UN World Conference against Racism, Racial Discrimination, Xenophobia, and Related Intolerance held in Durban declared slavery and the slave trade as crimes against humanity, with Switzerland as a signatory state.
22   Thomas David, Bouda Etemad, and Janick Maria Schaufelbuehl, *La Suisse et l'esclavage des noirs*, Lausanne 2005, pp. 47–51; Niklaus Stettler, Peter Haenger, and Robert Labhardt, *Baumwolle, Sklaven und Kredite. Die Basler Welthandelsfirma Christoph Burckhardt & Cie. in revolutionärer Zeit (1789–1815)*, Basel 2004, p. 222. Also, my own research in the Trans-Atlantic Slave Trade Database, edited by Emory University, which can be found at www.slavevoyages.org/voyage/database.

Saint-Domingue (now Haiti), Grenada, as well as in British North America/USA.[23] Third, mercenaries, military officers, and mercenary regiments from Switzerland played a significant role in maintaining slavery. They served as troops to keep order, were deployed to suppress slave uprisings, and bolstered colonial armies, for example, in Ceylon.[24] Finally, Swiss intellectuals and intellectuals in Switzerland have made significant contributions to the emergence and perpetuation of colonial racism.[25] They gave lectures, published books and articles in scientific journals, wrote letters to their families, engaged in networking, wrote travel reports, and popularized the racist ideas of other scholars. They spread the ideology that white people (who had only learned to see themselves as "white" through the oppression of Black people) were superior and destined to dominate the world. From 1835 to the mid-twentieth century, so-called "ethnographic exhibitions" or "human zoos"[26] in Switzerland also played their part in spreading the belief, well beyond intellectual circles, that Black people, people of color, and the so-called "colored peoples" were of a lower status, incapable or barely capable of civilization, and therefore needed to be forced into work due to their alleged inherent laziness.

This colonial racism or anti-Black racism was cultivated, "scientifically" researched, and justified up until World War II, and it was disseminated through various means—including posters and commercials—until the 1970s (some would argue even until today)[p. 137]. It was only when confronted with the abyss of the extermination of the European Jews out of racial hatred that

23   An extensive directory of plantations with Swiss connections can be found in the Caricom Compilation Archive, by Hans Fässler, at www.louverture.ch/cca.

24   The involvement of the Karrer/Hallwyl Regiment (1719–1763) in Saint-Domingue and Martinique (against enslaved individuals), as well as in Louisbourg and French Louisiana (against indigenous peoples); the deployment of individual officers and the 1st Battalion of the 3rd Helvetic Half Brigade in 1803 against the "Haitian Revolution" in Saint-Domingue (1802/1803); the deployment of the Neuchâtel Regiment de Meuron in the service of the Dutch East India Company in the Cape Colony (from 1783) and in Ceylon, as well as in British service in India against the Kingdom of Mysore (1799); the involvement of numerous Swiss mercenaries in the Dutch colonies in what is now present-day Indonesia, as well as in suppressing the slave uprising in Berbice (1763) and in the Boni Maroon Wars in Suriname and French Guiana (1765–1793).

25   Well-known Swiss individuals and intellectuals from Switzerland or associated with Switzerland who have been questioned regarding their contributions to racism or rather are still being questioned (in alphabetical order): Louis Agassiz, ichthyologist and glaciologist; Jacob Burckhardt, cultural historian; Alfred Ernst, botanist; Friedrich Fischer, philosopher; Auguste Forel, psychiatrist and brain researcher; Christoph Girtanner, physician and chemist; Jakob Laurenz Gsell, merchant and railway pioneer; Adolf Guyer-Zeller, cotton entrepreneur and railway pioneer; Arnold Guyot, geologist and geographer; Carl Ludwig von Haller, constitutional jurist and politician; Isaak Iselin, philosopher of history; C. G. Jung, psychiatrist; Johann Caspar Lavater, physiognomist; Adolphe Pictet, linguist; Henri Louis Frédéric de Saussure, mineralogist and entomologist; Edmund von Schumacher, diplomat; Ferdinand Karl Rudolf von Steiger, plantation owner in Brazil; Rudolf Steiner, anthroposophist; Johann Jakob von Tschudi, natural scientist and explorer; Carl Vogt, natural scientist and politician.

26   Rea Brändle, *"Wilde, die sich hier sehen lassen." Jahrmarkt, frühe Völkerschauen und Schaustellerei*, edited by Andreas Bürgi with a foreword by Hilke Thode-Arora, Zurich 2023.

27 There is currently a debate about whether racism can still exist when the non-existence of "races" has been proven and generally acknowledged: *Racism Without Races?* (Stuart Hall and Etienne Balibar), *Race and Ethnicity?*, *Racism Without Racists?* Associated with this is the question as to how to differentiate xenophobia in migrant societies from racism or how to theoretically locate xenophobia within racism. These academic debates are sometimes commented by saying that it is equally bad and unacceptable if, for example, someone is denied housing due to being a person of color or Black, or due to a surname that sounds "Balkan."

28 In the United States, there is neither a national museum of slavery nor a national memorial. The American-Jewish philosopher Susan Neiman has put forward the thesis that Germany's remembrance of the Holocaust and its having been and being addressed in the GDR/FRG should serve as a model for the United States: Susan Neiman, *Learning from the Germans: Confronting Race and the Memory of Evil*, London 2019.

29 Johann Friedrich Blumenbach (1752–1840) postulated from 1779 onwards the existence of, in addition to Europeans ("Caucasians"), Asians, Africans, and Americans, a fifth "Black-Brown" variety called "Malay." This category included Australia, Southeast Asia, and Polynesia, discovered in 1770. In the map "Distribution of the Primary Races" by American racist Lothrop Stoddard (1883–1950), Ceylon/Sri Lanka is part of the "Brown race." However, in a world map based on the 1905 skin color scale created by Austrian anthropologist Felix von Luschan (1854–1924), Sri Lanka appears rather dark brown, while Australia and Sub-Saharan Africa are assigned different categories. The concept of "Brown" skin color is also a subject of discussion for you, dear Max. We often refer to your family as the "M&Ms" due to your somewhat alliterative first names, and it is noteworthy that the name and the picture on the package of an M&M product called "Brownies" was criticized in 2021 as racist and sexist. After World War II, the term "Brown Babies" was used to refer to children of German mothers and African American soldiers. Depending on the language and the shade ("dark chocolate brown," "light chocolate brown," "visage d'or," "teint de safran," "beige tendre," "café au lait," "peau aux nuances olive"), and depending on the sociocultural context, "Brown" has a varied meaning, often derogatory. See Trina Jones, "Shades of Brown. The Law of Skin Color," in: *Duke Law Journal*, vol. 49 (2000), no. 6, pp. 1487–1557.

30 The Liberation Tigers of Tamil Eelam were a liberation movement in the Sri Lankan civil war (1983–2009).

this theoretical framework collapsed. However, even though it is now proven that there are no "races," racist thinking and actions persist to this very day.[27]

Maybe it's like in the Swiss mountains: the glaciers have receded and are no longer visible, but the moraines are still there, and they are large, not pleasing to look at, and difficult to traverse. The moraines of racism include racial profiling, racial discrimination, white supremacy, cultural appropriation, culturalism, and commodity racism. Most of these terms derived from so-called "critical race theory" stem from the bitter Black-white confrontation in a country that has never truly addressed its legacy of slavery and racism—the USA.[28]

Can you even position yourself in this debate about race, whiteness, "skin color," discrimination and violence, as well as the legacy of slavery with its extreme forms of exploitation? I have always had the impression that—ever since the writings of the German anthropologist Johann Friedrich Blumenbach—your distant "partial homeland" Sri Lanka, the Ceylon of Portuguese and Dutch colonizers, has existed in a no-man's land between "Indo-Aryans," the "Mongolian race," and the "Malayan race". The latter was invented as the "Brown race" because the discovery of Australia disrupted the neat and simple "order" of Europe (white), Africa (Black), America (Red), and Asia (Yellow).[29]

I would love, at some point, to talk to you about all of this, dear Max. I would also tell you that you sometimes had nicknames in the family: Brownie and Tamil Tiger.[30] The latter especially when you were wild ("wild") and full of vibrant energy. What do you think, are we allowed to make jokes

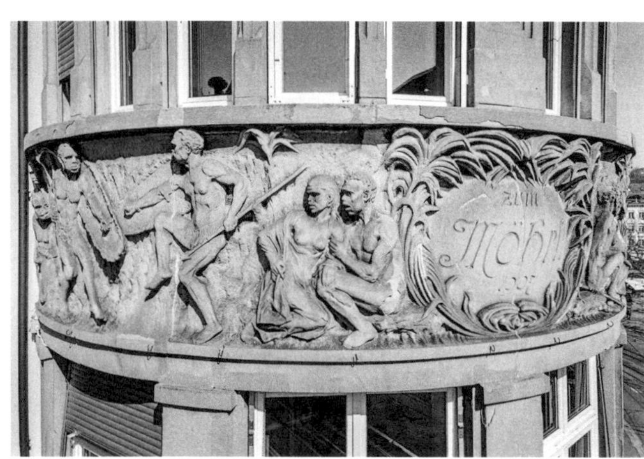

in this area? Or in doing so, does one, without thinking, reinforce problematic assumptions?

I want to return to the concept mentioned earlier, commodity racism, which often appears in advertising posters and ads for "colonial goods" (tobacco, chocolate, coffee, tea, rice), circuses, washing powder,[31] and airlines ^(p. 173). In advertisements for "colonial goods" and air travel, Black people are particularly often exoticized, eroticized, or portrayed as "noble savages." Despite the fact that in ancient times, for example, an African civilization flourished (Egypt);[32] there were libraries in Africa during the Middle Ages with thousands of manuscripts on natural science, philosophy, theology, and law (Timbuktu); African fighters armed with modern rifles defeated European armies at the close of the nineteenth century (defeat of the Italians in the Battle of Adwa); in the first half of the twentieth century an innovative urban Black music culture developed in South Africa (Mbube, Zulu Acapella, Bantu Radio, Kwela, Township Jazz) along with a record industry and performance practices (Shebeens, Sophiatown) and, around the turn of the millennium, roughly the

31   I belong to that generation that grew up with laundry detergent Dash ("Washes white, whiter than white!"). The brands known as Persil, Ariel, Dash, Weisser Ritter, and Omo, along with housewives from Germany and Switzerland, were part of what became known in economic history and in the history of whiteness as the *Washing Powder Wars*.
32   Egypt was long seen as a Eurocentric, white Mediterranean culture and served as an ideological bridge between the first advanced civilizations in Mesopotamia and classical antiquity (Greece and Rome). When Senegalese physicist Cheikh Anta Diop (1923–1986) demonstrated in his 1951 dissertation that Egypt was a Black African civilization, it was rejected by the Sorbonne and finally accepted only after nine years of revision.

same number of people lived in African cities as in rural areas—despite all of these things, it's not uncommon to see older buildings painted with murals [33] and modern advertising posters still depicting halfnaked, drumming "primitives" against a backdrop of deserts, seas, and palm trees.

In 1898, one of those "ethnographic exhibitions" or "human zoos" took place in St. Gallen, in the concert hall of the St. Leonhard Hotel. It provided entertainment for an audience consisting of men, women, schoolchildren and teachers, allowing them to engage with the "Other" and reinforce their superior white self-image. A "Singhalese troupe from the Royal Theater of Ceylon" performed, showcasing songs and dances of warriors (p. 138).[34] Back then, the organizers and the press were not very precise about ethnicities, so it's possible there were also Tamils among the twenty-one performers.

"Ethnographic exhibitions" or "human zoos," which involve the white gaze upon exoticized, "wild," or eroticized Black bodies, have never completely disappeared. In Switzerland, they continued until at least the 1960s in the Circus Knie. And, in the era of increasingly affordable mass air travel, these exhibitions have shifted to advertising posters and to the Global South, where tourists enjoy watching the "cheerful" and "colorful" lives of so-called "natives" in neighborhoods, villages, and markets. For example, in South Africa, which was already a Swissair destination by 1948 and advertised by posters featuring a half-naked female drummer in front of a mask and surrounded by palm trees and a village (p. 179). In the same area, ironically, where Bernese Albrecht Herport had already encountered the Other in

33 See: Haus zum Möhrli ("Blackamoor House") on Marktplatz 24 in St. Gallen. The commercial building, erected in 1909 on the property of the Hotel zum Möhrli, displays a frieze of figures on the rounded bay window on Augustinergasse / Marktplatz, depicting combat scenes of semi-naked African men and women with bows and arrows against a backdrop of palm trees.

34 Achim Hoop, *Völkerschauen in St. Gallen: Eine Analyse der Berichterstattung zu den St. Galler Völkerschauen zwischen 1870 und 1905*, Master's thesis, Pädagogische Hochschule St. Gallen, 2018.

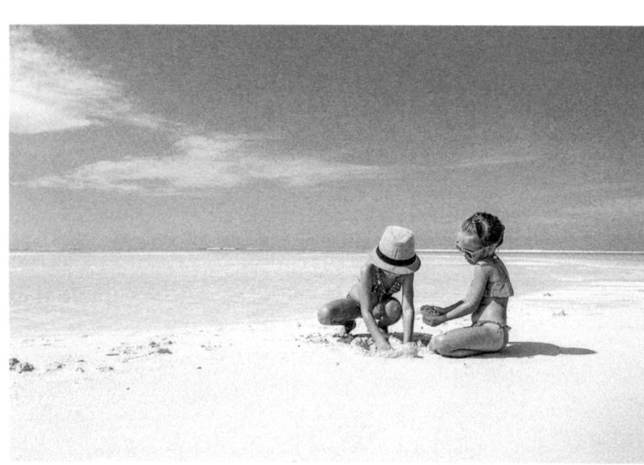

the form of a scantily clad Khoikhoi woman.[35]

For many, the preferred destination today is the Caribbean. Members of the same cultures that in the eighteenth and nineteenth centuries explicitly defined themselves as white and distiguished themselves from Black people now wish to vacation there. These white people are ironically depicted in a Helvetic Tours advertisement for Caribbean vacations, where a blonde woman tries to get a tan resembling the blackness of the Black population [(p. 146)]. Perhaps everyone could meet somewhere in the "tanned" middle: some after skin bleaching, skin lightening, and skin whitening,[36] others after spray tanning, tanning showers, and tanning beds. Possibly, one could then start talking to each other about what has gone wrong over the past few centuries.

We could also discuss the language of advertising. In 2022, in an ad for Switzerland's fourth-largest tour operating company, there's a caption accompanying a picture of two white children on a white beach: "Sand and sea—but something is missing." What is missing? The Black bodies of the so-called

35   Herport, *Reiss-Be-schreibung*, (note 16), p. 12.
36   Yaba Amgborale Blay, "Skin Bleaching and Global White Supremacy. By Way of Introduction," in: *Journal of Pan African Studies*, vol. 4 (2011), no. 4, pp. 4–46.

37   Knecht Reisen, Caribbean Travel with Children, www. knecht-reisen.ch/kari bik/reisen-mit-kindern.
38   Hildesheimer, *Mitteilungen* (note 1), p. 40.

"Ways of seeing": Who's sitting together there by the water? Illustration from *Der Ausflug. Eine Wimmelbilder-Geschichte*, 2022

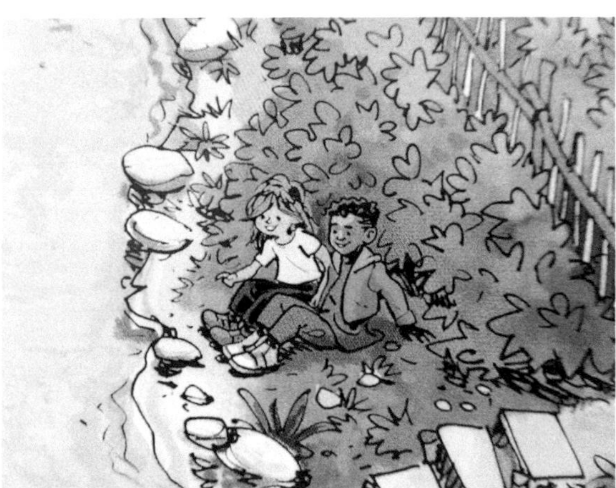

"locals?" No! The correct answer is: "That's right: sunshine! You won't need an umbrella on your Caribbean vacation."

Nevertheless, the question shall be asked once again: Where are the Black bodies, the people of this archipelago that stood at the beginning of colonial exploitation and Europe's rise through the capitalization of Black bodies? Where have the descendants of those people stacked in slave ships disappeared to? The answer can be found in the text of the advertisement: "In the various islands of the region that you know as the Caribbean Sea, a total of 38 million people live, many of whom work in the service industry of hotels. No wonder the Caribbean enjoys an excellent reputation in international tourism, especially in terms of Caribbean vacations with children!"[37] No wonder we don't see them, the Black service providers.

This reminds me, dear Max, of a passage from *Mitteilungen an Max*. Wolfgang Hildesheimer writes to Max Frisch that he now lives a very withdrawn life and then continues: "Recently, I have even attended a society meeting. I immediately saw that society needed to be transformed, so I made the transformations and went home early."[38] I like that and it gives me hope. Just like that image from the children's book *Der Ausflug*, which we used to look at together, and about which you never said anything. Back then when you proudly held up three fingers when someone asked your age. In the picture, a white girl and a Black boy are sitting closely together by the bank of a stream, joyfully gazing out at the water. Well, when all is said and done, dear Max, it's just a girl and a boy, right?

The Body, the Gaze, and the Creation of the Extraordinary

Markus Dederich

There have always been bodies that have been perceived as extraordinary—different, peculiar, eerie, or captivating. These bodies have been objects of fascination, igniting both a profound sense of awe and deep-seated fear. They have attracted mockery, disgust, and contempt, while also evoking pity and compassionate impulses. They were objects of fascination, igniting a profound horror in others; they attracted ridicule, disgust, and contempt, aroused pity and nurturing impulses, were interpreted as monstrous and sparked a wide range of efforts to control them: through removal from public spaces, attempts at healing and education, technical handling, and at times, even annihilation. Among the archetypal bodies that fit into this category are those labeled today as "disabled," individuals of advanced age, or those who do not conform to the gender binary.

In recent decades, numerous social, political, and scientific initiatives have emerged with the aim of challenging the gaze which, at least in Western societies, is both normalized and normative, particularly as it pertains to human bodies and their evaluation. Broadly speaking, these initiatives share a common goal: to loosen the grip of narrow aesthetic, health-centric, and functional evaluation frameworks and contribute to the acceptance of the diverse manifestations of human bodies—their appearances, forms, functionalities, desires, and ways of engaging with the world. This aspiration is documented by a range of posters presented in this book, including those created by organizations like Pro Infirmis or Insieme [p. 127, p. 169, p. 177], as well as those driven by commercial interests, such as Dove's "Fat? Fit?" campaign [p. 130].

However, despite these endeavors, the power of normalized perception and normative judgment regarding the human body remains largely unchallenged. Therefore, it is essential to explore the reasons behind the persistently negative assessments, rejection, and marginalization of certain bodies that continue to prevail today. Within this framework, bodies are not regarded as natural or pre-social entities, but rather as socially and culturally embedded. This understanding is crucial for two main reasons: firstly, bodies are shaped by their social origins and the associated practices of care, as well as the availability or lack of health-related resources and other influencing factors. Secondly, their perception and interpretation are always contingent upon social and cultural frameworks within which they are symbolically encoded and represented through images or texts. Extraordinary bodies, therefore, refer to those that fail to conform to historically changing and culturally diverse expectations, standards, and norms. They are bodies that disrupt the clarity and purity of socially and culturally constructed (functional, morphological, aesthetic, moral) orders. By transgressing the boundaries set by prescribed orders, these bodies trigger a sense of disquietude that calls for responses and measures to be taken.

In light of this backdrop, it is important to question how bodies affect us, how we gaze upon them and through our gaze imbue them with meaning, what image we construct of them, how we symbolically encode them, and the practices we employ to enclose the issue of their extraordinariness. This examination will be conducted using the example of "disability" based on a theoretical perspective developed within the context of cultural disability studies.[1]

Stigma and the Power of Gazes

To begin with, the interaction between bodies and gazes can be described through a phenomenon identified by sociologist Erving Goffman as "stigma."[2] It refers to specific characteristics of individuals that are perceived and evaluated as "deeply discrediting"[3] in certain social contexts. Examples include visible burn scars, malformed hands, spasms, as well as prostheses, white canes, or wheelchairs. These unexpected and extraordinary physical attributes draw attention, particularly when they are unfamiliar, and usually bring the individuals in question into focus in a highly unpleasant manner. At the same time, these stigmas evoke varying degrees of emotional response,

1 Anne Waldschmidt, "'Behinderung' neu denken: Kulturwissenschaftliche Perspektiven der Disability Studies," idem (ed.), *Kulturwissenschaftliche Perspektiven der Disability Studies*, Conference Proceedings, Kassel 2003, pp. 11–22; Markus Dederich, *Körper, Kultur und Behinderung: Eine Einführung in die Disability Studies*, Bielefeld 2007.
2 Erving Goffman, *Stigma: Notes on the Management of Spoiled Identity*, New York 1963, p. 3.
3 Ibid.

such as irritation, disgust, aversion, or pity. It is worth noting, as highlighted by Lennard J. Davis,[4] that stigmatization is not primarily triggered by the specific physical characteristic itself, but rather by the negative social reaction that transforms a particular quality or attribute into a stigma. Thus, it is the act of looking, the way of perceiving something, that allows the observed to emerge as strange, repulsive, uncanny, in need of repair, or subject to destruction. Cultural scholar Rosemarie Garland-Thomson, in her study on staring,[5] argues that staring is a mode of vision that generates meaning and significance in a particular manner. Staring can take various forms: it can be a detached observation, fixating, intrusive, exposing, or subjugating.

Staring occurs when something unexpected forcefully captures our visual attention, something unfamiliar that cannot be immediately categorized. Unfamiliar and unexpected occurrences are often simultaneously intriguing and unsettling. They interrupt our perceptual and interactive routines and are associated with intense emotions such as shock, empathy, anger, fear, uncertainty, or disgust.[6] Through these affects or emotions, others are perceived as "enemies, special cases, strangers," as "embodiments of impurity,"[7] and they are represented in their otherness as "evil, uncanny, threatening, contemptible, repulsive, and pitiable."[8]

Stigmas represent prototypes of what, in everyday situations—on the subway, at the market, in a pedestrian zone—directs negatively charged attention towards bodies which can then trigger staring. Goffman elucidates the central mechanism of stigmas as follows: "An individual who might have been received easily in ordinary social

4 Lennard J. Davis, *Enforcing Normalcy: Disability, Deafness and the Body*, London / New York 1995.
5 Rosemarie Garland-Thomson, *Staring: How We Look*, Oxford / New York 2009.
6 Rosemarie Garland-Thomson, *Extraordinary Bodies: Figuring Physical Disability in American Culture and Literature*, New York 1997, p. 37.
7 Bill Hughes, "Fear, Pity and Disgust: Emotions and the Non-Disabled Imaginary," in: Nick Watson, Alan Roulstone, and Carol Thomas (eds.), *Routledge Handbook of Disability Studies*, London / New York 2012, pp. 67–77; here p. 75.
8 Ibid.

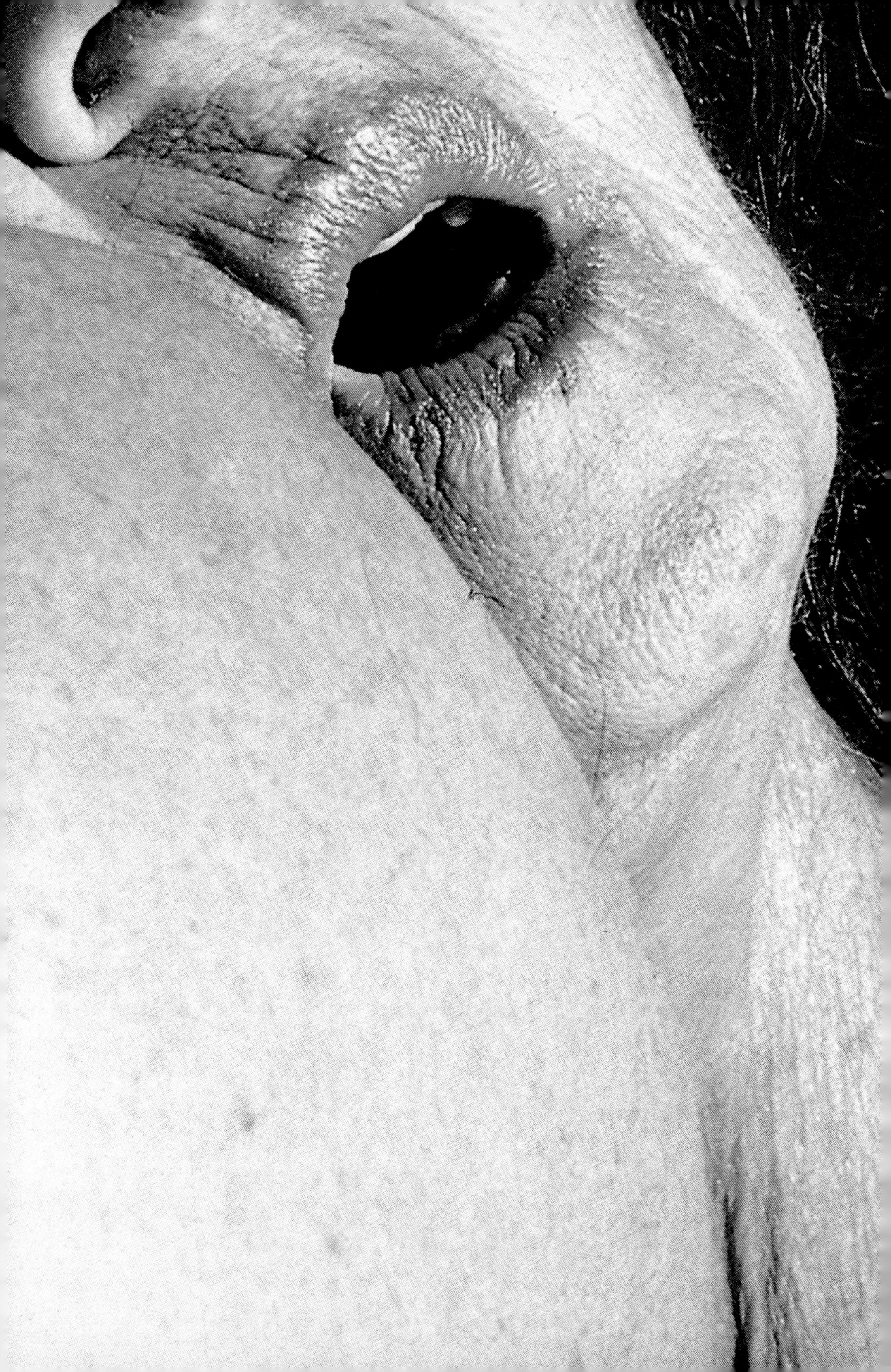

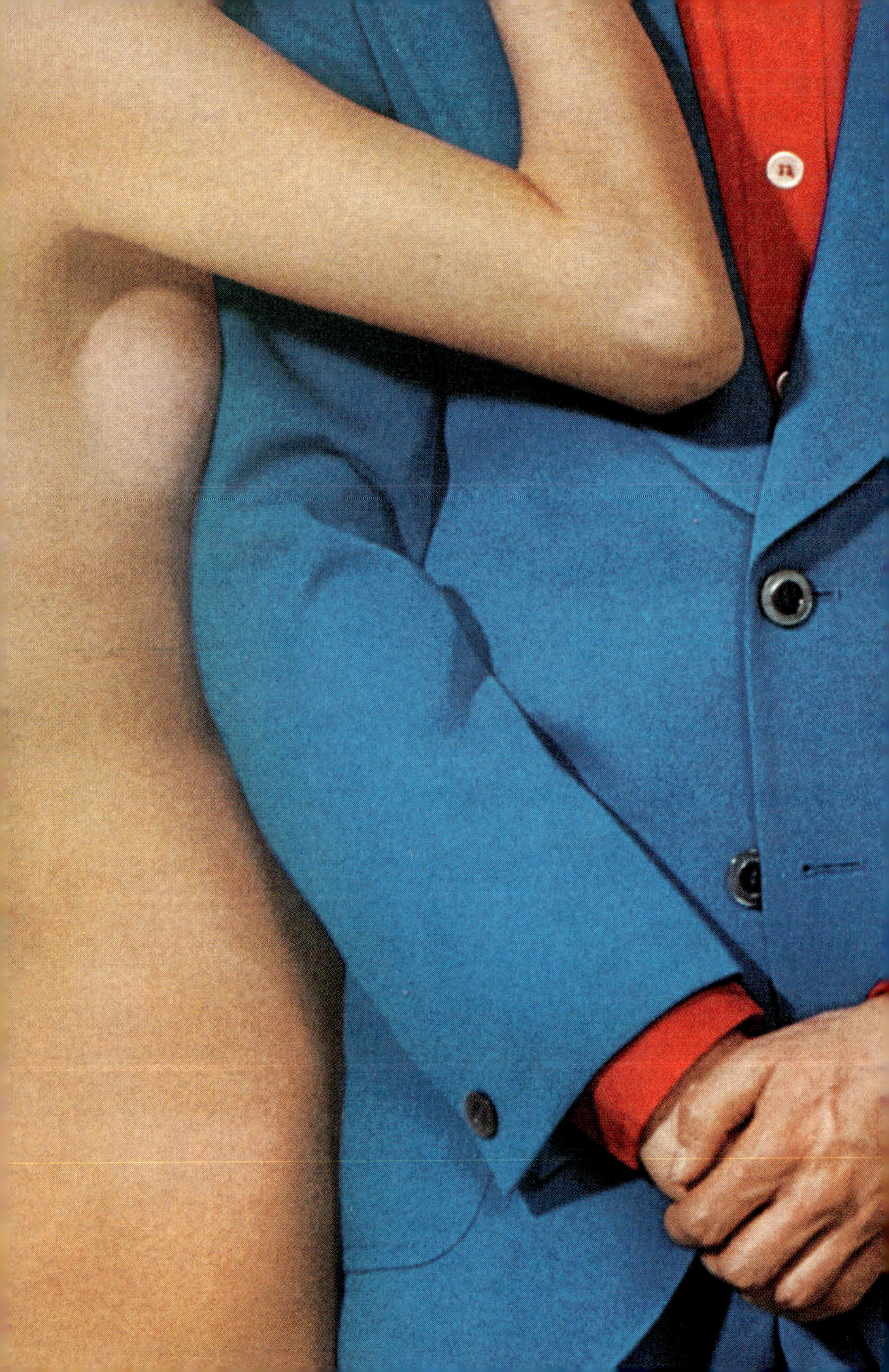

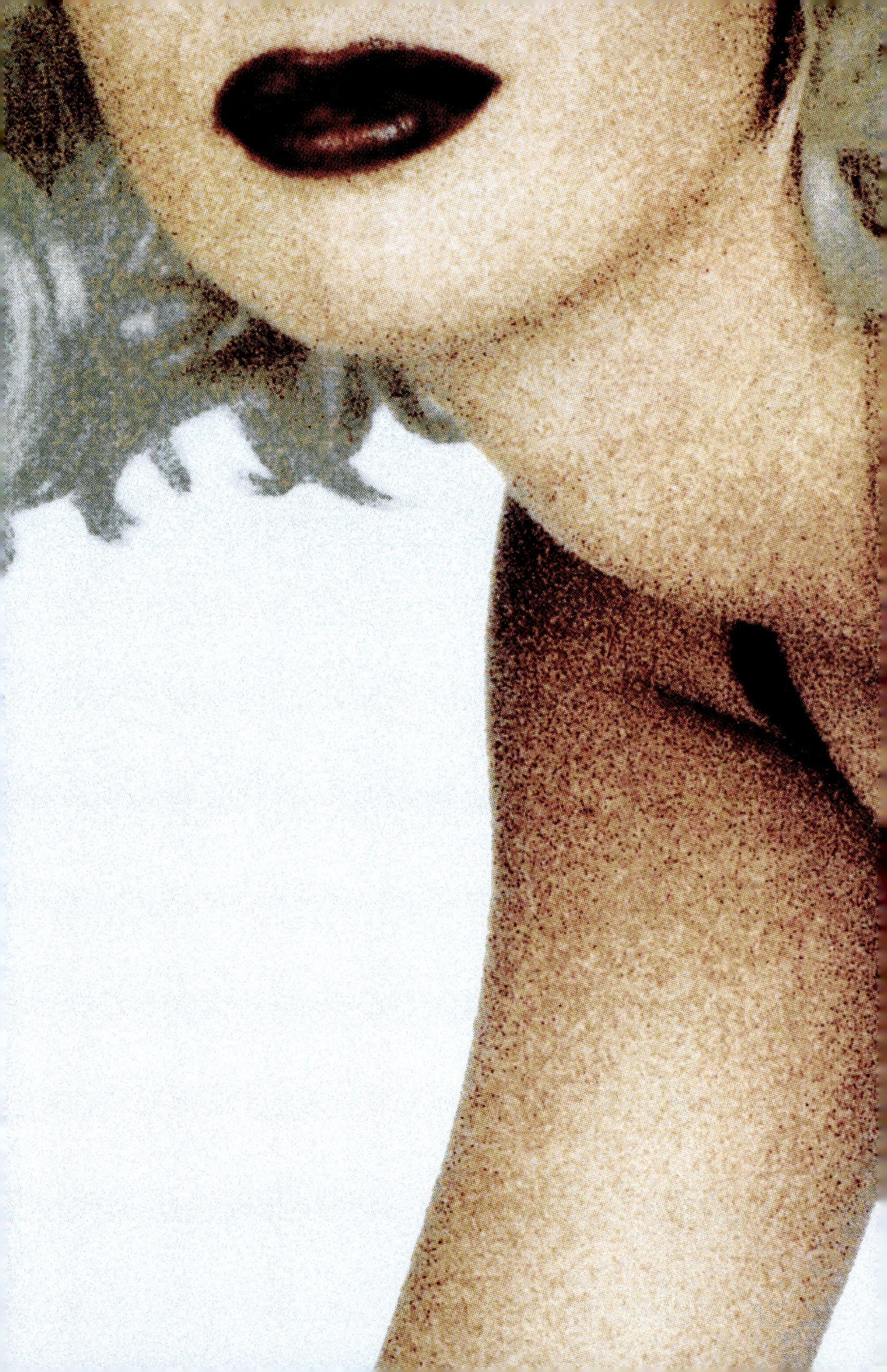

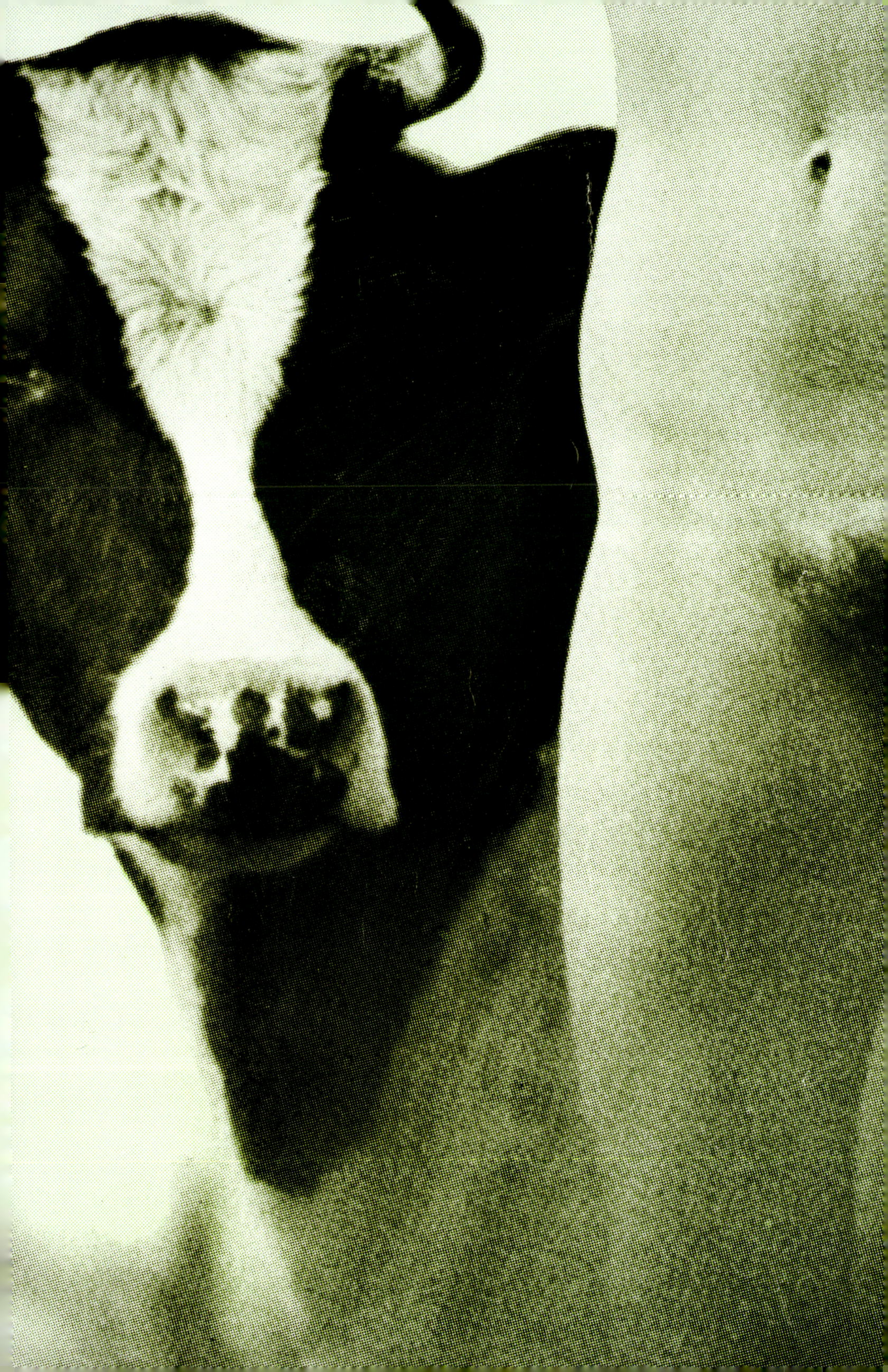

intercourse possesses a trait that can obtrude itself upon attention and turn those of us whom he meets away from him … He possesses a stigma, an undesired differentness from what we had anticipated."[9] One category of stigmas examined by Goffman is "physical deformities."[10] Through social reactions to stigmas, such as staring or awkwardly averting one's gaze, bodies become marked as extraordinary.

The potency of gazes, as Garland-Thomson writes, does not solely rely on an "economy of visual difference;"[11] gazes also reproduce the very economy that classifies bodies as superior or inferior, beautiful or ugly, perfect or grotesque, or expressions of integrated or damaged human beings.

It is important to note that staring is not just a social occurrence that produces meaning by making something stand out in a particular way. It is also culturally encoded and subject to rules. Many forms of staring are considered inappropriate and socially frowned upon. Staring embarrassingly magnifies specific attributes, characteristics, or actions of the person being stared at; however, under certain circumstances, it also reveals the inappropriate curiosity or lack of boundaries of the starer themself.

The pattern of marking and categorizing bodies mentioned above has persisted through the centuries. For instance, the "integrity" of individuals is not solely determined by their physicality; rather, the body is interpreted in a way that reveals and manifests moral and psychological aspects, and thus, the value of a person, as described by Maren Lorenz: "A central axiom remained unchanged throughout the ages: the conflation of beauty with goodness, nobility, and therefore, worth. Conversely, ugliness and wickedness, often coupled with weakness and inferiority … An entire chain of associations and causal connections on the axes of valuable / worthless and high-quality / low-quality, as well as good / evil, has rarely been questioned over the centuries or millennia, linking the visual realm with spheres of psychology and character."[12]

The "Clinical Gaze" and the Normalization of the Body

The previous discussion focused primarily on an everyday mode of perceiving bodies. This can be distinguished from the "clinical gaze," which started to take shape

9 Goffman, *Stigma* (note 2), p. 13.
10 Ibid., p. 15.
11 Garland-Thomson, *Extraordinary Bodies* (note 6), p. 7.
12 Maren Lorenz, *Menschenzucht: Frühe Ideen und Strategien 1500–1870*, Göttingen 2018, p. 50.

during the "early modern period" and, in the "classical age," became recognized as a way of perceiving and understanding associated with knowledge and truth.

As Davis demonstrates in his study on the power of normality and its significance in the construction of disability, a work referring to American and European cultural spheres, the process of scientifically marking certain individuals as "damaged," "invalid," "disabled," and so on begins at the level of body perception.[13] Unlike the intrusiveness of staring, the clinical gaze is analytical and precise, aiming to decipher the logic and structure of its subjects. As Michel Foucault emphasizes, the clinical gaze is guided by the intention to refrain from any intervention that could alter its subject: "Observation leaves things as they are; there is nothing hidden to it in what is given."[14] At the same time, this way of looking, which became more prominent in the eighteenth and nineteenth centuries, moves away from simply examining the surface for symptoms. It penetrates the depths of the body using microscopes, scalpels, and other technical devices, burns "things to their furthest truth."[15] At this point, the clinical gaze takes on the form of an intervention that makes its subject accessible and arranged in a particular way, not only based on theory but also supported by technology. The purported neutrality and objectivity of the clinical gaze become active and intertwined in shaping its subjects.[16]

The clinical gaze produces more than just medical knowledge; simultaneously, this knowledge influences the gaze and directs it in specific paths. The dual premise of such medical knowledge is that, on the one hand, there are objectively damaged, dysfunctional, and defective bodies, body parts, or bodily functions that, on the other hand, require intervention and repair. This perception, shaped by scientific expertise, focuses on a particular phenomenon as something that comes before actual experience. Simultaneously, because this phenomenon contradicts the assumed "natural order of things" or at least presents an exceptional and irregular case, it is placed within a selectively and exclusively structured context of practical action. In this context, visual perception serves as a truth-bearing organ through the analytical and measured assessment and diagnosis of the body's form and function. However, the clinical-diagnostic evaluation of what is revealed to such a methodically oriented gaze is only possible when some form of comparative and evaluative pattern exists. This pattern is the *normalized* body.[17] The

13   Davis, *Enforcing Normalcy* (note 4).
14   Michel Foucault, *The Birth of the Clinic: An Archaeology of Medical Perception*, transl. A.M. Sheridan, New York 1989, p. 131.
15   Ibid., p. 147.
16   Lorraine Daston and Peter Galison, *Objectivity*, Cambridge, MA 2007.
17   Davis, *Enforcing Normalcy* (note. 4); Jürgen Link, *Versuch über den Normalismus: Wie Normalität produziert wird*, Opladen 1997.

normalized body, an achievement of the nineteenth century, is the result of a scientific interpretation of the body primarily based on statistics.

Statistical values related to the body (which define, on a theoretically framed basis, what can be considered "typical" or not) serve a dual function. On the one hand, they empirically capture the shape, anatomy, function, and so on of bodies, including variations. This allows us to understand how bodies normally are, that is to say, in most cases. On the other hand, they form an evaluative matrix that determines how bodies should be.

Consequently, anomaly becomes a secondary, derived phenomenon that presupposes the measurement and normalization of the body. Only within the conceptual framework of differentiating physical normality from anomaly does it become possible to perceive certain deviations as unacceptable problem cases that, therefore, require specific interventions (such as medical, psychological, or educational). In the process, the originally descriptive concept of normality becomes normatively charged; by using statistical normality as a benchmark for evaluation, it transforms into an ideal that dictates how bodies should be.

Extraordinary Bodies and the Production of Social Inequality

Based on the preceding considerations, "disabilities" (as a form of extraordinary bodies) can be understood as a double negation: they are "attributed as a discrediting characteristic to all 'deviant' bodily variations, and on the other hand, they serve as a tangible marker of inferiority itself."[18] In the sense of this theory, a "disability" proves to be a fundamental motif of human disqualification: Sociohistorical norms or norms-turned-into-expectations of normality are not only physically encoded and thus naturalized but they assume also the function of a "barometer" through which all bodies are judged and compared.[19]

The process of standardizing bodies has multiple consequences. One historically powerful and significant consequence is that the statistically constructed body is not an individual body, but rather a collective body. Influenced by eugenicists and social Darwinists in the second half of the nineteenth century, it became associated with the idea of a unified population. Key distinctions such as normal-anomalous and superior-inferior were also incorporated into the body politic. This allowed for the identification of various other physical collectives, whose differences

18   David T. Mitchell and Sharon L. Snyder: *Narrative Prosthesis: Disability and the Dependencies of Discourse*, Ann Arbor, MI 2000, p. 3 (trans. MD).
19   David T. Mitchell and Sharon L. Snyder, "Representation and Its Discontents: The Uneasy Home of Disability in Literature and Film," in: Gary L. Albrecht, Katherine D. Seelman, and Michael Bury (eds.), *Handbook of Disability Studies*, Thousand Oaks, CA 2001, pp. 195–218; here p. 204.

were seen as biologically rooted and thus their societal inequality justified as biologically legitimate. Foremost among these were the bodies of women, the working class, migrant workers, people of color, and many others.

One consequence of the normalizing categorization of bodies, as Judith Butler writes, is that "certain kinds of bodies will appear more precariously than others, depending on which versions of the body, or of morphology in general, support or underwrite the idea of the human life that is worth protecting, sheltering, living, mourning. These normative frameworks establish in advance what kind of life will be a life worth living, what life will be a life worth preserving, and what life will become worthy of being mourned."[20]

According to the theoretical perspective of disability studies, extraordinary bodies have a series of important functions in the production and reproduction of social equality and inequality. By examining how extraordinary bodies are perceived, represented, and evaluated, we can discern what matters in our society, which values prevail, what people fear, the criteria by which belonging and non-belonging are organized, and also which lives are considered worth living and which are not. As Garland-Thomson writes, the reactions to people with disabilities are often so intense because, due to their (actual or presumed) greater limitations, dependence, and fragile social status, they reflect back to us our own fears, such as the fear of losing control, being controlled by others, dependency, vulnerability, loss of integrity, and so on.[21]

Here, a central aspect is addressed: people with disabilities undermine the modern understanding of intact and

20   Judith Butler
Frames of War: When Is Life Grievable?, London/ New York 2009, p. 53.

21   Garland-Thomson, *Extraordinary Bodies* (note 6), p. 6.

self-determined subjectivity. At least in the modern West, growing up means gradually overcoming the feeling of dependence, imperfection, and vulnerability through awareness of one's own sovereignty. Simone Danz speculates that the non-disabled subject who resists becoming aware of their own fragile and precarious constitution has limited possibilities to consider "people who are different, due to physical, mental, or psychological characteristics, as equal. The subject, which only constitutes itself as autonomous and capable of action under very ambivalent conditions, favors … certain processes of normalization that protect against perceiving disability as a potentially applicable condition for the self."[22]

For this reason as well, the history of extraordinary bodies is always connected to social practices that serve to cope with them. These range from pity, charitable care, and responsible concern to assimilation and exclusion tendencies, technological and prosthetic compensations, and even violent dehumanization and desires for annihilation. The specifically modern form of coping with extraordinary bodies was to establish a highly differentiated and specialized system of care, support, and education, such as special schools and therapeutic institutions.

An Ethical Outlook

Extraordinariness in bodies does not exist per se, as it is not an inherent property of bodies. Rather, extraordinariness indicates a relationship: it assumes selective and exclusive social and cultural patterns of order, systems for organizing experience, a specific knowledge along with difference-generating categorical concepts, unplanned and institutionalized social practices in response to unexpected and foreign situations, and more.

The historical, social, and cultural contexts that enable extraordinariness also highlight the uncertainty of this extraordinariness. In this context, "uncertainty" simply means that it is not inevitable or unalterable for us to keep distancing ourselves from individuals who appear different or foreign, or to confine them to a diminished sense of humanity. In contrast to processes that solidify and simplify what it means or should mean to be human in relation to corporeality, Julia Kristeva and Charles Gardou propose: "The indeterminate and ever-open nature of human beings calls for the refusal of mechanistic and final determinations, the rejection of simplifying dualisms (ability / disability, normality / anomaly, etc.), and the

22   Simone Danz, *Vollständigkeit und Mangel: Das Subjekt in der Sonderpädagogik*, Bad Heilbrunn 2015, p. 14.

questioning of categorizations that impede the recognition of personhood."[23]

Thus, the question of how we want to relate to people with disabilities, the elderly, and chronically ill individuals, ultimately emerges within an ethical framework. In such a framework, recognition would always involve refraining from exerting hierarchical control, appropriation, and subjugation over other individuals, regardless of who they are. This would require avoiding conceptual identifications that assign a defined value to people based on specific criteria and place them in a hierarchy. Only through such a mode of recognition will it be possible for highly diverse individuals to coexist in interconnectedness.

23   Julia Kristeva and Charles Gardou, "Behinderung und Vulnerabilität," in: Otto Braun and Ulrike Lüdtke (eds.), *Sprache und Kommunikation: Enzyklopädisches Handbuch der Behindertenpädagogik*, Stuttgart 2012, pp. 39–48; here p. 41.

Identification and Illusion— Body Images on Social Media

Maria Schreiber

The promise of disembodied identities in cyberspace, which has existed since the early days of the Internet, needs to be reconsidered, especially with the advent of the networked smartphone camera. On social media today, we are surrounded by body images in an almost endless range, from close-ups of stretch marks to manga-like avatars. But what does it mean when the body gets turned into pixels? What sociocultural and media-technological conditions come into effect?

Digitalization, Interconnection, and a Turn Towards the Self

A significant prerequisite for the omnipresence of body images on social media was the digitalization of photography and the progressive democratization and individualization of photographic practices, beginning in the late 1990s.[1] Storage capacity became the only limitation of the medium, so people began taking more photos of their everyday lives. Since the release of the first iPhone in 2007, smartphones with high-resolution cameras have become ubiquitous. The interconnected camera is now constantly present, usually carried close to the body, and always online. The camera sensor is also directly integrated into various apps and platforms, allowing for (more or less) real-time sharing and showcasing of photos. What is shown is what is important at the moment or what fits the desired image. For example, running shoes in the early morning can suggest athletic commitment, or an Aperol Spritz in the evening sun can convey a milieu-specific lifestyle. Along with this development comes a culture of theatricalization and aestheticization of everyday life.[2]

1   Wolfgang Reißmann, *Mediatisation visuell: Kommunikationstheoretische Überlegungen und eine Studie zum Wandel privater Bildpraxis,* Baden-Baden 2015.
2   Ulla Patricia Autenrieth, "Bilder in medial vermittelter Alltagskommunikation," in: Katharina Lobinger (ed.), *Handbuch Visuelle Kommunikationsforschung,* Wiesbaden 2019, pp. 249–268.

Practices of private photography are becoming increasingly diverse,[3] even though only a small fraction of photos is actually shared on social media.[4]

Bodies, too, are constantly being photographed and displayed on social media. Even the unborn body is already on view as a pregnant mother's belly or as a photographed ultrasound image,[5] while the deceased body can be presented as a corpse hidden in a coffin[6] or as an iconic symbol of a protest cause.[7] However, it is primarily the living body that has become an omnipresent subject. The face, as the most distinctive body part and marker of identity, holds a special significance. While self-portraiture has a longstanding tradition in art history and photography, this subject was once reserved for those who had means and resources. With the high-resolution front-facing camera of the smartphone, it became possible to take selfportraits and observe oneself in real-time. Poses, gestures, and facial expressions are perceived from the exact perspective of potential viewers and can be positioned accordingly. In combination with social media, selfies have become an established genre of visual communication, but above all, they serve as an "identity performance:"[8] the desired image (in the truest sense of the word) is embodied through facial expressions, clothing, hairstyle, and so on, and visually constructed through camera perspective, framing, background, and more. Additionally, it is continually updated, altered, and adapted depending on the target audience.[9] One presents oneself differently on a professional networking platform, for example LinkedIn, as compared to in a group chat with close friends.[10]

3 Asko Lehmuskallio and Edgar Gómez Cruz, "Why Material Visual Practices?," in: idem (eds.), *Digital Photography and Everyday Life: Empirical Studies on Material Visual Practices*, New York 2016, pp. 1–16; Jonas Larsen and Mette Sandbye, "The New Face of Snapshot Photography," in: idem (eds.), *Digital Snaps: The New Face of Photography*, London 2013, pp. xv–xxxiii.

4 T. J. Thomson, "Exploring the Life Cycle of Smartphone Images from Camera Rolls to Social Media Platforms," in: *Visual Communication Quarterly*, vol. 28 (2021), no. 1, pp. 19–33.

5 Katrin Tiidenberg, "Odes to Heteronormativity: Presentations of Femininity in Russian-Speaking Pregnant Women's Instagram Accounts," in: *International Journal of Communication*, vol. 9 (2015), pp. 1746–1758.

6 Martin Gibbs, James Meese, Michael Arnold, Bjorn Nansen, and Marcus Carter, „#Funeral and Instagram: Death, Social Media, and Platform Vernacular," in: *Information, Communication & Society,* vol. 18 (2015), no. 3, pp. 255–268.

7 This became visible, for example, with George Floyd's portrait in the context of #blacklivesmatter, see Ricarda Drüeke, Corinna Peil, and Maria Schreiber, "How do Black Lives Matter? The Visual Construction of Protest in German-language Newspapers and on Instagram," in: *Studies in Communication Sciences*, vol. 22 (2022), no. 1, pp. 129–147.

8 Edgar Gómez Cruz and Helen Thornham, "Selfies Beyond Self-Representation: The (Theoretical) F(r)ictions of a Practice," in: *Journal of Aesthetics & Culture,* vol. 7 (2015), no. 1, pp. 1–10, here p. 7.

9 Maria Schreiber, *Digitale Bildpraktiken: Handlungsdimensionen visueller vernetzter Kommunikation*, Wiesbaden 2020, pp. 208–210.

10 Maria Schreiber and Gerit Götzenbrucker, "Körperbilder—Plattformbilder? Bildpraktiken und visuelle Kommunikation auf Social Media," in: Elke Grittmann, Katharina Lobinger, Irene Neverla, and Monika Pater (eds.), *Körperbilder—Körperpraktiken*, Cologne 2018, pp. 29–50.

11   Michel Foucault, "Technologies of the Self," in: Luther H. Martin, Huck Gutman, and Patrick H. Hutton (eds.), *Technologies of the Self*, London, 1988, pp. 16–49, here p. 18. Discussed in the context of digital media by Jill Walker Rettberg, *Seeing Ourselves Through Technology*, London 2014.
12   Anne Burns, "Self(ie)-Discipline: Social Regulation as Enacted Through the Discussion of Photographic Practice," in: *International Journal of Communication*, no. 9 (2015), pp. 1716–1733, here p. 1716.
13   Michael R. Müller, "Das Körperbild als Selbstbild," in: Michael R. Müller, Hans-Georg Soeffner, and Anne Sonnenmoser (eds.), Körper Haben. *Die symbolische Formung der Person*, Weilerswist 2011, pp. 87–106, here p. 95.
14   Susan Sontag, *On Photography*, New York 2001, p. 90.
15   Maria Schreiber, "Digitale Ambivalenz? Übergegensätzlichkeiten in Bildkommunikation auf Social Media," in: Roswitha Breckner, Karin Liebhart, and Maria Pohn-Lauggas (eds.), *Sozialwissenschaftliche Analysen von Bild- und Medienwelten*, Berlin/Boston 2021, pp. 55–78; Shayla Thiel-Stern, "Collaborative, Productive, Performative, Templated: Youth, Identity, and Breaking the Fourth Wall Online," in: Rebecca Ann Lind (ed.), *Produsing Theory in a Digital World*, New York 2012, pp. 87–103.

Digital cameras, especially smartphone cameras, fit into a series of practices and technologies throughout media history that allow individuals to reflect upon, alter, and sometimes optimize their bodies or their thoughts about their bodies. These include confession, diary writing, but also the use of pedometers or menstrual cycle apps. With the digital camera as a visually photographic "technology of the self,"[11] the focus shifted to body images, both individually and collectively. Therefore, it is not surprising that with the increased presence of selfies, a culture-pessimistic debate emerged, branding the trend of self-portrayal solely as narcissism.[12] The question of potential consequences remains intriguing.

Images of our bodies enable us to "perceive the expressivity of our own bodies from the (assumed) external perspective of others and thus control this body as a socially symbolic medium."[13] Susan Sontag already observed, "We learn to see ourselves photographically."[14] This implies and promotes not only a reflexive attitude towards our own bodies ("seeing ourselves"), but another essential element as well, that of the manner of mediatization ("photographically") in which this reflexive perception takes place. Today, one could supplement Sontag's statement with "through the digital, networked camera" or "on social media." The photographic mediatization of images is expanded by the context of a specific (semi) public visibility on social media: One's own body is shown to often diffuse or anonymous audiences, thereby subjecting it to debate.[15] The spectrum of possible images and recipients is vast, ranging from exchanging intimate snapshots within a romantic relationship on apps like

Snapchat, which make the images visible only temporarily, to publicly presenting glossy portraits to millions of followers. The realm of body images on social media is characterized by a great deal of diversity, as it encompasses a wide range of practices that are closely connected to the capabilities and opportunities provided by different hardware and software platforms.

Media Technological Structures and Digital Masquerade

The development of social media platforms since the early 2000s has contributed to a low-threshold participation in (visual) content production. Facebook, YouTube, and Twitter were among the first social networks that allowed users to disseminate their own content using simple means. The different interfaces, functions, and algorithms contribute significantly to shaping the cultures of the respective platforms.[16] The rise of image-centric platforms like Instagram, Pinterest, and Snapchat began around 2010, when the focus in posting shifted clearly to photos. Instagram emerged from the app Hipstamatic, which imparted a nostalgic appearance to photos, sometimes even simulating analog materiality: scratches appeared on the photo, or filmstrips and Polaroid-style paper framed the image. This specific aesthetic also entailed a kind of anticipatory nostalgia for everyday life, as lived experiences were constantly evaluated for their potential as photographed past.[17]

The close connection between technical possibilities and social practices in the production and reception of body images continues at present. All popular image and video apps offer filters, which are based on specific presets for hue, saturation, or contrast, transforming the "raw" image into the desired aesthetic style. Designers, photographers, and influencers also develop their own presets, allowing their followers to present their lives, at least formally, in a similar fashion to their idols. Furthermore, starting with the development of the augmented reality application Looksery,[18] face filters have made their way into various apps. The program scans distinctive facial features and precisely adjusts various types of masks. Companies and fan communities also use filters for marketing and community building.[19] For example, with a filter from Sephora and Givenchy, customers can digitally try on a new lipstick. Who needs a billboard when advertising can be shown directly on and around the customers' bodies?

16   Taina Bucher and Anne Helmond, "The Affordances of Social Media Platforms," in: Jean Burgess, Thomas Poell, and Alice Marwick (eds.), *The SAGE Handbook of Social Media*, London 2017, pp. 30–44.

17   Nathan Jurgenson, "The Faux-Vintage Photo," *The Society Pages*, 2011, www.thesocietypages.org/cyborgology/2011/05/14/the-faux-vintage-photo-full-essay-parts-i-ii-and-iii

18   https://youtu.be/Pc2aJxnmzh0

19   www.newfacedigital.co.nz/blog/5-best-branded-instagram-story-ar-filters-of-2021

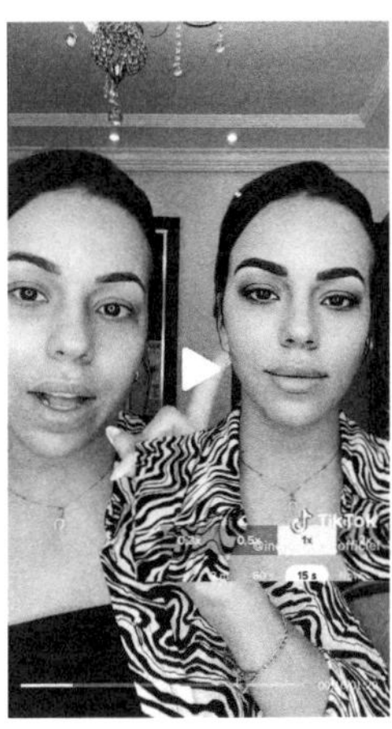

The ability to manipulate and reflect on one's own body image through digital photography is further intensified by face filters and their forms of digital masquerade. Bodies are no longer merely captured in photographs; their digital representations are directly transformed, shaped, and filtered. Filters that contribute to the normative "enhancement" of faces, such as smooth skin, long lashes, and full lips, are particularly popular, creating these features on the smartphone screen and on one's own face. As a result, it is no longer just images of famous Hollywood stars that serve as references for corrections in cosmetic surgery but increasingly, individuals are using their own filtered images for these references.[20] The broader societal implications of this trend are still difficult to assess. Recently, the TikTok filter "Bold Glamour" attracted both fascination and criticism due to its technical perfection and seamless adaptation to the face.

While there are efforts to mark retouched or manipulated images as such, these labels are often subtle and therefore mostly ineffective. Moreover, image editing is not universally

20   Mona Harfmann, "Teenager in der Schönheits falle," *ORF*, 2023, www.orf.at/stories/3306 994/?fbclid=PAAaakq RQVU1W1h4rkMhvBzdO 9YmylgkFbEji5FzpXx AqLvDxBCX5RGdwwac

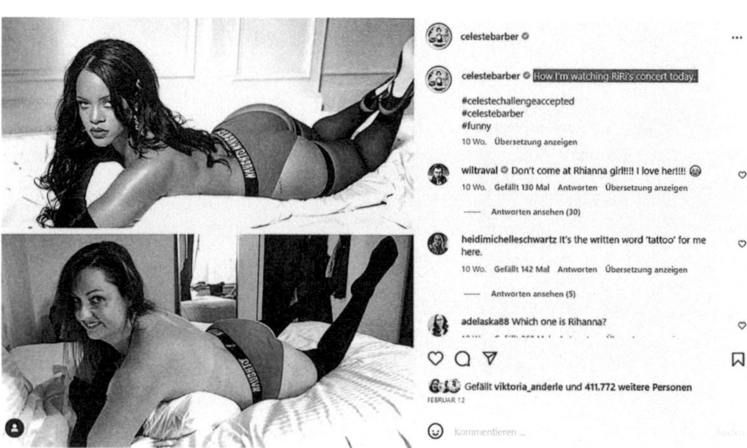

perceived as artificial or unrealistic, particularly among young people.[21] Nevertheless, there are explicit counter-movements that share unfiltered images or images with unflattering poses under hashtags like #nofilter or #fürmehrrealitätaufinstagram (for more reality on Instagram). There are also ironic takes which have caught on globally, such as those by Celeste Barber, which serve to expose filtered body images and prevailing beauty ideals on social media.

Related to these developments, the body positivity movement has gained significantly higher visibility through social media as compared to traditional print media. However, the movement has since been complemented by the concept of body neutrality, which fundamentally questions the emphasis placed on the body and appearance.[22] This concept is promoted by Jameela Jamil's "i_weigh" campaign and community, for instance.[23]

Body Images on Social Media as Agents of Socialization

In the realm of visually-oriented social media, influencers play a central role in mediating body images: these are

21   Brigitte Naderer, Christina Peter, and Kathrin Karsay, "This Picture Does Not Portray Reality: Developing and Testing a Disclaimer for Digitally Enhanced Pictures on Social Media Appropriate for Austrian Tweens and Teens," in: *Journal of Children and Media*, vol. 16 (2022), no. 2, pp. 149–167, here p. 162.
22   Elisabeth Lechner, *Riot, Don't Diet! Aufstand der widerspenstigen Körper*, Vienna 2021, p. 59; Poppy Noor, "What Is Body Neutrality, the New Trend Loved by Beautiful Celebs?," *The Guardian*, 2019. www.theguardian.com/fashion/2019/oct/31/body-neutrality-taylor-swift-jameela-jamil-latest-trend
23   www.iweighcommunity.com

"Realtalk": Screenshot of an Instagram story
by @anna_strigl, 2023

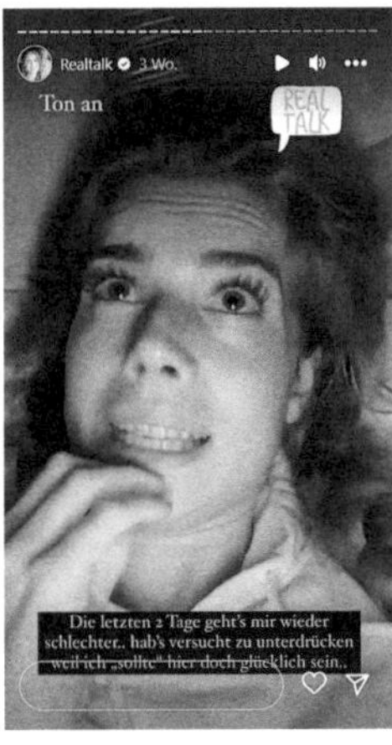

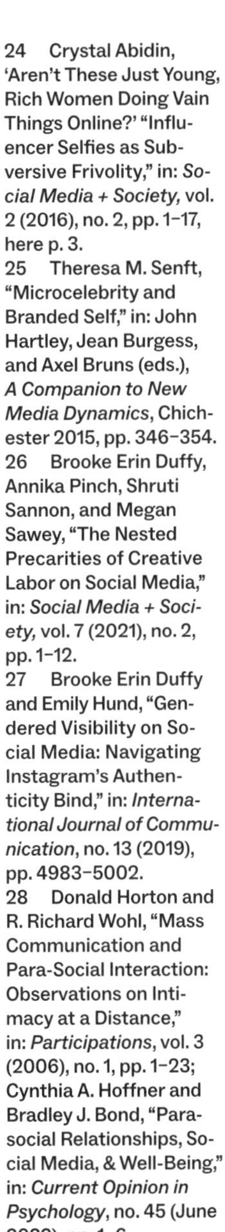

24   Crystal Abidin, 'Aren't These Just Young, Rich Women Doing Vain Things Online?' "Influencer Selfies as Subversive Frivolity," in: *Social Media + Society,* vol. 2 (2016), no. 2, pp. 1–17, here p. 3.
25   Theresa M. Senft, "Microcelebrity and Branded Self," in: John Hartley, Jean Burgess, and Axel Bruns (eds.), *A Companion to New Media Dynamics*, Chichester 2015, pp. 346–354.
26   Brooke Erin Duffy, Annika Pinch, Shruti Sannon, and Megan Sawey, "The Nested Precarities of Creative Labor on Social Media," in: *Social Media + Society,* vol. 7 (2021), no. 2, pp. 1–12.
27   Brooke Erin Duffy and Emily Hund, "Gendered Visibility on Social Media: Navigating Instagram's Authenticity Bind," in: *International Journal of Communication*, no. 13 (2019), pp. 4983–5002.
28   Donald Horton and R. Richard Wohl, "Mass Communication and Para-Social Interaction: Observations on Intimacy at a Distance," in: *Participations*, vol. 3 (2006), no. 1, pp. 1–23; Cynthia A. Hoffner and Bradley J. Bond, "Parasocial Relationships, Social Media, & Well-Being," in: *Current Opinion in Psychology*, no. 45 (June 2022), pp. 1–6.

Internet users who attract a large number of followers by documenting and staging their everyday lives and lifestyles.[24] Through entrepreneurial self-promotion,[25] brand collaborations, sponsored posts, media appearances, and sometimes even their own products, influencers generate revenue, with earnings ranging from very little[26] to multimillion-dollar incomes. The struggle for visibility takes the form of competition not just with other accounts, but primarily with the platform's algorithm, which favors and makes certain video content and selfies more visible.[27] Users develop parasocial relationships[28] with "their" influencers as they gain daily insights into their private lives, sometimes even being live witnesses. Proximity is established through intimate glimpses and physical proximity to the camera lens. Particularly through video formats where content creators speak directly into the camera, viewers have the impression of being addressed personally.

Professionally composed and curated photos are usually showcased in a user's Instagram feed, while Instagram Stories and TikTok videos are reserved for more spontaneous snapshots and blurry impressions from everyday life. The ultimate goal is to create a sense of perceived authenticity since credibility fosters a loyal community and, consequently, commercial success. However, for someone like Beyoncé, different expectations of authenticity exist as compared to a local mommy blogger. The emergence of "ordinary" people as figures of identification and projection alongside pop stars and top models on social media hardly serves to diversify the spectrum of body

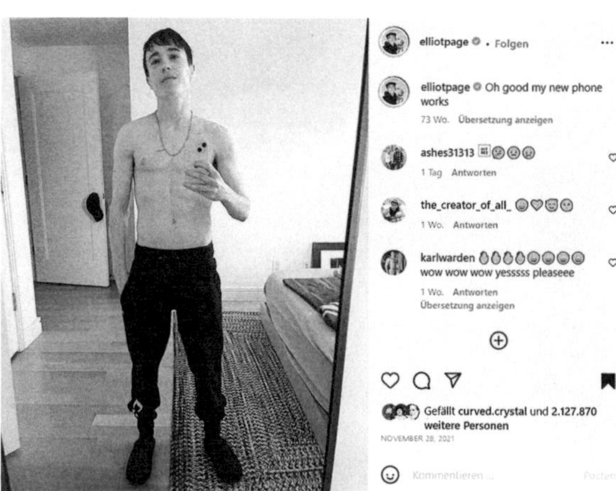

images. Their presence reinforces the late capitalist notion that on social media, everyone can have their "fifteen minutes [now rather: seconds] of fame" and achieve commercial success as long as they are attractive (women, rarely men) or funny (men, rarely women).[29]

What Beyoncé and the mommy blogger have in common is their contribution to the repertoire of body images in the visual memory of their followers. The strong presence of perfect bodies and lives on social media has already been widely problematized and criticized.[30] This trend can be particularly burdensome for teenagers who are preoccupied with a rapidly changing body, as well as questions of gender identity, attractiveness, and a sense of belonging to youth culture. Young women in particular feel subjected to complex and sometimes contradictory pressures in the context of social media, as shown by a recent study[31] where a beautiful photo is characterized as looking natural, as if it were taken spontaneously and effortlessly, despite the fact that a lot of work actually went into creating it.

Nevertheless, social media platforms, due to their openness and accessibility, offer the potential for resistance by marginalized bodies.[32] Social media platforms provide spaces for representation and identification for a wide range of body shapes, gender identities, and clothing styles. Alternative body images are given room for visibility and inspiration. Disabled or trans bodies, which are more or less absent in mainstream media contexts, gain new visibility, even though it may not always be free from beauty ideals. For instance, the actor Elliot Page revealed his slim and muscular bare

29 Theresa M. Senft, "Microcelebrity and Branded Self," in: Hartley / Burgess / Bruns, *A Companion* (note 25), pp. 346–354, here p. 349.
30 Angela McRobbie, "Notes on the Perfect. Competitive Femininity in Neoliberal Times," in: *Australian Feminist Studies*, vol. 30 (2015), no. 83, pp. 3–20; Georgia Wells, Jeff Horwitz, and Deepa Seetharaman, "Facebook Knows Instagram Is Toxic for Teen Girls, Company Documents Show," *The Wall Street Journal*, September 14, 2021, www.wsj.com/articles/facebook-knows-instagram-is-toxic-for-teen-girls-company-documents-show-11631620739
31 Rosalind Gill, "Being Watched and Feeling Judged on Social Media," in: *Feminist Media Studies*, vol. 21 (2021), no. 8, pp. 1387–1392, here p. 1388.
32 Lechner, *Riot, Don't Diet!* (note 22).

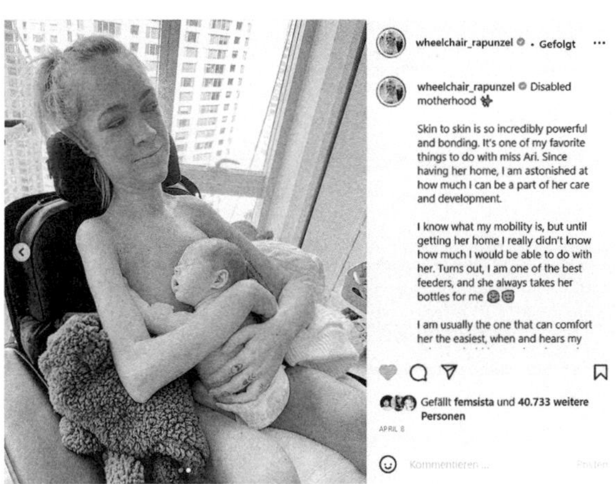

33   Stine Eckert, "Fighting for Recognition. Online Abuse of Women Bloggers in Germany, Switzerland, the United Kingdom, and the United States," in: *New Media & Society*, vol. 20 (2018), no. 4, pp. 1282–1302; George Veletsianos, Shandell Houlden, Jaigris Hodson, and Chandell Gosse, "Women Scholars' Experiences with Online Harassment and Abuse: Self-Protection, Resistance, Acceptance, and Self-Blame," in: *New Media & Society*, vol. 20 (2018), no. 12, pp. 4689–4708; Ellie Morrissey, "Gender, Power and Technology: Is Trolling a Man's Sport?," in: *Trinity Women's Review*, vol. 3 (2019), no. 1, pp. 25–38; Rebecca Mardon, Hayley Cocker, and Kate Daunt, "When Parasocial Relationships Turn Sour: Social Media Influencers, Eroded and Exploitative Intimacies, and Anti-Fan Communities," in: *Journal of Marketing Management*, January 2023, pp. 1–31.
34   Shristi Marwah, "Who is Wheelchair Rapunzel? TikToker Attempts to Get Reddit 'Snark Page' Removed Following 'Cyber Bullying,'" *Sportskeeda*, 2023, www.sportskeeda.com/pop-culture/who-wheelchair-rapunzel-tiktoker-attempts-get-reddit-snark-page-removed-following-cyber-bullying

chest on Instagram after his mastectomy, and the post received more than two million likes.

Visibility on social media can be fundamentally shaped and staged by the actors themselves. No editor, graphic designer, or editorial guidelines need determine which body images are acceptable or attractive enough to be published—although advertising clients naturally choose influencers whose body image they perceive as fitting their brand. Additionally, platforms reserve the right to act as control authorities, which is necessary to prevent the display of violence, pornography, and abuse, but also perpetuates social norms and values. This is especially true of those (partially automated) controls that often go beyond their intended purpose and censor, for example, female nipples.

Despite the potential for resistance that social media offers to marginalized bodies, being visible also means making oneself vulnerable. Minorities, in particular, are increasingly subjected to intrusive and discriminatory comments, hostility, and cyberbullying on social media.[33] For example, Alex Dacy, a disabled influencer who documented her pregnancy and motherhood on Instagram as @wheelchair_rapunzel, was confronted by cyberbullying.[34]

The legal options to address such issues are gradually being developed. Some influencers seek support in moderating comments, while others sometimes use criticism to educate and contextualize their positions. However, the platforms themselves almost always fall behind when it comes to providing critical information or raising awareness. For instance, although action has been taken against communities that promote anorexic bodies[35] so that searching for the hashtag on Instagram redirects users to a page with support services and contacts,[36] users often simply resort to other hashtags to continue networking.

The body images we are confronted with on social media are ultimately linked to the decision of which accounts and hashtags we choose to follow. But when highly algorithmically sorted platforms like TikTok and YouTube impose normatively beautiful filters on us, is it enough to curate our own feed in order to be diverse? The abilities and resources to intervene are unequally distributed, especially as long as commercial actors control who is made visible, where, and how. Ultimately, massive profits are generated from the insecurities surrounding our own body images.[37] Or, as Velvet D'Amour, photographer and plus-size model, has succinctly summarized, "If everyone accepted themselves, just as they are, imagine how sales would go down."[38]

35   Debbie Ging and Sarah Garvey, "'Written in these Scars Are the Stories I Can't Explain': A Content Analysis of Pro-Ana and Thinspiration Image Sharing on Instagram," in: *New Media & Society*, vol. 20 (2018), no. 3, pp. 1181–1200.
36   http://help.instagram.com
37   Lechner, *Riot, Don't Diet!* (note 22), p. 37.
38   Velvet D'Amour in an interview with sociologist Amanda Czerniawski, cited in: Amanda M. Czerniawski, "Beauty Beyond a Size 16," in: *Contexts*, vol. 15 (2016), no. 2, pp. 70–73, cited in Lechner, *Riot, Don't Diet!* (note 22), p. 27.

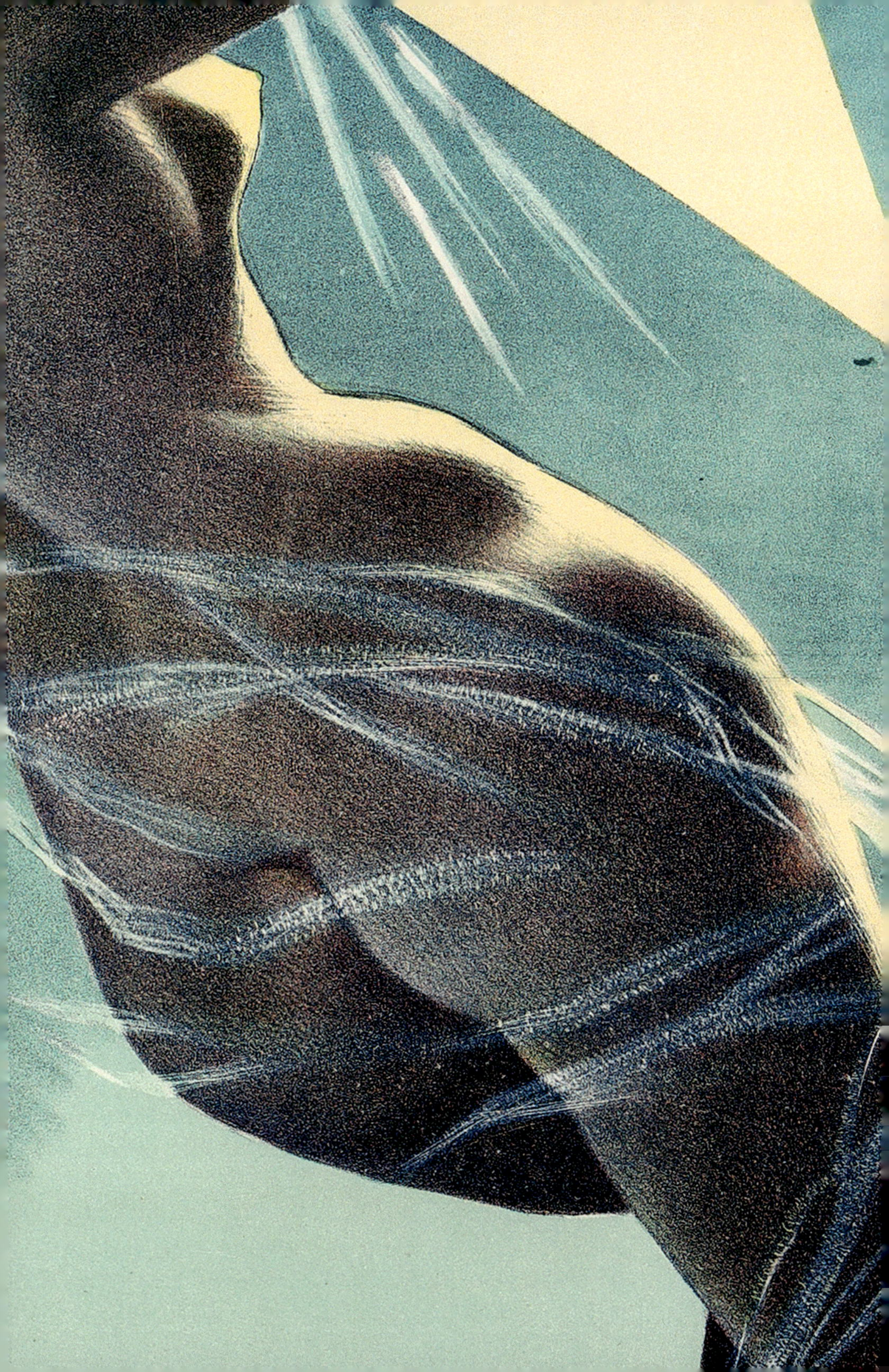

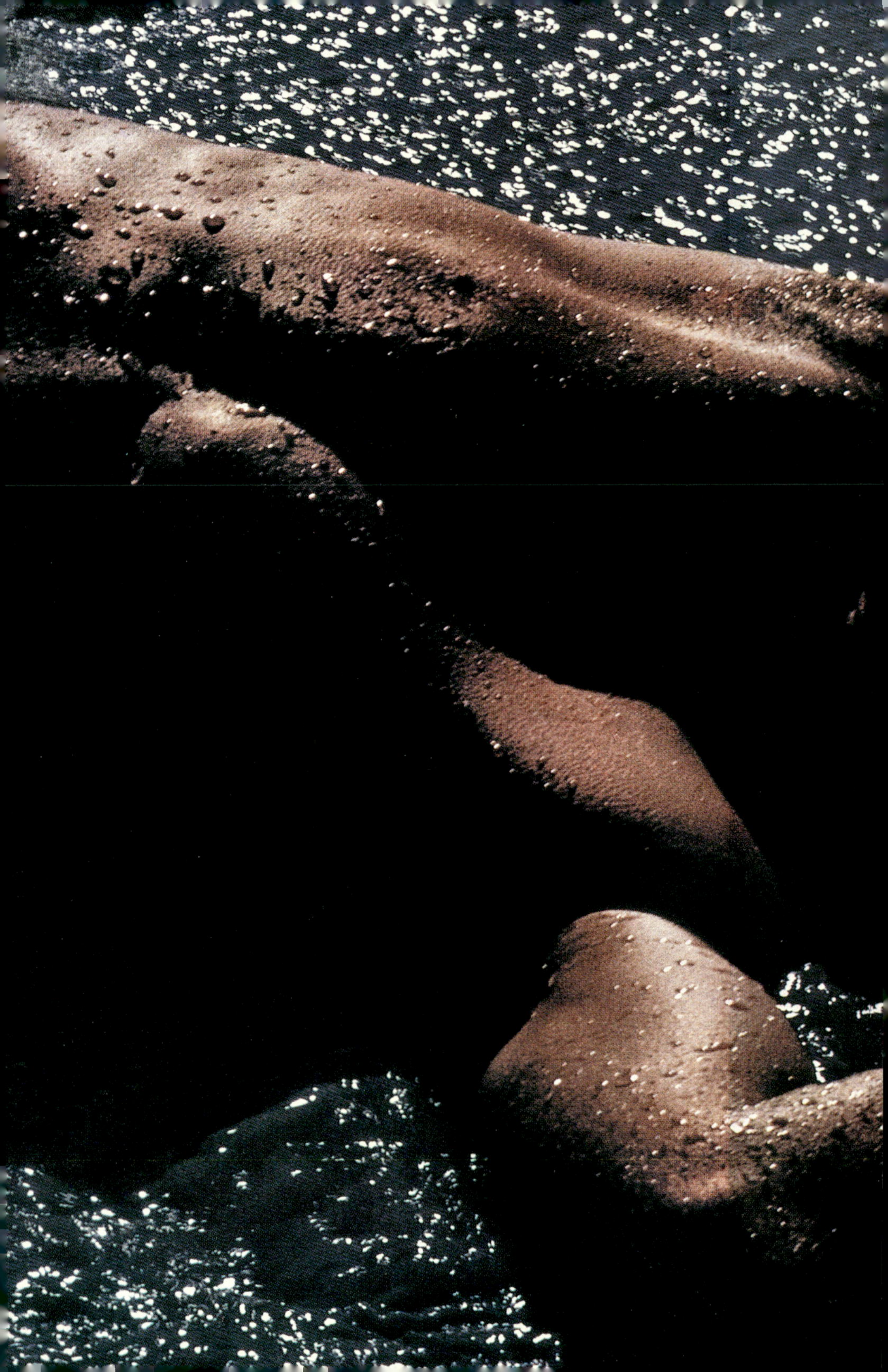

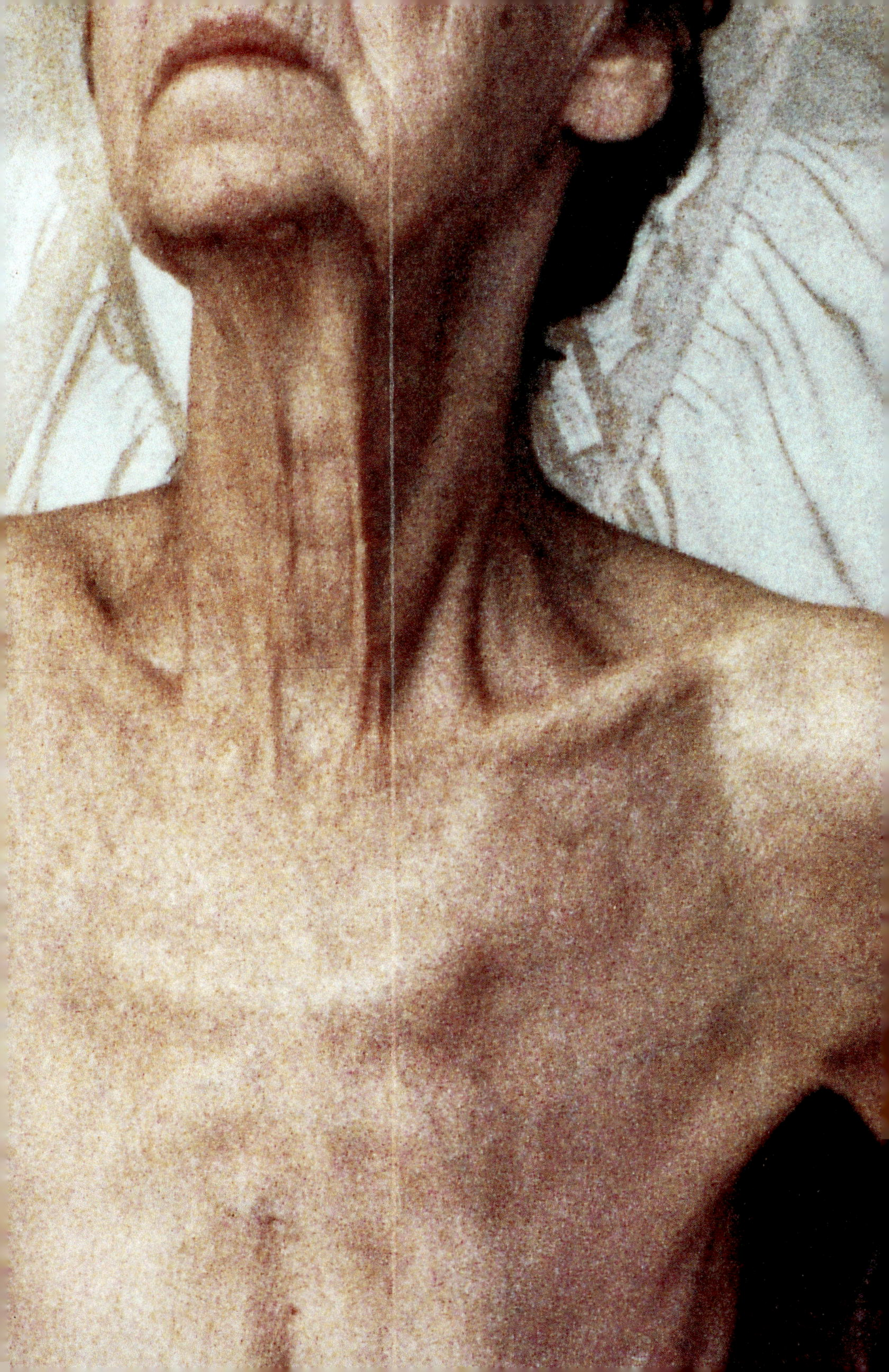

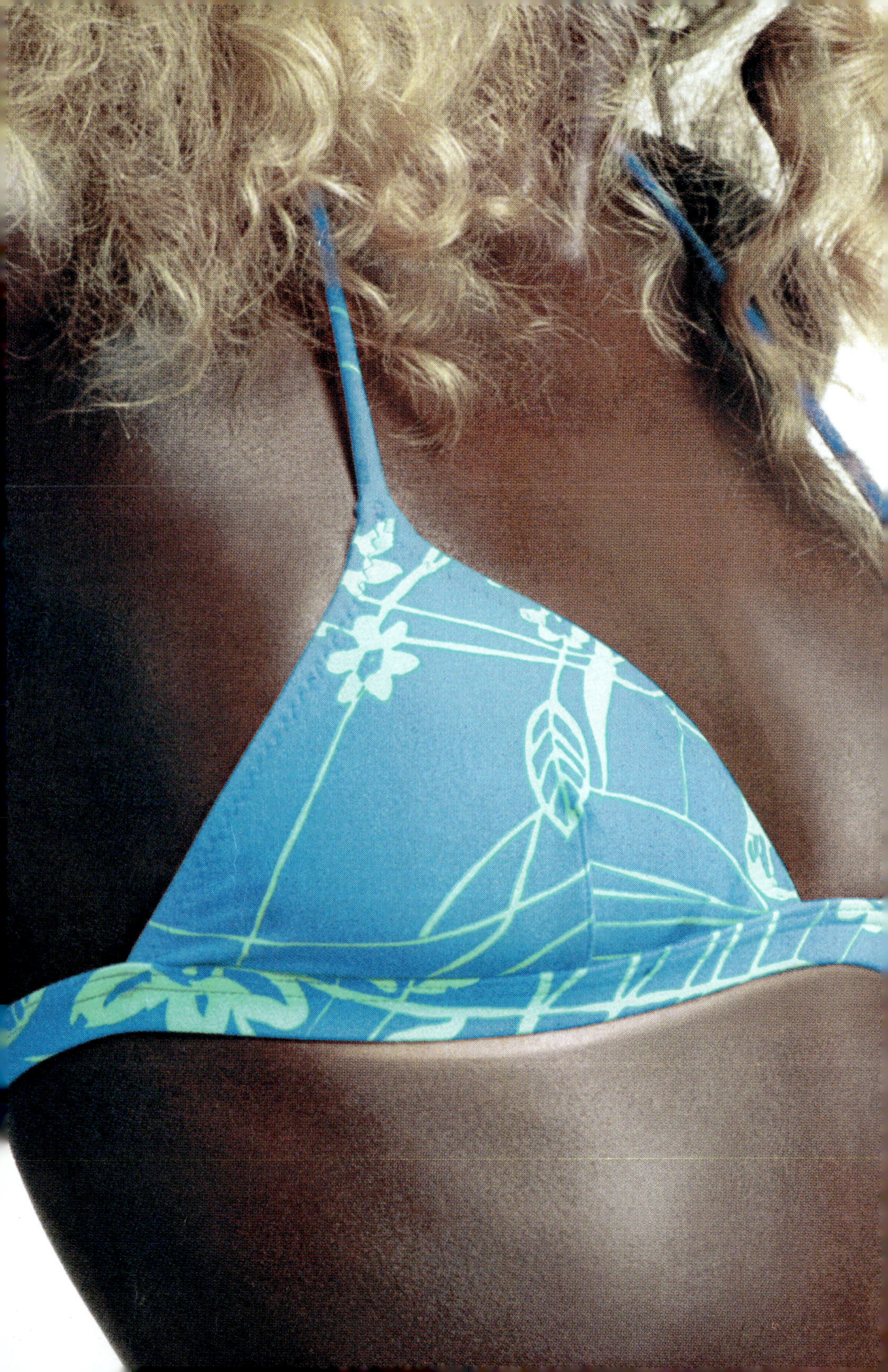

Diversity Management:
New Perspectives or a Thriving Business?

Bettina Richter

Calls for diversity have become louder and more specific in recent years, forcing numerous companies to respond. Today, most corporations and institutions have adopted and actively communicate diversity concepts and policies. The activist community has, in turn, revived the term "pinkwashing," coined over a decade ago, to expose these efforts as a marketing ploy that often fails to produce a real and lasting impact on corporate culture. Consistent commitment to the rights of social minorities and the promotion of diversity in everyday corporate life remains, for the most part, mere lip service. In her book *No Logo: Taking Aim at the Brand Bullies,* globalization critic Naomi Klein sharply criticizes the capitalist logic of the appropriation of diversity, which is particularly manifest in advertising: "The market has seized upon multiculturalism and gender-bending in the same ways that it has seized upon youth culture in general—not just as a market niche but as a source of new carnivalesque imagery."[1]

International fashion group Benetton took a pioneering role when it made multiculturalism its trademark in the early 1980s. Celebrating a utopian world of ethnic diversity, Oliviero Toscani's staged, emblematic photographs were highly innovative in the advertising industry of the day (p. 155). However, Toscani's first campaigns also affirmed stereotypical role attributions, which he sought to refract through humorous visual representation (p. 147). It was particularly in 1992 that Benetton stirred up controversy with provocative, polemical pictorial rhetoric. Toscani only served as the creative director of this campaign, the pictures themselves were taken by other reportage photographers. They depicted, among other things, unsettling scenes of tightly

1 Naomi Klein, *No Logo: Taking Aim at the Brand Bullies*, Toronto 2000, p. 115.

packed groups of refugees stripped of their individuality, or David Kirby as he lay dying of AIDS, surrounded by his family (p. 153, p. 163). The Benetton posters of the early 1990s brought highly charged sociopolitical issues into a public realm of shared image consumption, thus breaking unwritten rules about which bodies had a right to make visual appearances in public spaces.

Furthermore, the direct juxtaposition of the smooth, aestheticized bodies depicted in advertising and the massed bodies of refugees also illustrated the utterly unequal value placed on human life. Exploring this disparity, Achille Mbembe developed the term necropolitics, which draws on and expands the work of Michel Foucault and Frantz Fanon.[2] It describes the use of social and political power to dictate how some people must be left to die or condemned to death. In light of current asylum policy, this notion has, tragically, only gained in relevance. As Jule Govrin notes, "Refugees in particular are identified as a vulnerable group, but such attributions, usually accompanied by media images of helpless masses, exacerbate the structural causes of vulnerability, as refugees are not recognized as political subjects capable of articulating themselves."[3]

Indeed, we have not seen a return of the radicalism of the Benetton campaigns to date. The negotiation of diversity in advertising is still focused on the female body, which attests to the fact that it remains the key public platform for beauty ideals and strictly binary gender discourses. A certain short-term expansion of the visual spectrum is occasionally achieved in that older women, women with natural body proportions or plus-size figures are brought into the picture. Even so, normative notions are never challenged on their basic assumptions, but are, at most, shifted ever so slightly. The idea remains untouched that a woman must invariably meet standards of attractiveness that are reduced to physical appearances. In 2012, two campaigns launched by Victoria's Secret and Dove created a visual dialogue that caused a sensation. Both brands ran slogans that promoted loving one's own individual body. But Victoria's Secret showcased perfect, ultra-slim models, while Dove featured women with highly diverse bodies, which likewise reinforced common beauty standards. Both campaigns had obviously endeavored to show women of different ethnicities.

Ten years later, Adidas ran a big billboard campaign featuring two well-known women as "other" role models:

2   Achille Mbembe, *Necropolitics*, Durham, NC 2019.
3   Jule Govrin, *Politische Körper: Von Sorge und Solidarität*, Berlin 2022, p. 204.

Victoria's Secret and Dove promote the love of one's own body: "The difference between Victoria's Secret and Dove," Reddit post by @aggibridges, 2012

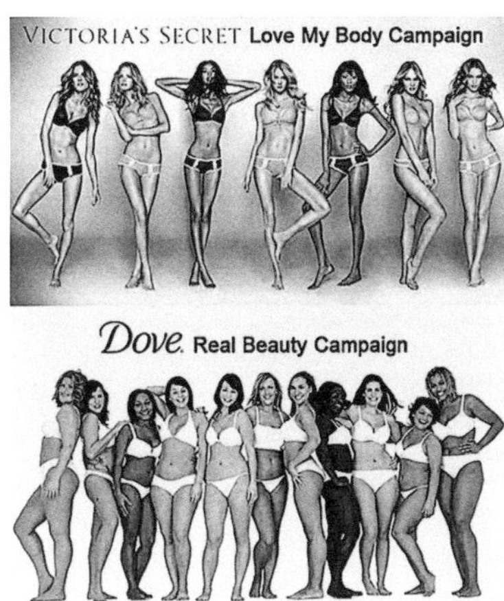

yoga instructor Jessamyn Stanley, whose body breaks with the stereotype of white, slender yoga devotees [p. 158], and model Ellie Goldstein, who was born with Down syndrome. The accompanying slogan, however, reads "Impossible Is Nothing," which emphasized the unusual and unconventional nature of these female advertising models and thus amounted to a reverse form of Othering.[4] Goldstein was the face of Gucci's 2019 beauty campaign and Victoria's Secret chose Sofía Jirau as its "own" model with Down syndrome in 2022. The upshot is that competition for diversity as a brand identity primarily seeks to generate attention and, hence, serves economic interests.

As of yet, a similar situation persists for Black models. Aside from a few famous figures such as Naomi Campbell, they were still largely unwelcome in the fashion industry in the aughts, before being discovered and marketed as a "trend," albeit a short-lived one. In terms of their numbers, they are still not on an equal footing with white models. By the same token, the media void created by the absence of older and elderly people has been filled in recent years. In light of demographic developments and their significance as consumers, somewhat euphemistic terms have been coined to put them back on the map, such as "best agers" or "silver generation." Nevertheless, some of their current depictions suffer from coming across as clichéd exaggerations. After decades they are certainly no longer invisible or presented on social posters solely as worn-out bodies, exhausted to death, or with hunchbacks and wrinkled hands. Elderly people are now portrayed as full of energy and zest for life and as boasting svelte, well-trained bodies as well as an alert mind. They

4   The term Othering refers to a social process in which individuals or groups assure themselves of their own identity by distinguishing themselves from other people or groups. This is achieved by turning them into Others. The distinction usually reflects the power relations and hierarchies of our society and thus results in a debasement of the Other.

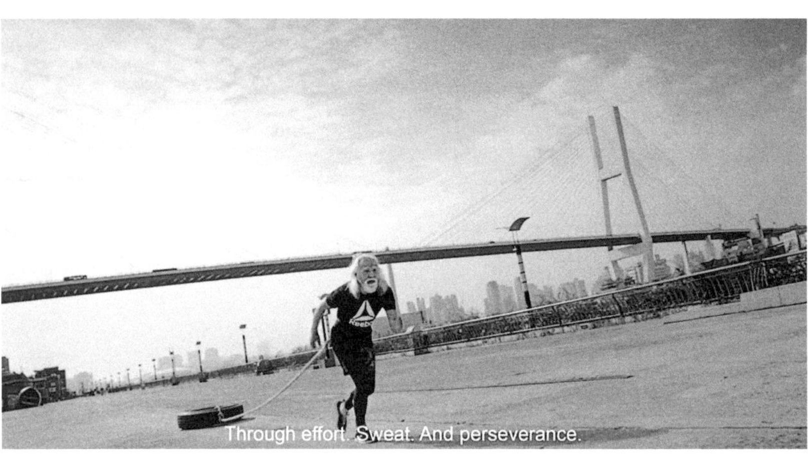

are thus included in the visual alphabet of market-driven images of optimized bodies, distinguished only by a difference in age.

Novel or more diverse body images are almost never formulated proactively in advertising communication. They are usually adopted in response to virulent social currents or as confirmation of already widely accepted representations, so as to highlight a company's tolerant, progressive stance. The most recent rediscovery on the "diversity market" is the LGBTQIA+ community. Presently, this is not so much about advocating for the rights of the gay community, which has been a fairly simple and long-standing practice via the appropriation of the rainbow flag as a lifestyle symbol. Rather, non-binary and trans bodies are now hesitantly brought into focus, too. In 2019, Starbucks won the UK's Diversity in Advertising Award with a commercial celebrating James's coming out at a Starbucks store.[5] Through perfidious simplification of sociopolitical structures and psychological processes and a purely emotional appeal, companies thus position themselves as progressive proponents of a diverse society. The award itself, which has been presented since 2016, exemplifies the extent to which diversity is now appropriated and controlled to serve the interests of the market. What appears particularly absurd is that every year, a different "specific diverse community" features as the theme of the competition announcement.[6]

As much as we need new and varied body images, especially in the public sphere, it has become clear how difficult it is to establish a commonly accepted representation of diversity. bell hooks has pointed out that creating

5   www.youtube.com/watch?v=pcSP1r9eCWw
6   www.diversityinadvertising.co.uk/about

innovative imagery always runs the risk of falling into inverted clichés that perfectly lend themselves to appropriation.[7] Advertising always reflects market power, as well. Ultimately, a paradigm shift can only be achieved if pictorial worlds are examined on a fundamental level with regard to the prevalent gaze and the outlook of their producers, and if they are permanently renewed and overwritten. Today's increased diversity in the representation of bodies has so far not had the power to erase fixed negative images in people's minds—especially since diverse bodies are always read as starkly contrasting stereotypical bodies that conform to market norms, which still dominate the public sphere.

Nevertheless, the fact that varied body images have increasingly made their appearance in today's advertising landscape and are conditioning the gaze of future generations in new ways is in itself a step forward. In the long term, they may also facilitate structural change towards increased equality. A diverse aesthetics "from above" creates an opportunity to critically interrogate its sincerity and sustainability. It is an invitation to consider counter-proposals by various communities "from below": fluid, fragile, changeable, versatile, irritating, and provocative images of the body, which elude fixed definition and dissolve commonly held codes of attribution.

7   bell hooks, *Black Looks: Race and Representation*, Boston, MA 1992, p. 71.

Markus Dederich
Born in 1960, he currently serves as Professor of General Curative Education, Theory of Curative Education and Rehabilitation at the Faculty of Human Sciences at the University of Cologne. His areas of research include ethical considerations in the context of disability, disability studies, inclusion and exclusion research as well as educational aspects of vulnerability. Notable publications: *Optimierung. Ein interdisziplinäres Handbuch* (co-edited with Jörg Zirfas 2023), *Glossar der Vulnerabilität* (co-edited with Jörg Zirfas 2022), *Körper, Kultur und Behinderung. Eine Einführung in die Disability Studies* (2009), *Behinderung, Medizin, Ethik* (2000).

Florian Diener
Born in 1986, he is Managing Director of the Study Center Campus Rothenburg, a research associate at the Ansbach University of Applied Sciences and lecturer at the Friedrich-Alexander-University Erlangen–Nuremberg (FAU). He studied theater and media studies, economics and psychology in Erlangen and Utrecht and received his doctorate from the Chair of Communication Studies at the FAU with a dissertation on stereotypical representations of age and gender in advertising. His research focuses on intersectionality, masculinity, beauty, and the double standard of aging in visual cultures, especially in advertising.

Hans Fässler
Born in 1954, he studied English language and literature as well as history in Zurich. He subsequently served as party secretary of the Social Democratic Party of Switzerland in St. Gallen and taught English at a high school in Trogen AR. Since 2000, he has researched the Swiss involvement in transatlantic slavery and colonialism. His book *Reise in Schwarz-Weiss. Schweizer Ortstermine in Sachen Sklaverei* (2005) was one of the first studies to explore this subject and bring it to the attention of the Swiss public. Now based in St. Gallen, he works as an author, speaker, activist, and city guide following the traces of colonialism, aiming to raise awareness of the part Switzerland played in this crime against humanity.

Bettina Richter
Born in 1964, she studied art history as well as German and Romance languages and literature in Heidelberg, Paris and Zurich, graduating with a dissertation on the anti-war graphics of Théophile-Alexandre Steinlen in 1996. From 1997 to 2006, Richter served as a research associate at the Poster Collection of the Museum für Gestaltung Zürich and was appointed its curator in 2006. In this capacity she has realized, among other exhibitions, *The Magic of Things* (2012), *Japanese Poster Artists—Cherry Blossom and Asceticism* (2014) and *Protest!* (2018). From 2000 to 2005, she taught at the Zurich University of the Arts. She has published and lectured extensively on subjects related to the history of art and literature, as well as on posters. Since 2007, she has served as the editor of the *Poster Collection* series, Museum für Gestaltung Zürich.

Maria Schreiber
Born in 1983, she serves as a postdoctoral researcher at the Department of Communication Studies at the University of Salzburg. As a DOC-team fellow of the Austrian Academy of Sciences, Schreiber was a guest at the Research Training Group "Visibility and Visualization" at the University of Potsdam and at the Digital Ethnography Research Center at RMIT University, Melbourne. In 2017, she earned her doctorate at the University of Vienna with a thesis on digital image practices (*Digitale Bildpraktiken*, Wiesbaden 2020). Her research focuses on visual communication, social media and digital image cultures. She is currently heading the Austrian team at the Chanse project "Travis—Trust and Visuality: Everyday digital practices."

Marilyn Umurungi
Born in 1985, she currently serves as a co-curator at the Swiss National Museum in Zurich. After earning her BA in Art & Media at the Zurich University of the Arts (specialization: theory), she received her MA from the Center for African Studies (ZASB) at the University of Basel, where she focused her research on intersections of Black activist art and feminist politics. She is a member of Bla*Sh, the network for Black women in German-speaking Switzerland. In her theoretical and artistic work, she explores Afrofuturist forms and spaces of poetry and their extension into post-colonial studies, as well as their intersections with racism studies, queer and gender studies and critical whiteness studies.

Paula-Irene Villa
Born in 1968, she serves as Professor of Sociology and Gender Studies at the Ludwig Maximilian University of Munich and, since 2021, as Chairwoman of the German Sociological Association. Her research focuses, among other things, on biopolitics (the relationship between society and the body), care & gender, gender in political mobilizations, popular culture, and social theory. She is the (co-)author or (co-)editor of eleven books and more than fifty-five scientific papers. She has been organizing the Gender Salon, a public science format, in Munich for more than ten years.

Abidin, Crystal, "'Aren't These Just Young, Rich Women Doing Vain Things Online?'. Influencer Selfies as Subversive Frivolity," in: *Social Media + Society*, vol. 2 (2016), no. 2, pp. 1–17.

Arndt, Susan and Nadja Ofuatey-Alazard (eds.), *Wie Rassismus aus Wörtern spricht: (K)Erben des Kolonialismus im Wissensarchiv deutsche Sprache: Ein kritisches Nachschlagewerk*, 4th ed., Münster 2021.

Autenrieth, Ulla Patricia, "Bilder in medial vermittelter Alltagskommunikation," in: Katharina Lobinger (ed.), *Handbuch Visuelle Kommunikationsforschung*, Wiesbaden 2019, pp. 249–268.

Bailey, David E., "Rethinking Black Representation," in: *Ten.8*, no. 31 (1988).

Bauman, Zygmunt, *Modernity and Ambivalence*, Cambridge 1991.

Beauvoir, Simone de, *The Second Sex*, London 1953.

Bellamy, Dodie, *When the Sick Rule the World*, Cambridge/London 2015.

Belting, Hans, *Menschenbild und Körperbild*, Münster 2000.

Bendix, Regina, "Of Mohrenköpfe and Japanesen: Swiss Images of the Foreign," in: *Journal of Folklore Research*, vol. 30 (1993), no. 1, pp. 15–28.

Berger, John, *Ways of Seeing*, London 1972.

Bischoff, Christine, "'Kommt die nächste Miss Schweiz aus dem Kongo?' Postkoloniale Blickregimes in den Medien," in: Patricia Purtschert, Barbara Lüthi and Francesca Falk (eds.), *Postkoloniale Schweiz: Formen und Folgen eines Kolonialismus ohne Kolonien*, Bielefeld 2012, pp. 65–88.

Blake, Christopher, *Wie mediale Körperdarstellungen die Körperzufriedenheit beeinflussen*, Wiesbaden 2015.

Blay, Yaba Amgborale, "Skin Bleaching and Global White Supremacy: By Way of Introduction," in: *Journal of Pan African Studies*, vol. 4 (2011), no. 4, pp. 4–46.

Body Politics. Zeitschrift für Körpergeschichte (Online-Open-Access-journal): http://bodypolitics.de/de

Bonorand, Conradin, "Hieronymus Sailer aus St. Gallen, Schwiegersohn des Augsburger Grosskaufherrn Bartholomäus Welser, und seine Tätigkeit im Lichte seines Briefwechsels mit Vadian," in: *Zwingliana*, vol. 20 (1993), pp. 103–125.

Borscheid, Peter, "Sparsamkeit und Sicherheit: Werbung für Banken, Sparkassen und Versicherungen," in: Peter Borscheid and Clemens Wischermann (eds.), *Bilderwelt des Alltags: Studien zur Geschichte des Alltags*, Stuttgart 1995, pp. 294–349.

Borstnar, Nils, *Männlichkeit und Werbung: Inszenierung—Typologie—Bedeutung*, Kiel 2002.

Bourdieu, Pierre, *Distinction: A Social Critique of the Judgement of Taste*, Cambridge, MA 1984.

Bourdieu, Pierre, "Forms of Capital," trans. Richard Nice, chapter 9 in John G. Richardson (ed.), *Handbook of Theory and Research for the Sociology of Education*, Westport, CN 1986, pp. 280–291.

Bourdieu, Pierre, *Masculine Domination*, Cambridge, MA 2001.

Boyer, Anne, *The Undying: A Meditation on Modern Illness*, New York 2019.

Brändle, Rea, *"Wilde, die sich hier sehen lassen". Jahrmarkt, frühe Völkerschauen und Schaustellerei*, ed. Andreas Bürgi and with a preface by Hilke Thode-Arora, Zurich 2023.

Brändli, Sabina, "'… die Männer sollten schöner geputzt sein als die Weiber': Zur Konstruktion bürgerlicher Männlichkeit im 19. Jahrhundert," in: Thomas Kühne (ed.), *Männergeschichte, Geschlechtergeschichte: Männlichkeit im Wandel der Moderne*, Frankfurt a. M./New York 1996, pp. 101–118.

Brücke-Museum (ed.), *Kirchner und Nolde: Expressionismus: Kolonialismus*, exh. cat. Brücke-Museum Berlin, Munich 2021.

Brun, Samuel, *Samuel Brun, des Wundartzet und Burgers zu Basel, Schiffarten: welche er in etliche newe Länder und Insulen, zu fünff underschiedlichen Malen, mit Gottes Hülff, gethan: an jetzo aber, auff Begeren vieler ehrlicher Leuthen, selbs beschrieben: und menniglichen, mit Kurtzweil und Nutz zu läsen, in Truck kommen lassen*, Basel 1624.

Brunner, Markus, "'Körper im Schmerz'—Zur Körperpolitik der Performancekunst von Stelarc und Valie Export," in: Paula-Irene Villa (ed.), *Schön normal: Manipulationen am Körper als Technologien des Selbst*, Bielefeld 2008, pp. 21–40.

Brunotte, Ulrike and Rainer Herrn (eds.), *Männlichkeiten und Moderne: Geschlecht in den Wissenskulturen um 1900*, Bielefeld 2008.

Bucher, Taina and Anne Helmond, "The Affordances of Social Media Platforms," in: Jean Burgess, Thomas Poell and Alice Marwick (eds.), *The SAGE Handbook of Social Media*, London 2017, pp. 30–44.

Burns, Anne, "Self(ie)-Discipline: Social Regulation as Enacted Through the Discussion of Photographic Practice," in: *International Journal of Communication*, no. 9 (2015), pp. 1716–1733.

Butler, Judith, *Gender Trouble: Feminism and the Subversion of Identity*, London 1990.

Butler, Judith, *Bodies That Matter: On the Discursive Limits of "Sex,"* London 1993.

Butler, Judith, "Imitation and Gender Insubordination" in: Henry Abelove, Michèle Aina Barale and David M. Halperin (eds.), *The Lesbian and Gay Studies Reader*, New York/London 1993, pp. 307–320.

Butler, Judith, *Frames of War: When is Life Grievable?*, London 2010.

CARAH, Collective for Anti-Racist Art History, www.khist.uzh.ch/de/research/projects/carah.html

Coates, Ta-Nehisi, *Between the World and Me*, New York 2015.

Connell, Raewyn, *Masculinities*, Cambridge 1995.

Connell, Raewyn, *Gender*, Wiesbaden 2013.

Corbin, Alain, Jean-Jacques Courtine, and Georges Vigarello (eds.), *L'Histoire de la virilité*, 3 volumes : 1. *L'invention de la virilité: De l'Antiquité aux Lumières*, 2. *Le triomphe de la virilité. Le XIXe siècle*, 3. *La virilité en crise ? Le XXe-XXIe siècle*, Montrouge 2011.

Crais, Clifton C. and Pamela Scully, *Sara Baartman and the Hottentot Venus: A Ghost Story and a Biography*, Princeton, NJ 2009.

Danz, Simone, *Vollständigkeit und Mangel: Das Subjekt in der Sonderpädagogik*, Bad Heilbrunn 2015.

Daston, Lorraine and Peter Galison, *Objectivity*, Princeton, NJ 2010.

David, Thomas, Bouda Etemad, and Janick Maria Schaufelbuehl, *La Suisse et l'esclavage des noirs*, Lausanne 2005.

Davis, Lennard J., *Enforcing Normalcy: Disability, Deafness and the Body*, London / New York 1995.

Dederich, Markus, *Körper, Kultur und Behinderung: Eine Einführung in die Disability Studies*, Bielefeld 2007.

Degele, Nina, *Gender/ Queer Studies: Eine Einführung*, Paderborn 2008.

Derra, Julia Maria, *Das Streben nach Jugendlichkeit in einer alternden Gesellschaft*, Baden-Baden 2012.

Deutsches Hygiene-Museum Dresden and Aktion Mensch e. V. (eds.), *Der (im-)perfekte Mensch: Vom Recht auf Unvollkommenheit*, Dresden 2001.

Deutsches Plakat Museum im Museum Folkwang and Museum Folkwang (eds.), *Afrika: Reflexionen im Plakat*, Göttingen 2012.

Diehl, Paula, *Macht— Mythos—Utopie: Die Körperbilder der SS-Männer*, Berlin 2005.

Diener, Florian, *Stereotype Darstellungen von Alter und Geschlecht in der Werbung: Eine quantitative Bildinhaltsanalyse ausgewählter Zeitschriftenanzeigen der Jahre 2000 und 2020*, dissertation Friedrich-Alexander-Universität Erlangen 2023.

Doppe, Blu and Daniel Holtermann (eds.), *Vom Scheitern, Zweifeln und Ändern: Kritische Reflexionen von Männlichkeiten*, Münster 2021.

Dreßler, Raphaela, "Vom Patriarchat zum androgynen Lustobjekt—50 Jahre Männer im *stern*," in: Christina Holtz-Bacha (ed.), *Stereotype? Frauen und Männer in der Werbung*, 2nd ed., Wiesbaden 2011, pp. 136–166.

Drüeke, Ricarda, Corinna Peil, and Maria Schreiber, "How do Black Lives Matter? Zur visuellen Konstruktion von Protest in deutschsprachigen Tageszeitungen und auf Instagram," in: *Studies in Communication Sciences*, vol. 22 (2022), no. 1, pp. 129–147.

DU, Die Zeitschrift der Kultur, Hautnah: Bilder und Geschichten vom Körper, no. 4, April 1998.

Duden, Barbara, *The Woman Beneath the Skin: A Doctor's Patients in Eighteenth Century Germany*, Cambridge 1991.

Duffy, Brooke Erin and Emily Hund, "Gendered Visibility on Social Media: Navigating Instagram's Authenticity Bind," in: *International Journal of Communication*, no. 13 (2019), pp. 4983–5002.

Duffy, Brooke Erin, Annika Pinch, Shruti Sannon, and Megan Sawey, "The Nested Precarities of Creative Labor on Social Media," in: *Social Media + Society*, vol. 7 (2021), no. 2, pp. 1–12.

Dufour, Annie (ed.), *Le modèle noir: De Géricault à Matisse*, exh. cat. Musée d'Orsay, Paris 2019.

Eckert, Martin, *Werbung mit Behinderung*, Bielefeld 2014.

Eckert, Stine, "Fighting for Recognition: Online Abuse of Women Bloggers in Germany, Switzerland, the United Kingdom, and the United States," in: *New Media & Society*, vol. 20 (2018), no. 4, pp. 1282–1302.

Edmonds, Anthony O., *Muhammad Ali: A Biography*, Westport, CT 2005.

Ellison, Ralph, *Invisible Man*, New York 1952.

Ensel, Angelica, *Nach seinem Bilde: Schönheitschirurgie und Schöpfungsphantasien in der westlichen Medizin*, Bern 1996.

Fässler, Hans, *Reise in Schwarz-Weiss: Schweizer Ortstermine in Sachen Sklaverei*, Zurich 2005.

Fanon, Frantz, *Black Skin, White Masks*, New York 1967.

Fansa, Mamoun (ed.), *Schwarzweissheiten – Vom Umgang mit fremden Menschen*, exh. cat. Landesmuseum für Natur und Mensch Oldenburg, Oldenburg 2001.

Federici, Silvia, *Beyond the Periphery of the Skin: Rethinking, Remaking, and Reclaiming the Body in Contemporary Capitalism*, Oakland, CA 2020.

Fend, Mechthild and Marianne Koos (eds.), *Männlichkeit im Blick: Visuelle Inszenierungen in der Kunst seit der Frühen Neuzeit*, Cologne / Weimar / Vienna 2004.

Foucault, Michel, *The Birth of Clinic: An Archaeology of Medical Perception*, New York 1994.

Foucault, Michel, *Discipline and Punish: The Birth of the Prison*, New York 1977.

Foucault, Michel, "Technologien des Selbst," in: Luther H. Martin, Huck Gutman, and Patrick H. Hutton (eds.), *Technologies of the Self*, London 1988, pp. 29–50.

Foucault, Michel, *The Birth of Biopolitics. Lectures at the Collège de France 1978/1979*, London 1978.

Fredrickson, George M., *Racism: A Short History*, Princeton, NJ 2015.

Frevert, Ute, "*Mann und Weib, und Weib und Mann*": Geschlechter-Differenzen in der Moderne, Munich 1995.

Frevert, Ute, "Soldaten, Staatsbürger: Überlegungen zur historischen Konstruktion von Männlichkeit," in: Thomas Kühne (ed.), *Männergeschichte, Geschlechtergeschichte: Männlichkeit im Wandel der Moderne*, Frankfurt a. M. / New York 1996, pp. 69–87.

Frisch, Max, *Schweiz ohne Armee? Ein Palaver*, Zurich 1989.

Fuchs, Eduard, *Die Juden in der Karikatur: Ein Beitrag zur Kulturgeschichte*, Munich 1921.

Garland-Thomson, Rosemarie, *Extraordinary Bodies: Figuring Physical Disability in American Culture and Literature*, New York 1997.

Garland-Thomson, Rosemarie, *Staring: How We Look*, Oxford / New York 2009.

Gaugele Elke and Kristina Reiss (eds.), *Jugend, Mode und Geschlecht: Die Inszenierung des Körpers in der Konsumkultur*, Frankfurt a. M. 2003.

Gibbs, Martin, James Meese, Michael Arnold, Bjorn Nansen, and Marcus Carter, "#Funeral and Instagram: Death, Social Media, and Platform Vernacular," in: *Information, Communication & Society*, vol. 18 (2015), no. 3, pp. 255–68.

Gill, Rosalind, "Being Watched and Feeling Judged on Social Media," in: *Feminist Media Studies*, vol. 21 (2021), no. 8, pp. 1387–1392.

Ging, Debbie and Sarah Garvey "'Written in these Scars Are the Stories I Can't Explain': A Content Analysis of Pro-Ana and Thinspiration Image Sharing on Instagram," in: *New Media & Society*, vol. 20 (2018), no. 3, pp. 1181–1200.

Goffman, Erving, *Stigma: Notes on the Management of Spoiled Identity*, Harmondsworth 1963.

Goffman, Erving, *Gender Advertisements*, London 1979.

Gojny, Tanja, Kathrin S. Kürzinger, and Susanne Schwarz (eds.), *Selfie—I like it: Anthropologische und ethische Implikationen digitaler Selbstinszenierung*, Stuttgart 2016.

Gómez Cruz, Edgar and Helen Thornham, "Selfies Beyond Self-Representation: The (Theoretical) F(r)ictions of a Practice," in: *Journal of Aesthetics & Culture*, vol. 7 (2015), no. 1, pp. 1–10.

Gordon, Terri J., "A 'Saxophone in the Movement': Josephine Baker and the Music of Dance," in: *Nottingham French Studies*, vol. 43 (2004), Nr. 1, pp. 39–52.

Govrin, Jule, *Politische Körper: Von Sorge und Solidarität*, Berlin 2022.

Grittmann, Elke, Katharina Lobinger, Irene Neverla, and Monika Pater (eds.), *Körperbilder—Körperpraktiken: Visualisierung und Vergeschlechtlichung von Körpern in Medienkulturen*, Cologne 2018.

Gugutzer, Robert, *Soziologie des Körpers*, 5th ed., Bielefeld 2015.

Härtel, Insa and Sigrid Schade (eds.), *Körper und Repräsentation*, Wiesbaden 2002.

Hall, Stuart, "The Spectacle of the Other," in: idem (ed.), *Representations: Cultural Representations and Signifying Practices*, London 1997, pp. 223–290.

Hall, Stuart, *Rassismus und kulturelle Identität*, Hamburg 2021.

Hammer-Tugendhat, Daniela, "Körperbilder – Abbild der Natur? Zur Konstruktion von Geschlechterdifferenz in der Aktkunst der Frühen Neuzeit," in: *L'Homme: Zeitschrift für feministische Geschichtswissenschaft*, vol. 5 (1994), no. 1, pp. 45–58.

Hammer-Tugendhat, Daniela, "Kunst, Sexualität und Geschlechterkonstruktionen in der abendländischen Kultur," in: Franz X. Eder and Sabine Frühstück (eds.), *Neue Geschichten der Sexualität: Beispiele aus Ostasien und Zentraleuropa 1700–2000*, Vienna 1999, pp. 69–92.

Hammer-Tugendhat, Daniela, *Kunstgeschichte als Kulturwissenschaft*, lecture series at the University of Applied Arts, Vienna 2018, www.youtube.com/playlist?list=PLjR8HTOEMQuf_tkFoVsadjWa5Ofqk_Y4e

Hepp, Frieder (ed.), *Frauenkörper: Der Blick auf das Weibliche von Albrecht Dürer bis Cindy Sherman*, Petersberg 2021.

Herport, Albrecht, *Eine kurtze Ost-Indianische Reiss-Beschreibung*, Bern 1669.

Hipfl, Brigitte, Elisabeth Klaus, and Uta Scheer (eds.), *Identitätsräume: Nation, Körper und Geschlecht in den Medien. Eine Topografie*, Bielefeld 2004.

Hoffmann, Dagmar (ed.), *Körperästhetiken: Filmische Inszenierungen von Körperlichkeit*, Bielefeld 2010.

Hoffner, Cynthia A. and Bradley J. Bond, "Parasocial Relationships, Social Media, & Well-Being," in: *Current Opinion in Psychology*, no. 45 (June 2022), pp. 1–6.

Holtz-Bacha, Christina (ed.), *Stereotype? Frauen und Männer in der Werbung*, Wiesbaden 2011.

Holzinger, Sarah, *Die Darstellung von Juden und Jüdinnen im humoristischen Volksblatt Kikeriki*, Master's thesis, Karl-Franzens-Universität Graz 2015.

hooks, bell, *Black Looks: Race and Representation*, 2015.

Hoop, Achim, *Völkerschauen in St. Gallen: Eine Analyse der Berichterstattung zu den St. Galler Völkerschauen zwischen 1870 und 1905*, Master's thesis, Pädagogische Hochschule St. Gallen 2018.

Horton, Donald and R. Richard Wohl, "Mass Communication and Para-Social Interaction: Observations on Intimacy at a Distance," in: *Participations*, vol. 3 (2006), no. 1, pp. 1–23.

Hürlimann, Annemarie, Martin Roth, and Klaus Vogel (eds.), *Fremdkörper—Fremde Körper: Von unvermeidlichen Kontakten und widerstreitenden Gefühlen*, exh. cat. Deutsches Hygienemuseum Dresden, Ostfildern-Ruit 1999.

Hughes, Bill, "Fear, Pity and Disgust: Emotions and the Non-Disabled Imaginary," in: Nick Watson, Alan Roulstone, and Carol Thomas (eds.), *Routledge Handbook of Disability Studies*, London / New York 2012, pp. 67–77.

Hund, Wulf D., *Wie die Deutschen weiss wurden: Kleine (Heimat)Geschichte des Rassismus*, Stuttgart 2017.

Jelloun, Tahar Ben, *Le racisme expliqué à ma fille*, Paris 1998.

Jones, Trina, "Shades of Brown: The Law of Skin Color," in: *Duke Law Journal*, vol. 49 (2000), no. 6, pp. 1487–1557.

Junge, Torsten and Imke Schmincke (eds.), *Marginalisierte Körper: Beiträge zur Soziologie und Geschichte des anderen Körpers*, Münster 2007.

Jurgenson, Nathan, "The Faux-Vintage Photo," *The Society Pages*, 2011, www.thesocietypages.org/cyborgology/2011/05/14/the-faux-vintage-photo-full-essay-parts-i-ii-and-iii

Kaufmann, Jean-Claude, *Frauenkörper – Männerblicke*, Konstanz 1996.

Keller, Reiner and Michael Meuser (eds.), *Alter(n) und vergängliche Körper*, Wiesbaden 2017.

Kelly, Natasha A., *Millis Erwachen—Milli's Awakening: Schwarze Frauen, Kunst und Widerstand—Black Women, Art and Resistance*, Berlin 2018.

Kirchhoff, Arthur (ed.), *Die akademische Frau: Gutachten hervorragender Universitätsprofessoren, Frauenlehrer und Schriftsteller über die Befähigung der Frau zum wissenschaftlichen Studium und Berufe*, Berlin 1897.

Klein, Naomi, *No Logo! Taking Aim at the Brand Bullies*, London 2000.

Klöppel, Ulrike, *XX0XY ungelöst: Hermaphroditismus, Sex und Gender in der deutschen Medizin: Eine historische Studie zur Intersexualität*, Bielefeld 2010.

Kollarz, Anika-Brigitte, *Aus dem Rahmen—Ein weisses Gedicht auf 'nem schwarzen Gesicht? Visuelle Repräsentationen Schwarzer Frauen zwischen der deutschen Kolonialzeit und der Weimarer Republik*, dissertation, Technische Universität Darmstadt 2012.

Krech, Hartmut, "Lichtbilder vom Menschen: Vom Typenbild zur anthropologischen Fotografie," in: *Fotogeschichte: Beiträge zur Geschichte und Ästhetik der Fotografie*, vol. 4 (1984), no. 14, pp. 3–15.

Krischel, Roland and Anja K. Sevcik, *Susanna: Bilder einer Frau vom Mittelalter bis MeToo*, exh. cat. Wallraf-Richartz-Museum Cologne, Petersberg 2022.

Kristeva, Julia and Charles Gardou, "Behinderung und Vulnerabilität," in: Otto Braun and Ulrike Lüdtke (eds.), *Sprache und Kommunikation: Enzyklopädisches Handbuch der Behindertenpädagogik*, Stuttgart 2012, pp. 39–48.

Annette Kuhn, *The Power of the Image: Essays on Representation and Sexuality*, London/ New York 1994.

Kühne, Thomas, "Staatspolitik, Frauenpolitik, Männerpolitik: Politikgeschichte als Geschlechtergeschichte," in: Hans Medick and Anne-Charlott Trepp (eds.), *Geschlechtergeschichte und Allgemeine Geschichte: Herausforderungen und Perspektiven*, Göttingen 1998, pp. 171–231.

Kunstmuseum Basel (ed.), *Kara Walker: A Black Hole Is Everything a Star Longs to Be*, exh. booklet, Basel 2022.

L'Alpe, Le sexe de l'alpe, no. 68, 2015.

Lang, Josef, *Demokratie in der Schweiz: Geschichte und Gegenwart*, Baden 2020.

Laqueur, Thomas, *Auf den Leib geschrieben: Die Inszenierung der Geschlechter von der Antike bis Freud*, Munich 1996.

Larsen, Jonas and Mette Sandbye, "The New Face of Snapshot Photography," in: idem (eds.), *Digital Snaps: The New Face of Photography*, London 2013, pp. xv–xxxiii.

Lechner, Elisabeth, *Riot, Don't Diet! Aufstand der widerspenstigen Körper*, Vienna 2021.

Leduc, Amanda, *Disfigured: On Fairy Tales, Disability and Making Space*, Toronto 2020.

Lehmuskallio, Asko and Edgar Gómez Cruz, "Why Material Visual Practices?," in: idem (eds.), *Digital Photography and Everyday Life: Empirical Studies on Material Visual Practices*, New York 2016, pp. 1–16.

Leipold-Schneider, Gerda, "Die inszenierte Frau in den Bergen: Das Bild der Frau in Fotografie und Tourismusplakat in Graubünden in der ersten Hälfte des 20. Jahrhunderts," in: Ursula Jecklin, Silke Redolfi, and Silvia Hofmann (eds.). *FrauenKörper: Beiträge zur Frauen- und Geschlechtergeschichte Graubündens im 19. und 20. Jahrhundert*, Zurich 2005, pp. 152–175.

Link, Jürgen, *Versuch über den Normalismus: Wie Normalität produziert wird*, Opladen 1997.

Lischka, Gerhard Johann (ed.), *Kunstkörper: Werbekörper*, Cologne 2000.

Lorenz, Maren, *Menschenzucht: Frühe Ideen und Strategien 1500–1870*, Göttingen 2018.

Maase, Kaspar, "Entblösste Brust und schwingende Hüfte: Momentaufnahmen von der Jugend der fünfziger Jahre," in: Thomas Kühne (ed.), *Männergeschichte, Geschlechtergeschichte: Männlichkeit im Wandel der Moderne*, Frankfurt a. M./New York 1996, pp. 193–217.

Maier, Tanja, "Feminismus, Gender und Queer," in: Andreas Hepp, Friedrich Krotz, Swantje Lingenberg, and Jeffrey Wimmer (eds.), *Handbuch Cultural Studies und Medienanalyse*, Wiesbaden 2015, pp. 49–58.

Malacrida, Claudia and Jacqueline Low (eds.), *Sociology of the Body*, Don Mills, CA 2016.

Mardon, Rebecca, Hayley Cocker, and Kate Daunt, "When Parasocial Relationships Turn Sour: Social Media Influencers, Eroded and Exploitative Intimacies, and Anti-Fan Communities," in: *Journal of Marketing Management*, January 2023, pp. 1–31.

Martschukat, Jürgen and Olaf Stieglitz, *Geschichte der Männlichkeiten,* Frankfurt a. M./New York 2018.

Martschukat, Jürgen, *Das Zeitalter der Fitness: Wie der Körper zum Zeichen für Erfolg und Leistung wurde*, Frankfurt a. M. 2019.

Marwah, Shristi, "Who is Wheelchair Rapunzel? TikToker Attempts to Get Reddit 'Snark Page' Removed Following 'Cyber Bullying'," *Sportskeeda*, 2023, www.sportskeeda.com/pop-culture/who-wheelchair-rapunzel-tiktoker-attempts-get-reddit-snark-page-removed-following-cyber-bullying.

Mbembe, Achille, *Critique of Black Reason*, Durham, NC 2017.

Mbembe, Achille, *Necropolitics*, Durham, NC 2019.

McRobbie, Angela, "Notes on the Perfect: Competitive Femininity in Neoliberal Times," in: *Australian Feminist Studies,* vol. 30 (2015), no. 83, pp. 3–20.

Mehlmann, Sabine and Sigrid Ruby (eds.), *"Für Dein Alter siehst Du gut aus!" Von der Un/Sichtbarkeit des alternden Körpers im Horizont des demographischen Wandels: Multidisziplinäre Perspektiven*, Bielefeld 2010.

Meuser, Michael, *Geschlecht und Männlichkeit. Soziologische Theorie und kulturelle Deutungsmuster*, Opladen 1998.

Michel, Noémie, *Quand les mots et les images blessent: Postcolonialité, égalité et politique des actes de discours en Suisse et en France,* dissertation, Université de Genève, 2014.

Michelberger, Melodie, *Body Politics*, Hamburg 2021.

Millett-Gallant, Ann, *The Disabled Body in Contemporary Art*, New York 2010.

Minder, Patrick, *La Suisse colonial: Les représentations de l'Afrique et des Africains en Suisse au temps des colonies (1880–1939)*, Bern 2011.

Mitchell, David T. and Sharon L. Snyder, *Narrative Prosthesis. Disability and the Dependencies of Discourse*, Ann Arbor, MI 2000.

Mitchell, David T. and Sharon L. Snyder, "Representation and Its Discontents: The Uneasy Home of Disability in Literature and Film," in: Gary L. Albrecht, Katherine D. Seelman and Michael Bury (eds.), *Handbook of Disability Studies*, Thousand Oaks, CA 2001, pp. 195–218.

Morrissey, Ellie, "Gender, Power and Technology: Is Trolling a Man's Sport?," in: *Trinity Women's Review*, vol. 3 (2019), no. 1, pp. 25–38.

Mosse, George L., *The Image of Man: The Creation of Modern Masculinity*, New York 1996.

Müller, Michael R., "Das Körperbild als Selbstbild," in: Michael R. Müller, Hans-Georg Soeffner, and Anne Sonnenmoser (eds.), *Körper Haben: Die symbolische Formung der Person*, Weilerswist 2011, pp. 87–106.

Naderer, Brigitte, Christina Peter and Kathrin Karsay, "This Picture Does Not Portray Reality: Developing and Testing a Disclaimer for Digitally Enhanced Pictures on Social Media Appropriate for Austrian Tweens and Teens," in: *Journal of Children and Media*, vol. 16 (2022), no. 2, pp. 149–167.

Neiman, Susan, *Learning from the Germans: Confronting Race and the Memory of Evil*, London 2019.

Nelson, Elyse and Wendy S. Walters, *Fictions of Emancipation: Carpeaux's Why Born Enslaved! Reconsidered*, exh. cat. Metropolitan Museum, New York 2022.

Neugebauer, Daniel (ed.), *Gegen_Lesungen des Körpers*, Leipzig 2021.

Nimmergut, Jörg, *Werben mit Sex*, Munich 1966.

Noor, Poppy, "What Is Body Neutrality, the New Trend Loved by Beautiful Celebs?," in: *The Guardian*, 2019, www.theguardian.com/fashion/2019/oct/31/body-neutrality-taylor-swift-jameela-jamil-latest-trend.

Nymoen, Ole and Wolfgang M. Schmitt, *Influencer: Die Ideologie der Werbekörper*, Berlin 2021.

Orbach, Susie, *Bodies,* London 2009.

Otele, Olivette, *African Europeans: An Untold History*, London 2020.

Oyěwùmí, Oyèrónkè, *The Invention of Women: Making an African Sense of Western Gender Discourses*, London 1997.

Pardo, Alona (ed.), *Masculinities: Liberation Through Photography*, exh. cat. Barbican Art Gallery, Les recontres de la Photographie und Gropius-Bau, Munich / London / New York 2020.

Paulus, Julia, Eva-Maria Silies, and Kerstin Wolff, "Die Bundesrepublik aus geschlechterhistorischer Perspektive," in: idem (eds.), *Zeitgeschichte als Geschlechtergeschichte: Neue Perspektiven auf die Bundesrepublik*, Frankfurt a. M. / New York 2012, pp. 11–29.

Pedretti, Erica, *Valerie oder Das unerzogene Auge*, Frankfurt a. M. 1986.

Penny, Laurie, *Meat Market: Female Flesh Under Capitalism,* Winchester, UK 2011.

Prommer, Elizabeth, "Der kühne Abenteurer, der fleissige Forscher und der geniale Denker. Das Männerbild in der Gartenlaube," in: Christiane Hackl, Elizabeth Prommer, and Brigitte Scherer (eds.), *Models und Machos? Frauen- und Männerbilder in den Medien*, Konstanz 1996, pp. 13–50.

Purtschert, Patricia, *Kolonialität und Geschlecht im 20. Jahrhundert: Eine Geschichte der weissen Schweiz*, Bielefeld 2019.

Reißmann, Wolfgang, *Mediatisierung visuell: Kommunikationstheoretische Überlegungen und eine Studie zum Wandel privater Bildpraxis*, Baden-Baden 2015.

Riegraf, Birgit, Dierk Spreen, and Sabine Mehlmann (eds.), *Medien—Körper—Geschlecht*, Bielefeld 2012.

Rousseau, Jean-Jacques, *Discours sur l'origine et les fondements de l'inégalité parmi les hommes*, Geneva 1755.

Said, Edward W., *Orientalism*, New York 1978.

Sarasin, Philipp, *Reizbare Maschinen: Eine Geschichte des Körpers 1765–1914*, Berlin 2001.

Sarasin, Philipp. "'Mapping the body': Körpergeschichte zwischen Konstruktivismus, Politik und 'Erfahrung'," in: idem, *Geschichtswissenschaft und Diskursanalyse*, Frankfurt a. M. 2003, pp. 100–121.

Schaffer, Johanna, *Ambivalenzen der Sichtbarkeit*, Bielefeld 2008.

Schaffer, Johanna and Barbara Paul (eds.), *Mehr(wert) queer—Queer Added (Value): Visuelle Kultur, Kunst und Gender-Politiken—Visual Culture, Art, and Gender Politics*, Bielefeld 2009.

Scheller, Jörg, *Body-Bilder*, Berlin 2021.

Schiebinger, Londa, *Nature's Body: Gender in the Making of Modern Science*, Boston 1993.

Schiebinger, Londa (ed.), *Feminism and the Body*, Oxford / New York 2000.

Schmale, Wolfgang, *Geschichte der Männlichkeit in Europa (1450–2000)*, Vienna 2003.

Schmerl, Christiane, "Kosmetische Zwangsjacken," in: idem (ed.), *Frauenfeindliche Werbung. Sexismus als heimlicher Lehrplan*, Reinbek bei Hamburg 1983, pp. 41–47.

Schmincke, Imke, *Körpersoziologie*, Paderborn 2021.

Schor, Gabriele (ed.), *Feministische Avantgarde. Kunst der 1970er-Jahre aus der Sammlung Verbund, Wien*, Munich 2015.

Schreiber, Maria and Gerit Götzenbrucker, "Körperbilder—Plattformbilder? Bildpraktiken und visuelle Kommunikation auf Social Media," in: Elke Grittmann, Katharina Lobinger, Irene Neverla, and Monika Pater (eds.), *Körperbilder – Körperpraktiken*, Cologne 2018, pp. 29–50.

Schreiber, Maria, *Digitale Bildpraktiken: Handlungsdimensionen visueller vernetzter Kommunikation*, Wiesbaden 2020.

Schreiber, Maria, "Digitale Ambivalenz? Übergegensätzlichkeiten in Bildkommunikation auf Social Media," in: Roswitha Breckner, Karin Liebhart, and Maria Pohn-Lauggas (eds.), *Sozialwissenschaftliche Analysen von Bild- und Medienwelten*, Berlin / Boston 2021, pp. 55–78.

Schroer, Markus (ed.), *Soziologie des Körpers*, Frankfurt a. M. 2005.

Schroeter, Klaus R., "Altersbilder als Körperbilder. Doing Age by Bodyfication," in: Frank Berner, Judith Rossow, and Klaus-Peter Schwitzer (eds.), *Individuelle und kulturelle Altersbilder: Expertisen zum Sechsten Altenbericht der Bundesregierung*, Wiesbaden 2012, pp. 153–230.

Senft, Theresa M., "Microcelebrity and Branded Self," in: John Hartley, Jean Burgess, and Axel Bruns (eds.), *A Companion to New Media Dynamics*, Chichester 2015, pp. 346–354.

Siebers, Tobin, *Disability Aesthetics*, Ann Arbor, MI 2010.

Siegele-Wenschkewitz, Leonore and Gerda Stuchlik (eds.), *Frauen und Faschismus in Europa: Der faschistische Körper*, Pfaffenweiler 1993.

Société des Amis de la Bibliothèque Forney (ed.), *NégriPub: L'image des Noirs dans la publicité depuis un siècle*, Paris 1987.

Sontag, Susan, "The Double Standard of Ageing," in: Vida Carver and Penny Liddiard (eds.), *An Ageing Population*, New York 1979, pp. 72–80.

Sontag, Susan, "In Plato's Cave," in: Sontag, Susan, *On Photography*, New York 1977, pp. 2–24.

Sontag, Susan, *On Photography*, New York 1977.

Spickernagel, Ellen, "Geschichte und Geschlecht: Der feministische Ansatz," in: Hans Belting et al. (eds.), *Kunstgeschichte: Eine Einführung*, Berlin 1985, pp. 264–282.

Staatsgalerie Stuttgart (ed.), *Das exotische Plakat*, Stuttgart 1987.

Stammberger, Birgit, *Monster und Freaks. Eine Wissensgeschichte aussergewöhnlicher Körper im 19. Jahrhundert*, Bielefeld 2011.

Stapferhaus Lenzburg (ed.), *Geschlecht: Jetzt entdecken,* Zurich 2020.

Steininger, Florian and Ekow Eshun (eds.), *The New Africain Portraiture: Shariat Collections*, exh. cat. Kunsthalle Krems, Cologne 2022.

Stettler, Niklaus, Peter Haenger, and Robert Labhardt, *Baumwolle, Sklaven und Kredite: Die Basler Welthandelsfirma Christoph Burckhardt & Cie. in revolutionärer Zeit (1789–1815)*, Basel 2004.

Tappe, Heinrich, "Der Genuss, die Wirkung und ihr Bild: Werte, Konventionen und Motive gesellschaftlichen Alkoholgebrauchs im Spiegel der Werbung," in: Peter Borscheid and Clemens Wischermann (eds.), *Bilderwelt des Alltags: Studien zur Geschichte des Alltags*, Stuttgart 1995, pp. 222–241.

Taubira, Christiane, *L'Esclavage raconté à ma fille*, Paris 2016.

Theweleit, Klaus, *Male Fantasies*, Cambridge, UK 1987.

Thiel-Stern, Shayla, "Collaborative, Productive, Performative, Templated: Youth, Identity, and Breaking the Fourth Wall Online," in: Rebecca Ann Lind (ed.), *Produsing Theory in a Digital World*, New York 2012, pp. 87–103.

Thomson, T. J., "Exploring the Life Cycle of Smartphone Images from Camera Rolls to Social Media Platforms," in: *Visual Communication Quarterly*, vol. 28 (2021), no. 1, pp. 19–33.

Tiidenberg, Katrin, "Odes to Heteronormativity: Presentations of Femininity in Russian-Speaking Pregnant Women's Instagram Accounts," in: *International Journal of Communication*, vol. 9 (2015), pp. 1746–1758.

Turner, Bryan S. (ed.), *Routledge Handbook of Body Studies*, London / New York 2012.

Ullrich, Bettina, *Das Alter in der Kunst: Die Darstellung des alten Menschen in der bildenden Kunst des 20. Jahrhunderts*, Oberhausen 1999.

Veletsianos, George, Shandell Houlden, Jaigris Hodson, and Chandell Gosse, "Women Scholars' Experiences with Online Harassment and Abuse: Self-Protection, Resistance, Acceptance, and Self-Blame," in: *New Media & Society*, vol. 20 (2018), no. 12, pp. 4689–4708.

Vergine, Lea, *Body Art and Performance: The Body as Language*, Milan 2007.

Villa, Paula-Irene, *Sexy Bodies: Eine soziologische Reise durch den Geschlechtskörper*, Wiesbaden 1999.

Villa, Paula-Irene (ed.), *Schön normal: Manipulationen am Körper als Technologien des Selbst*, Bielefeld 2008.

Villa, Paula-Irene, "Zygmunt Bauman und die Geschlechterforschung: Eine viel versprechende Liaison?" in: *Österreichische Zeitschrift für Soziologie*, vol. 33 (2008), no. 4, pp. 45–61.

Waldschmidt, Anne, "'Behinderung' neu denken: Kulturwissenschaftliche Perspektiven der Disability Studies," in: idem (ed.), *Kulturwissenschaftliche Perspektiven der Disability Studies*, Tagungsdokumentation, Kassel 2003, pp. 11–22.

Walker King, Debra, *African Americans and the Culture of Pain*, Charlottesville, VA 2008.

Walker Rettberg, Jill, *Seeing Ourselves Through Technology*, London 2014.

Walters, Margaret, *Der männliche Akt: Ideal und Verdrängung in der europäischen Kunstgeschichte*, Berlin 1979.

Wells, Georgia, Jeff Horwitz, and Deepa Seetharaman,

"Facebook Knows Instagram Is Toxic for Teen Girls, Company Documents Show," in: *The Wallstreet Journal*, Sept. 14, 2021, www.wsj.com/articles/facebook-knows-instagram-is-toxic-for-teen-girls-company-documents-show-11631620739

Willems, Herbert and York Kautt, *Theatralität der Werbung: Theorie und Analyse massenmedialer Wirklichkeit: Zur kulturellen Konstruktion von Identitäten*, Berlin 2003.

Wolter, Stefanie, *Die Vermarktung des Fremden: Exotismus und die Anfänge des Massenkonsums*, Frankfurt a. M. 2005.

Yancy, George, *Black Bodies, White Gazes: The Continuing Significance of Race*, Lanham, MD 2008.

Young, Stella, "Inspiration Porn and the Objectification of Disability," TEDxSydney, 2014, www.youtube.com/watch?v=SxrS7-I_sMQ.

Zeller, Joachim, *Weisse Blicke, schwarze Körper: Afrikaner im Spiegel westlicher Alltagskultur*, Erfurt 2010.

Zurstiege, Guido, *Mannsbilder—Männlichkeit in der Werbung: Zur Darstellung von Männern in der Anzeigenwerbung der 50er, 70er und 90er Jahre*, Opladen 1998.

www.louverture.ch/cca
www.slavevoyages.org/voyage/database

Image Credits

All posters depicted are from the collection of the Museum für Gestaltung Zürich: Museum für Gestaltung Zürich, Poster Collection / Zurich University of the Arts. All rights (including copyright) belong to the creators and/or their assignees.

We have made every effort to identify all relevant rights holders. In those instances where we have not been able to locate and / or notify the rights holder(s), we ask that they contact the publisher.

The cropped details depicted in the book are taken from the poster images on the following pages:
Cover   136 upper right / 137 lower left / 126 right / 164 left
Contents   1 > 148 upper left / 2 > 124 lower left / 19 > 159 lower left / 20 > 149 lower left / 21 > 133 upper right / 22 > 175 right / 39 > 166 right / 40 > 140 lower right / 41 > 139 left / 42 > 155 left / 59 > 156 lower left / 60 > 165 right / 61 > 154 upper right / 62 > 163 right / 79 > 154 left / 80 > 174 upper right / 81 > 135 left / 82 > 174 lower right / 99 > 156 right / 100 > 128 left / 101 > 165 left / 102 > 146 right / 119 > 123 lower right / 120 > 148 right

13   University Library of Erlangen-Nürnberg
15   Private collection
17   John A. McAllister Collection: Civil War Envelopes (Library Company of Philadelphia)
18   Bayerische Staatsbibliothek, Image Archive
24   Christen Sveaas Art Collection. Courtesy of the artist and Galerie Nordenhake, Berlin, Stockholm, Mexico City. Photo: Matthias Lindner
30   Alice Salomon Archive, Alice Salomon University of Applied Sciences, Signature 7-PK-1
33   Wikimedia Commons
43 left   Henkel Corporate Archives © Konzernarchiv Henkel AG & Co. KGaA
43 right   From: Paul Ruben, *Die Reklame: Ihre Kunst und Wissenschaft* (vol. 1), Berlin, 1913, p. 224
44   Mercedes-Benz Classic
45   Deutscher Sparkassenverlag
46   https://www.theconcertposter.com/Prince-Parade-Frankfurt-1986-Konzertplakat
56   Neil Leifer / Neil Leifer Collection via Getty Images
67   Excerpt from: Rotraut Susanne Berner, *Frühlings-Wimmelbuch* © 2004 Gerstenberg Verlag, Hildesheim
69   Princeton University Library
72   Kulturmuseum St. Gallen. Photo: Urs Bucher / ubupix.com
74   Photo: Dmitrii Travnikov
75   Excerpt from: Doro Göbel and Peter Knorr, *Der Ausflug* © 2022, 2010 Beltz & Gelberg, Verlagsgruppe Beltz, Weinheim Basel
93   https://www.tiktok.com/@inesbeauty_officiel/video/7207870123292642565?q=Ines.beauty&t=1682496863668
94   https://www.instagram.com/p/CokzmbWS8PZ/?hl=de
95   https://www.instagram.com/stories/highlights/17906047622728348/
96   https://www.instagram.com/p/CW02-kvIBuV/
97   https://www.instagram.com/p/CqxwhmFOLsn/?hl=de
105   https://www.businessinsider.com/victorias-secret-angels-vs-dove-models-2012-12?r=US&IR=T
106   Excerpt from: https://www.youtube.com/watch?v=IYmXMvYZuYg
123 lower right / 126 right / 154 upper right
        © Benetton Group / Terry Richardson
126 upper left / 159 right
        © Musée Ruzo
127 right   Martin Peikert © 2023, ProLitteris, Zurich
130 right   © Bill Graham Archives, LLC, all rights reserved
134 lower left / 136 lower right
        © Guerrilla Girls, courtesy http://guerrillagirls.com
143 right / 158 right
        Karl Bickel-Stiftung, Walenstadt

144 left / 147 lower left / 155 lower right / 167 upper left / 168 upper left © Benetton Group / Oliviero Toscani © 2023, ProLitteris, Zurich
145 left   Roman Cieślewicz © 2023, ProLitteris, Zurich
148 right / 164 upper right / 176 lower right   Kabushiki Kaisha Tanaka Ikko Design Shitsu / DNP Foundation for Cultural Promotion / Shigenori Tanaka
150 upper left   © hansfalksuccession
150 upper right / 173 lower right   Otto Baumberger © 2023, ProLitteris, Zurich
153 right   © Benetton Group / Patrick Robert
163 left   © René Burri / Magnum Photos / Fondation René Burri, Museum für Gestaltung Zürich
163 right   © Benetton Group
164 lower right   © Verein "Celestino Piatti – das visuelle Erbe," Basel
166 right   © Benetton Group / Yves Gellie
178 right   Albert Brenet © 2023, ProLitteris, Zurich

Donors

124 upper right   Gigant Kino Markt, Basel, CH
125 upper right / 167 lower left / 173 upper right   Graphis Verlag, Zurich, CH
125 lower right   Palmers Textil AG, Wiener Neudorf, AT
127 lower left / 128 left / 130 lower left / 133 lower right / 135 left / 137 lower left / 145 lower right / 146 right / 146 lower left / 148 lower left / 153 upper left / 154 left / 154 upper right / 157 lower left / 159 upper left / 168 upper left / 177 left / 177 lower right / 178 upper left / 178 lower left / 179 upper left / 180 upper left   Allgemeine Plakatgesellschaft, APG, Zurich, CH
127 right   Suzanne Marie Peikert-Borboën
129 left   Switzerland Tourism, Zurich, CH
130 upper left / 175 right / 179 lower left   Clear Channel Switzerland PLC, Hünenberg, CH
133 upper right   Publicis Group Austria, Vienna, AT
143 upper left   Unifontes AG, Rheinfelden, CH
143 lower left   Publicis Werbeagentur AG, BSW, Zurich, CH
147 upper left   Ina Hattenhauer
148 upper left   Karl Duschek
148 right / 164 upper right / 176 lower right   DNP Foundation for Cultural Promotion, Tokyo, JP / Kabushiki Kaisha Tanaka Ikko Design Shitsu, Tokyo, JP
148 lower left   Frieder Grindler
154 lower right   Serge Libiszewski
155 left   Eram, Saint-Pierre-Montlimart, FR
160 right   JRP Ringier Kunstverlag AG, Zurich, CH
164 left   André Hoinkes
167 right   Daniele Buetti

168 lower left   Cyan, Berlin, DE
169 lower left   Pro Infirmis, Zurich, CH
174 lower right   Art Ringger
175 left   Jonathan Ellery
176 left   Wieden & Kennedy, Portland, US
176 upper right   Heidy und Louis Lambelet, Basel, CH
179 right   Flughafen Zürich AG, Kloten, CH
180 right   Ruf Lanz Werbeagentur AG, Zurich, CH

**Museum
für Gestaltung
Zürich**

Talking Bodies—Image, Power, Impact

A Publication of the
Museum für Gestaltung Zürich
Christian Brändle, Director

Editors:
Museum für Gestaltung Zürich, Bettina Richter
Texts:
Bettina Richter, Markus Dederich, Florian Diener,
Hans Fässler, Mara Yağmur Richter, Maria
Schreiber, Marilyn Umurungi, Paula-Irene Villa
Concept and editing:
Bettina Richter, Petra Schmid
Design:
Studio Krispin Heé (Krispin Heé, Katya Lupanova)
Project management:
Petra Schmid
Project management publisher:
Kristina Lemke, Fanny Rakeseder
Translation (Ger.–Eng.):
Matthias Goldmann, Michael Hacker
Copyediting:
Camilla Nielsen
Photography:
Umberto Romito, Ivan Šuta
Image research:
Simone Hellmüller
Image editing:
prints professional, Germany
Printing and binding:
DZA Druckerei zu Altenburg, Germany
Paper:
Munken Print White 15, 115 g/qm;
Artogloss, 135 g/qm
Typeface:
ABC Social, Dinamo

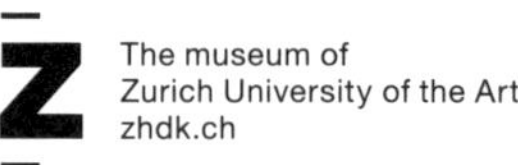

The museum of
Zurich University of the Arts
zhdk.ch

Museum für Gestaltung Zürich
Postfach
CH–8031 Zürich
museum-gestaltung.ch

ISBN: 978-3-03778-734-2

Printed in Germany

With the kind support of

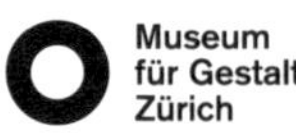

Museum
für Gestaltung
Zürich
Circle of Friends

Lars Müller Publishers is supported by
the Swiss Federal Office of Culture with a
structural contribution for the years
2021–2024.

Lars Müller Publishers
CH–8005 Zürich
lars-mueller-publishers.com

Distributed in North America, Latin America,
the Caribbean by ARTBOOK | D.A.P.
www.artbook.com

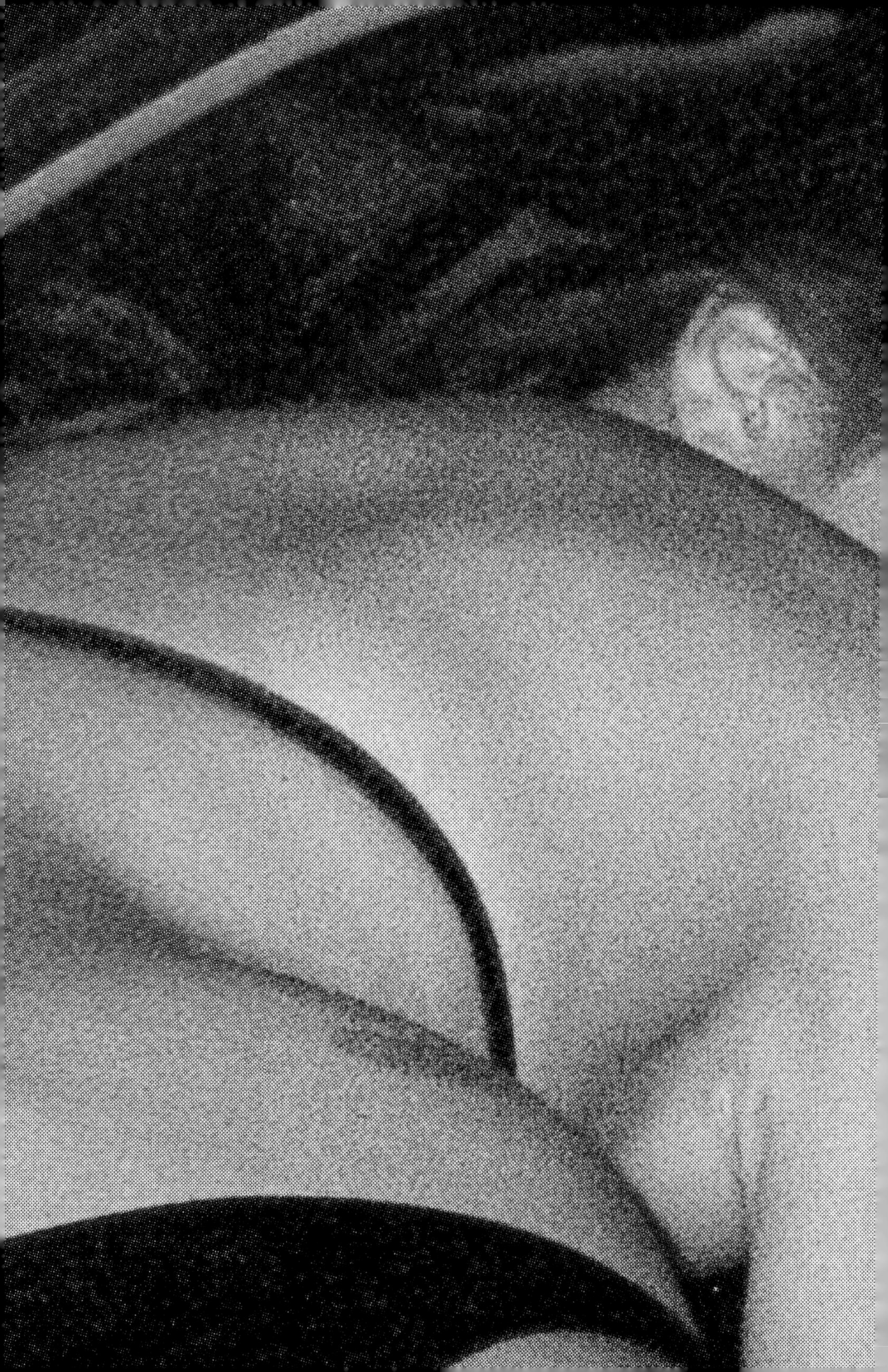

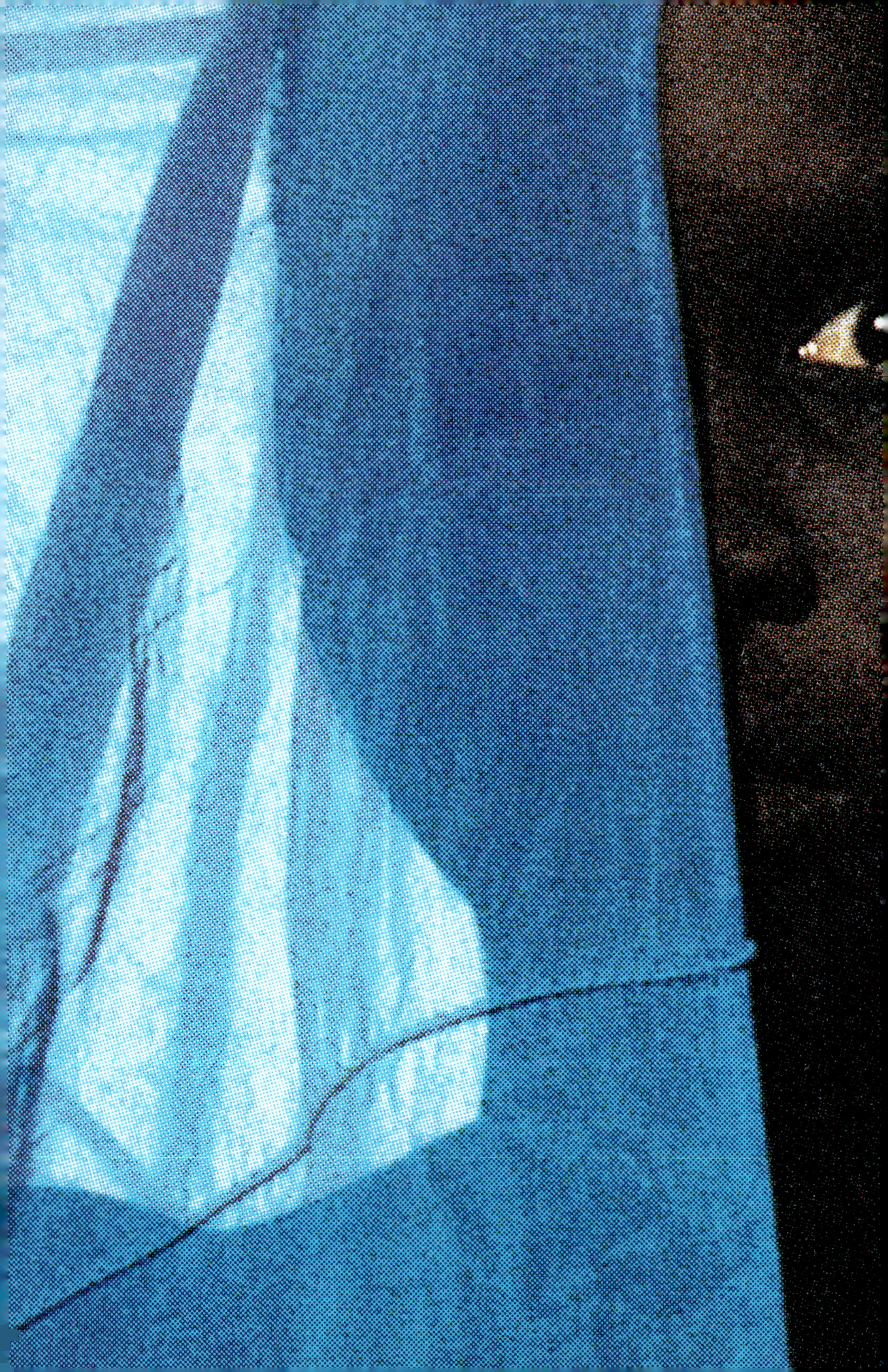

Dichotomies are also conveyed by omission, in that certain bodies are not, or hardly ever, brought into the picture: old or sick bodies or ones that are considered less attractive. This is a testament to the fact that images of the body are never just external images, but that they are always charged with essentialist notions and cultural positing.

A naked female* body, presented as "beautiful" according to prevailing conventions, does not quite escape heteronormative objectification, no matter how "feminist" the intent may be. Conversely, the supposedly most stereotypical image of hypersexualized women can also be interpreted as drag, as a queer implosion.

Hennes & Mauritz Advertising Department
Bikini 24.90 / H & M, 1996
Hennes & Mauritz, H & M AB, Stockholm, SE

Anonymous
Terry Richardson (photo)
Sisley, 1999
Benetton Group S.p.A., Ponzano Veneto, IT

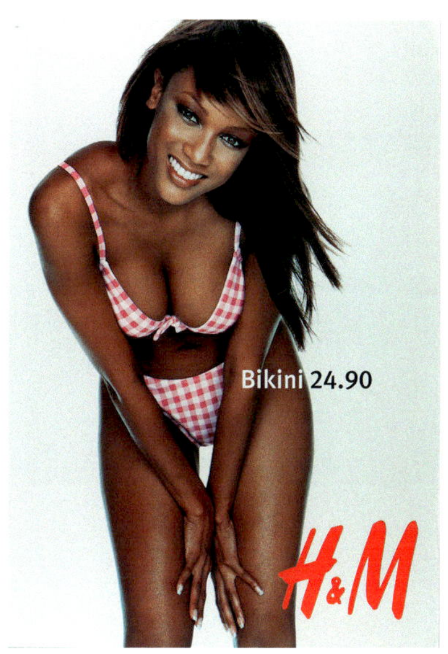

p.16

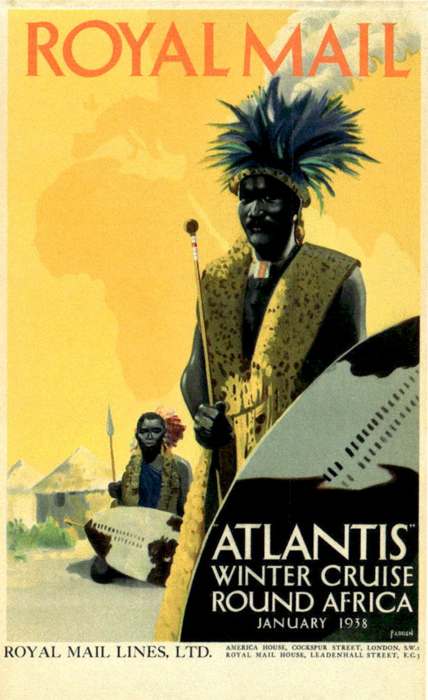

p.28

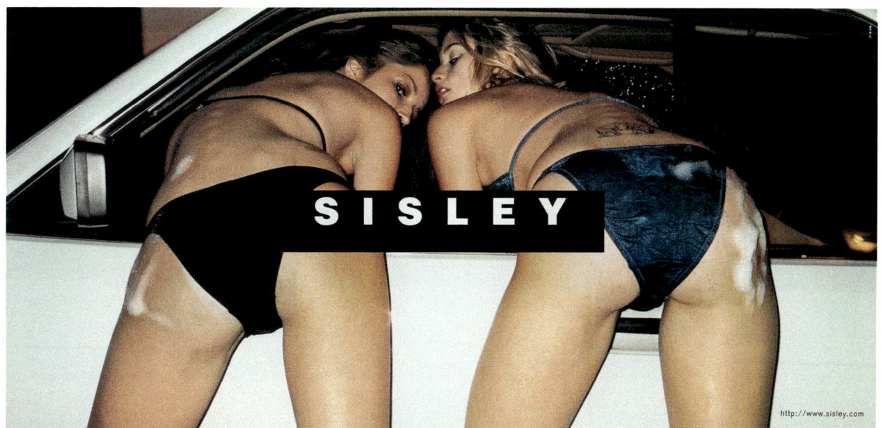

Armando González
Junta suprema / Ruptura con Franco!
(Break with Franco!), 1944
Unión Nacional Española, UNE, ES

Anonymous
Stallone / First Blood / This Time He's Fighting
for His Life, 1982
Orion Pictures Corporation, US

Seiler DDB Needham/cR Werbeagentur AG
Wir schützen uns, weil wir uns lieben (We Protect
Ourselves Because We Love Each Other), 1994
Federal Office of Public Health FOPH, Bern, CH

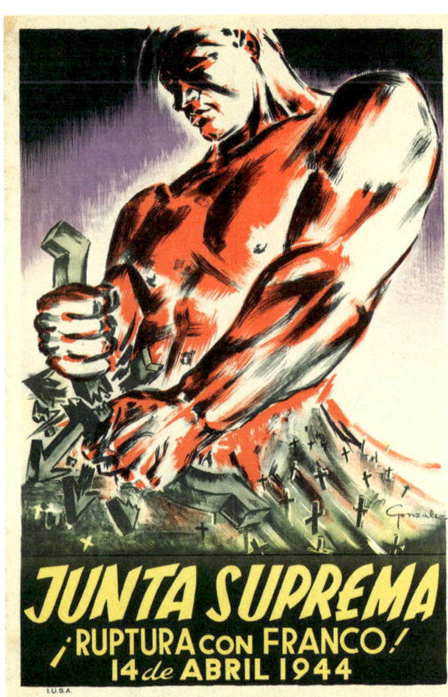

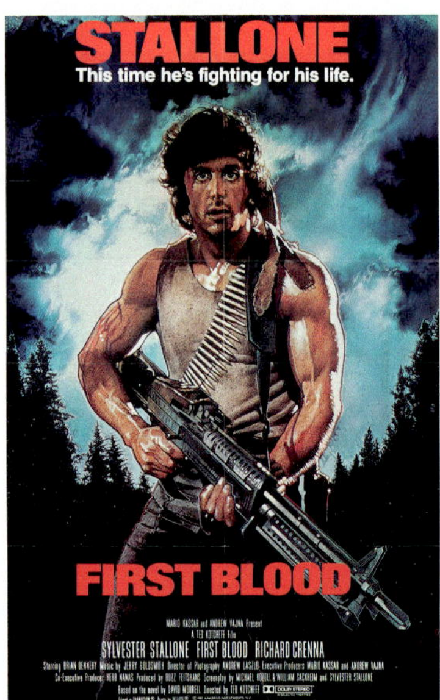

p. 46

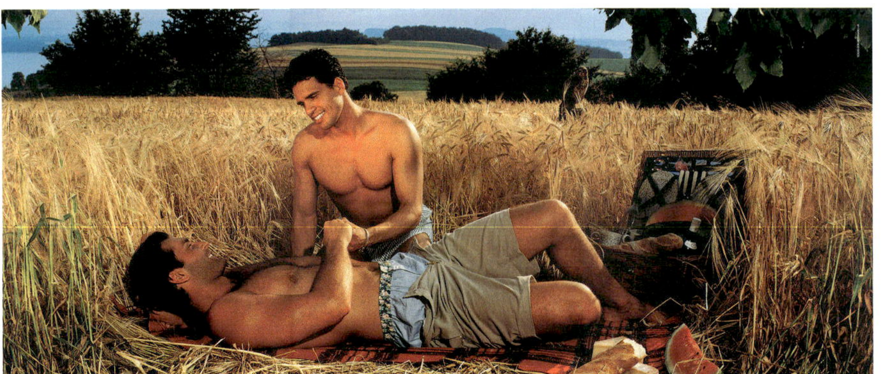

Solá
Mes homes! Mes armes! Mes municions!
(More Men! More Weapons! More
Ammunition!), 1937
Unión General de Trabajadores, UGT, ES

Political posters have frequently presented the male body as a "fighting machine" and continue to do so today. Here, muscular arms under rolled-up shirtsleeves reference the stereotypical image of the worker that inspired this design. The poster calls on its viewers to defend the Republic in the Spanish Civil War and turns the gun into an extension of the arm. The repetition of the ever-same silhouettes renders the individual body anonymous and merges it into a *Volkskörper,* the single shared body of a people. In his book *Male Fantasies*, Klaus Theweleit described the ideal of the impenetrable body armor as constitutive of the fascist ego. When it comes to the staging of the man as a symbol of internalized fortitude, on the other hand, there is not much difference between fascist and socialist posters.

Anonymous
Budweiser / Bikeweek 1994 /
Daytona Beach, 1994
Anheuser-Busch Inc., St. Louis, MO, US

GGK Wien
Raphael Just (photo)
Palmers, 2000
Palmers Textil AG, Wiener Neudorf, AT

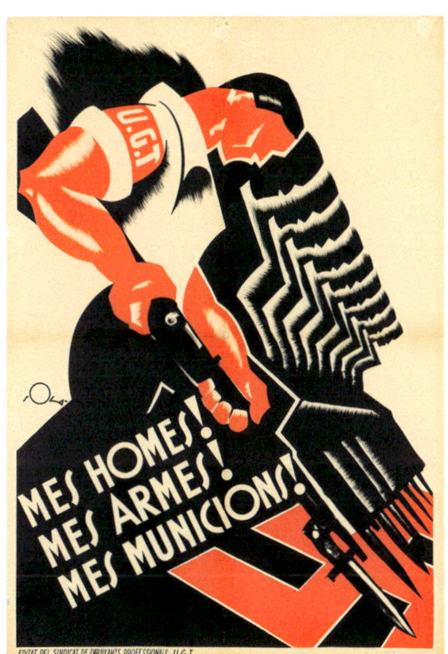

p.38

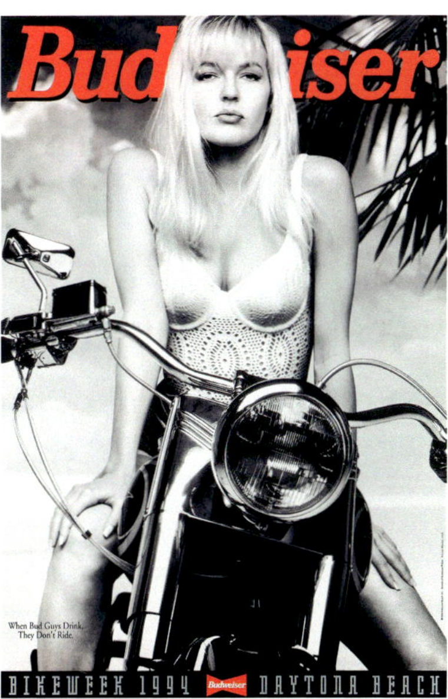

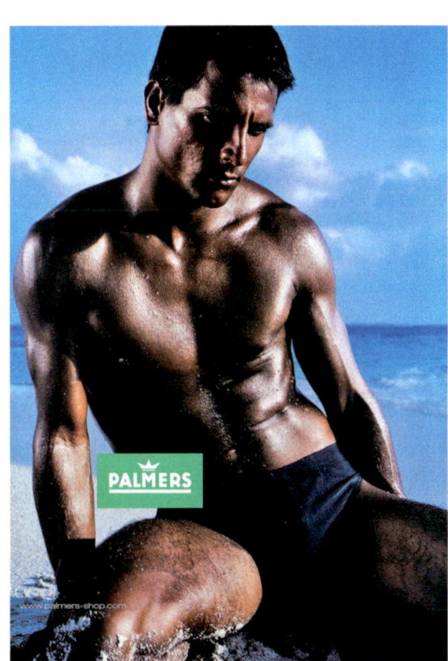

Viktor Rutz
Herrliches Arosa (Magnificent Arosa), 1935
Verkehrsverein Arosa, CH

Charles Kuhn
PKZ, 1937
PKZ Burger-Kehl & Co. AG, Zurich, CH

Anonymous
Terry Richardson (photo)
Sisley, 1998
Benetton Group S.p.A., Ponzano Veneto, IT

This ironically exaggerated picture of a Sisley model epitomizes a straight-out masculine self-image through his posture, gestures, facial expressions and clothes. The position of his hands and the oversized belt buckle, which is adorned with a Texas flag, immediately draw attention to the man's crotch. His cropped face flashes a challenging grin that adds to the provocation of the leg posture. Nearly two decades later, the pejorative term "manspreading" was coined, which refers to the socialized male habit of sitting with legs wide apart in public spaces, thereby encroaching on others. Here, the man's body again breaks the confines of the poster format. Individual women artists documented and inverted this form of physically dominating behavior early on. Notable examples include Valie Export and her *Action Pants: Genital Panic* and Marianne Wex's studies of male and female postures.

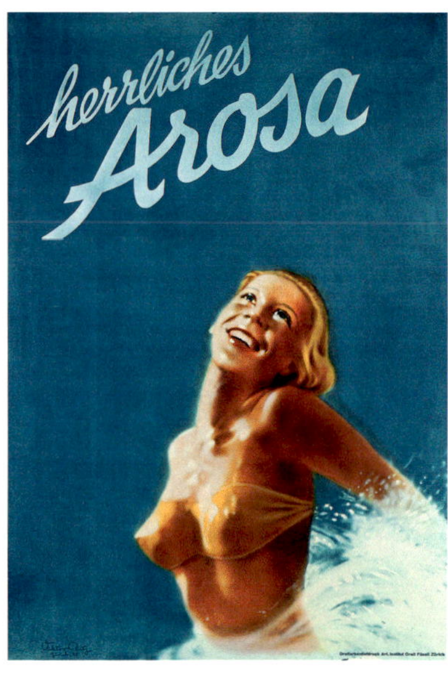

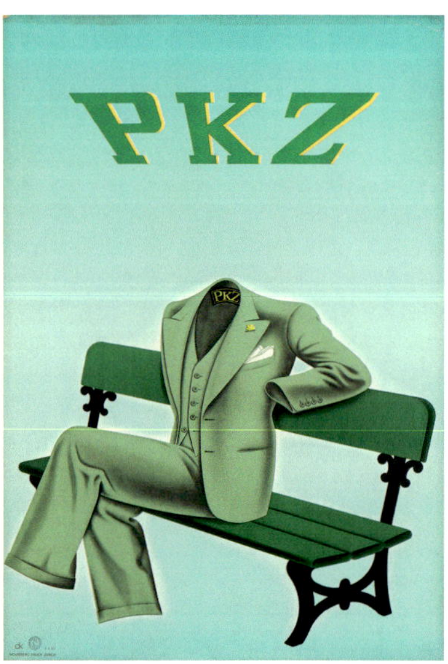

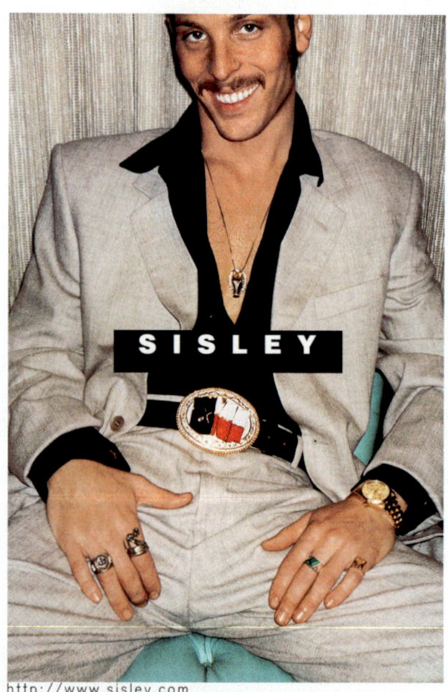

p. 28

http://www.sisley.com

Dr. Rudolf Farner Werbeagentur AG
Renault 5 / Aus Lebensfreude
(Out of Zest for Life), 1977
Renault (Suisse) SA, Geneva, CH

Sulzer, Sutter AG / Florian Bachofen,
Sebastian Krayer
Jos Schmid (photo)
Schraube locker? Für mich keine Behinderung.
(Screw Loose? Doesn't Disable Me.), 2010
Insieme Schweiz, Bern, CH

Martin Peikert
Champéry / Téléférique (Cable Car) /
Planachaux / Valais / Suisse, 1945
Chemin de fer Aigle-Monthey-Champéry, CH

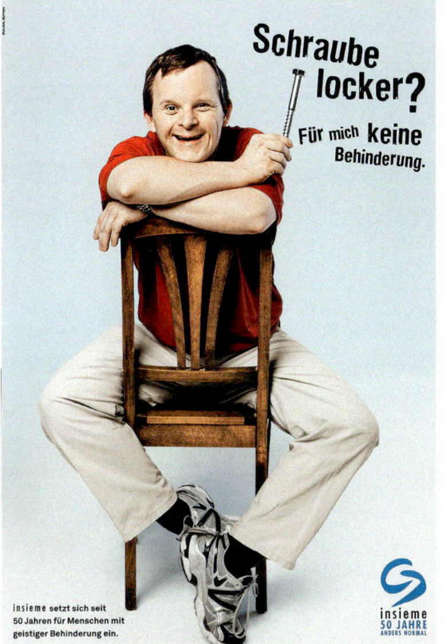

p. 76

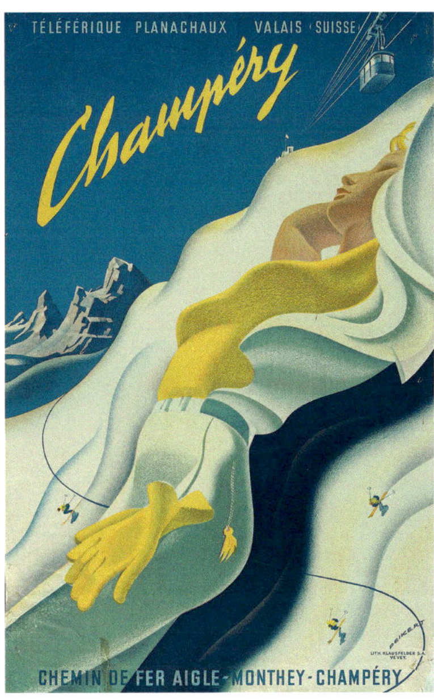

p. 29

Damm
Cool Water / Davidoff / Eau de Toilette, 1994
Lancaster Group Schweiz AG, Zug, CH

Viktor Borisovič Koreckij
My trebuem mira! (We Demand Peace!), 1950
Unknown assignment

This perfect male body is presented as if washed
up from the sea to promote the Eau de Toilette
Cool Water. The seductively glittering drops on
his skin increase his sensual appeal; his eyes
are closed. The model's entire posture is reminiscent of the centuries-old tradition of female nudes.
The depiction of men as passive erotic objects
was a late arrival in the world of advertising. Yves
Saint Laurent kicked off this development in
1971 when he posed for photographer Jeanloup
Sieff to promote his eau de toilette. Already in
the fourth century BC, the nude figure of Eros
adorned scented oil jars. Even though the male
body here corresponds to classical ideals of
beauty, its vulnerability and its naked exposure
to the environment create a new narrative.

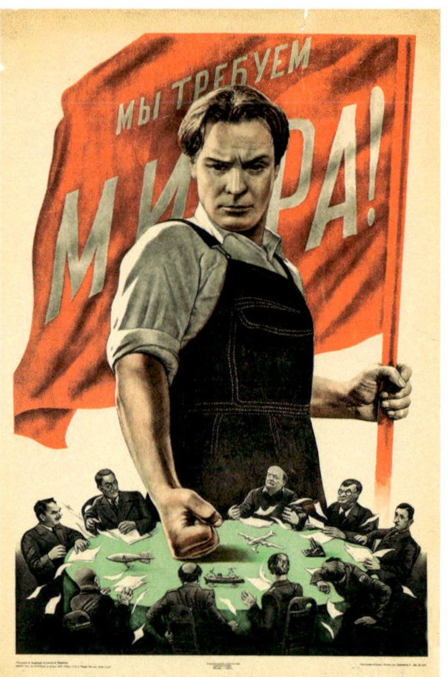

p. 18

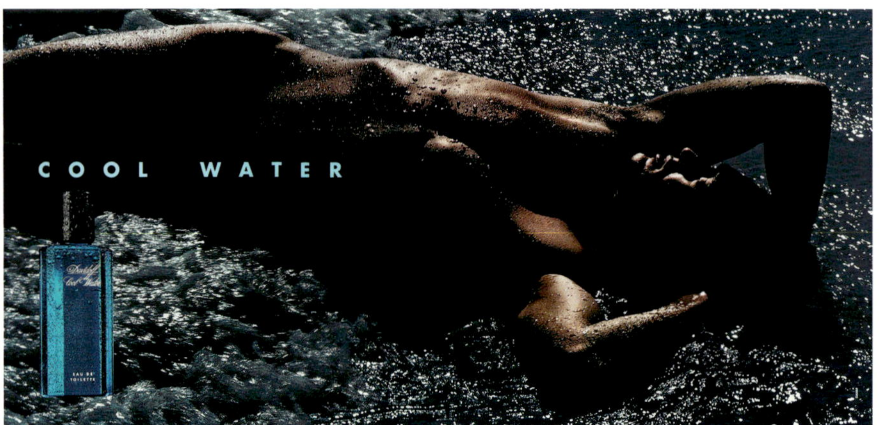

p. 47

Anonymous
Lötschberg, ca. 1912
Unknown assignment

Construction of the Lötschberg tunnel was launched in 1906 and the last separating wall of rock fell in 1911. In a symbolic depiction of this feat, a nude man breaks through the stone masses by the sheer strength of his body. His muscular arms and his hands clenched into fists hark back to the later stages of socialist worker posters of the 1930s. His appearance is also inspired by ancient heroes: it is modeled after Prometheus, the Titan who in modern times came to symbolize scientific and technological progress, embodying man's putative dominion over the natural world. The workers' strikes, accidents and fatalities that accompanied the construction of the tunnel are glossed over and the focus is firmly set on technical feasibility and achievement.

Menschlichkeit ist ansteckend. Mit HIV-Positiven arbeiten nicht. (Humanity is Contagious. Working with HIV Positive People Is Not.), ca. 1997
Aids-Hilfe Österreich, AT

Werner von Axster-Heudtlass
Reichswettkämpfe der SA (Reich Sports Competitions of the SA), 1937
National Socialist German Workers' Party, NSDAP, Main Propaganda Office, Hamburg, DE

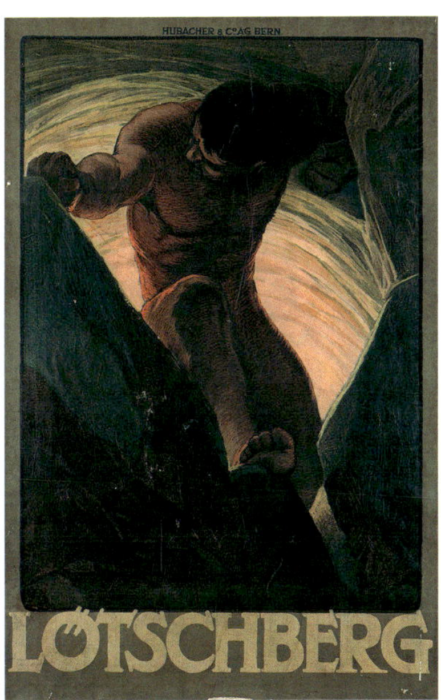

p. 45

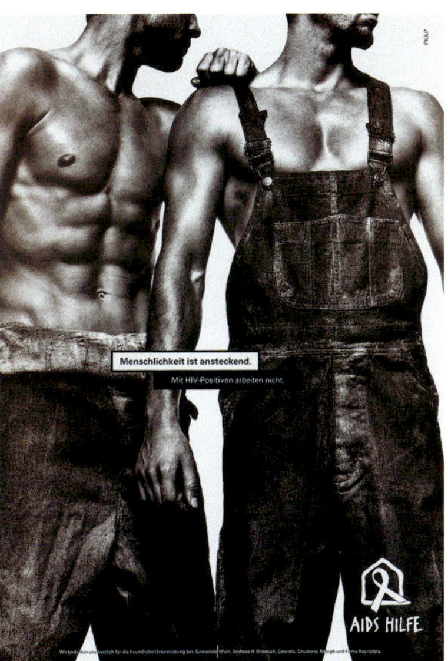

p. 47

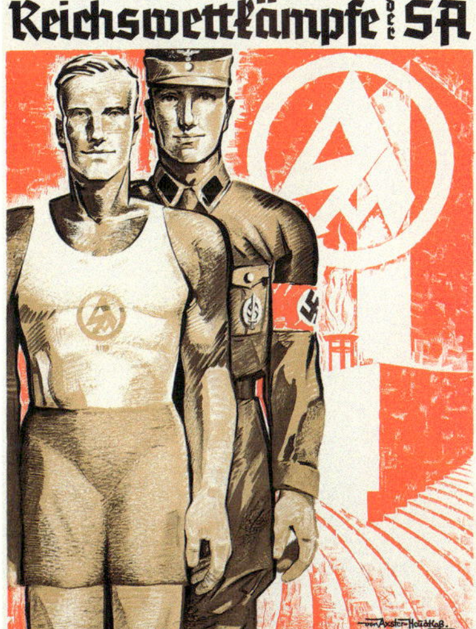

Anomaly Berlin
Dan Beleiu (photo)
Zalando / Every. Body. Here to Stay. / Charlotte
und Beate. Neue Perspektiven eröffnen
(Opening Up New Perspectives), 2021
Zalando SE, Berlin, DE

Ogilvy & Mather AG
Fett? Fit? Passt wahre Schönheit nur in Grösse
36? Reden Sie mit bei der Schönheitsdebatte.
Dove (Fat? Fit? Does True Beauty Only Fit in Size
36? Join in the Beauty Debate. Dove), 2005
Lever Fabergé GmbH, Zug, CH

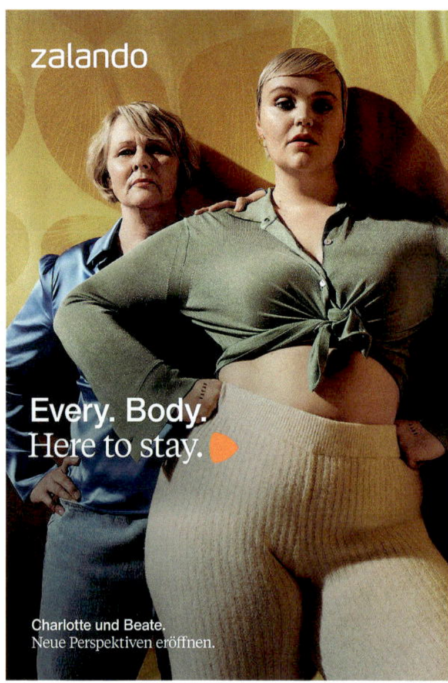

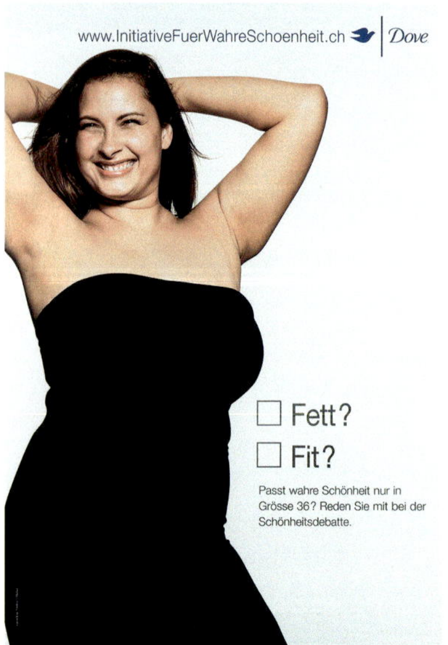

Wes Wilson
Bill Graham Presents in San Francisco /
Dance Concert / The Sound / Jefferson
Airplane / Muddy Waters / Butterfield Blues
Band / Winterland / Fillmore Auditorium, 1966
Bill Graham

The summer of 1967 went down in history as
the Summer of Love. Progressive political movements also revolutionized music in the mid-
sixties. The San Francisco hippie scene had its
heyday and rock 'n' roll was celebrated as an
emerging subculture. The modern, liberal body
politics that manifested itself in experiments
around unbureaucratic and unbiased "free clin-
ics" were radically at odds with the traditional
role and gender images conveyed in the San Francisco rock poster. Stylistic devices such as flow-
ing forms, undulating warped spaces and ornamental embellishments harked back to Art
Nouveau. The movement's idealized, eroticized
portrayal of women was embraced uncritically, especially by Wes Wilson, the most important designer on the scene.

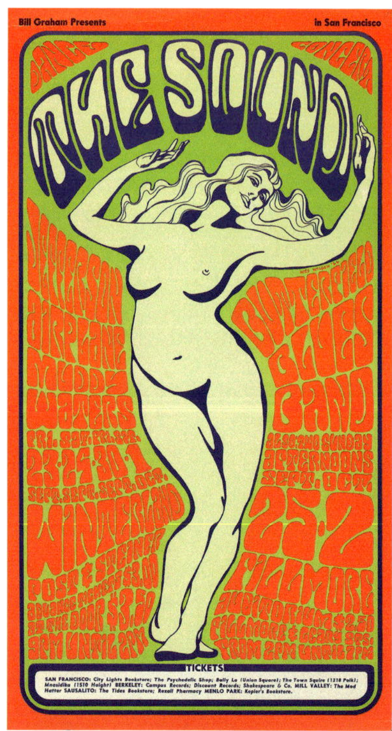

The negotiation of diversity in advertising is still focused on the female body, which attests to the fact that it remains the key public platform for beauty ideals and strictly binary gender discourses.

Mass media depictions of male, female, or even racialized bodies directly draw on Christian culture and a Eurocentric historiography of art, whose images are deeply inscribed in our collective memory. Their powerful impact is evident precisely in the fact that they have remained unquestioned and unchallenged for so long.

Temptations—Body Narratives in Art

Bettina Richter

Adolfo de Karolis
Turin 1911 / Internationale Industrie- und
Gewerbe-Ausstellung / Zum fünfzigjährigen
Jubiläum der Proklamation des Königreichs
Italien (International Industry and Trade
Exhibition / On the Fiftieth Anniversary of the
Proclamation of the Kingdom of Italy), 1911
Esposizione Internazionale dell'Industria
e del Lavoro, Turin, IT

Anonymous
Ein paar Frauen sind Supermodels. 3 Milliarden
nicht. Alles über Selbstachtung und wahre
Schönheit erfahren Sie bei The Body Shop.
(A Few Women Are Supermodels. Three Billion
Are Not. Learn All About Self-Esteem and True
Beauty at The Body Shop.), 1997
The Body Shop Levy AG, Uster, CH /
Tamedia AG, Zurich, CH

Publicis Group Austria
Peter Paul Rubens (pictorial reference)
Orangenhaut ist Geschichte.
(Orange Peel Syndrome is History.), 2007
L'Oréal Österreich GmbH, Vienna, AT

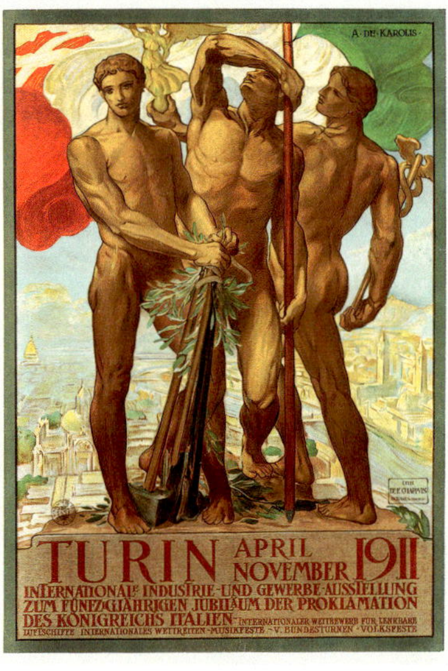

p. 37

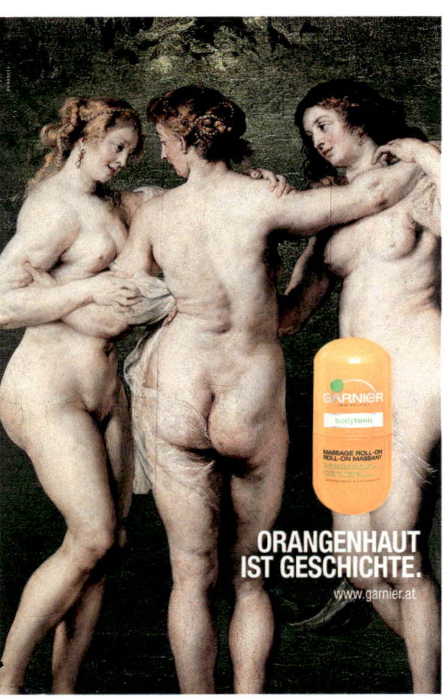

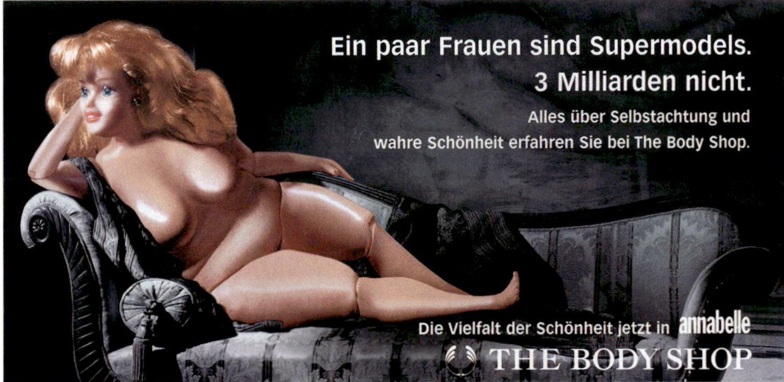

Ogilvy
Hep, garçon! Perrier, ca. 1980
Perrier S.A., Vergèze, FR

Guerrilla Girls
A Major Hollywood Studio Presents the Birth of
Feminism / Equality Now! / They Made Women's
Rights Look Good. Really Good, 2017
Private project

Anonymous
Paul Colin (pictorial reference)
Paul Colin et les spectacles
(Paul Colin and the Shows), 1994
Musée des Beaux-Arts, Nancy, FR

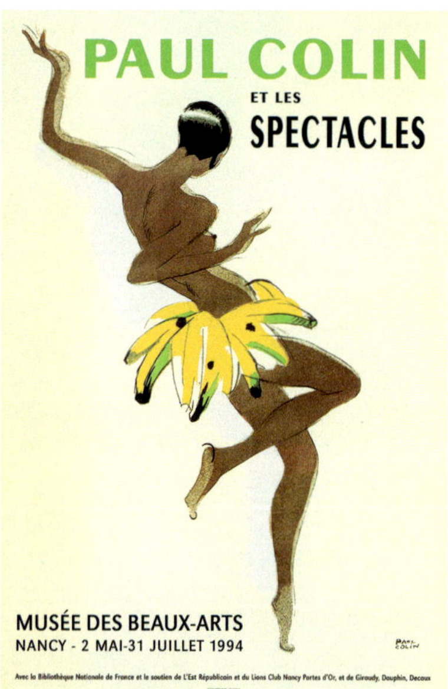

p. 53

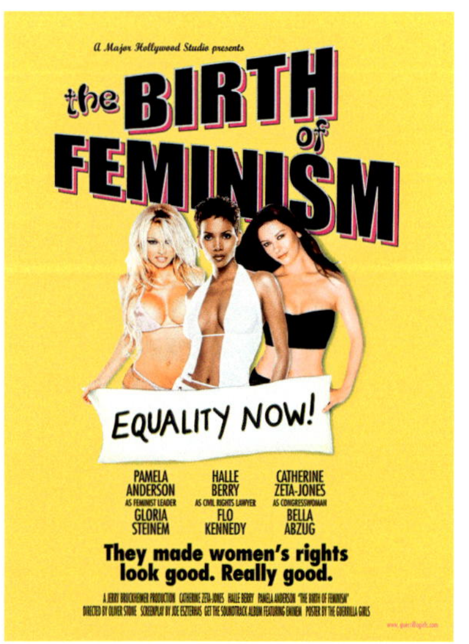

p. 29

Advico Young & Rubicam AG
Produkt / So liest man sonntags Zeitung (This
Is How You Read Sunday's Newspaper), 1995
Tamedia AG, Zurich, CH

In this poster, a woman's body is intentionally
staged as the ultimate sex object. Her self-
confident look and animal-like pose increase
the erotic appeal of her body. Her skimpy
dress highlights her body contours; her hairstyle is reminiscent of Marilyn Monroe, who
is marketed as a "sex icon" to this day. In a direct and undisguised manner, the female
body itself is labeled and promoted as a "product." Only the small print reveals that this
is an advertisement for a Sunday newspaper.
With this campaign, the advertising agency
sought to expose consumer perceptions
shaped by patriarchal social structures and,
in a provocative manner, to emphasize the
sexualization of the female body.

Hans Looser AG Werbeagentur Zürich /
Dominik L. Burckhardt
N. Bosshard (photo)
Fogal / Keinen Strumpf, den es nicht gibt
(No Stocking That Doesn't Exist), 1971
Fogal AG, Zurich, CH

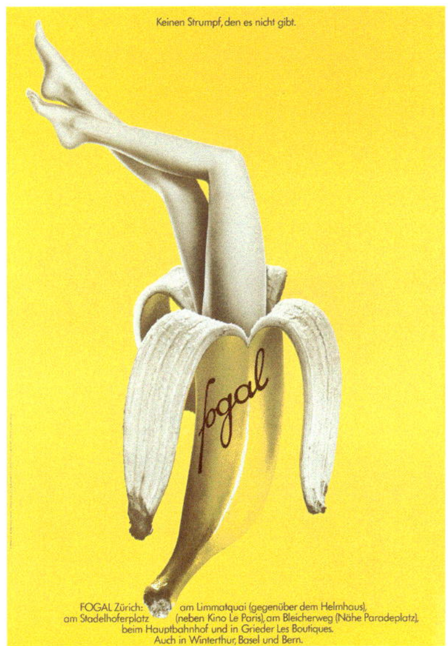

p. 29

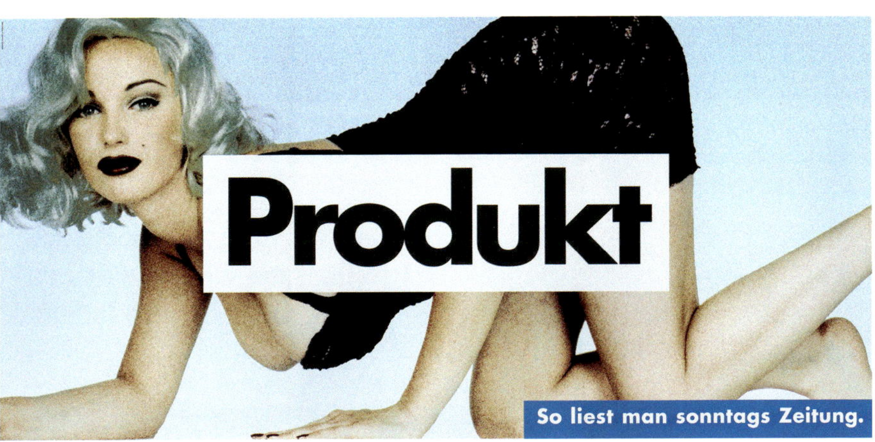

Anonymous
Canada Dry / Durststillend
(Quenches Your Thirst), 1954
Canada Dry Produkte AG, Zurich, CH

Peter Marti
Traumjeans Rifle (Dream Jeans Rifle), 1982
Rifle Schweiz, Denges, CH

Guerrilla Girls
Jean-Auguste-Dominique Ingres (pictorial reference)
Do Women Have to Be Naked to Get into the Met.
Museum? Less than 4 % of the Artists in the Modern
Art Sections Are Women, but 76 % of the Nudes Are
Female, 2011
Private project

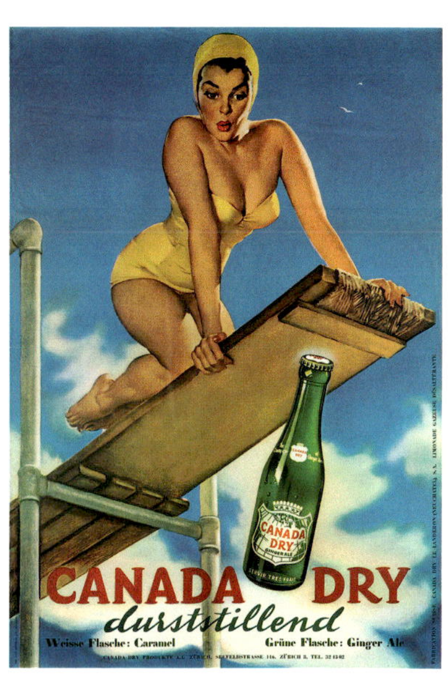

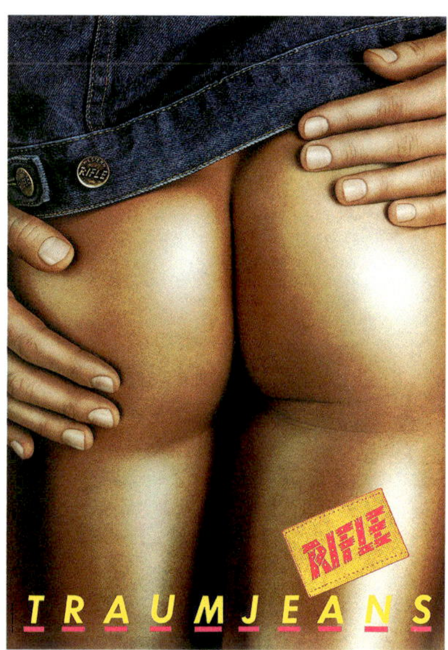

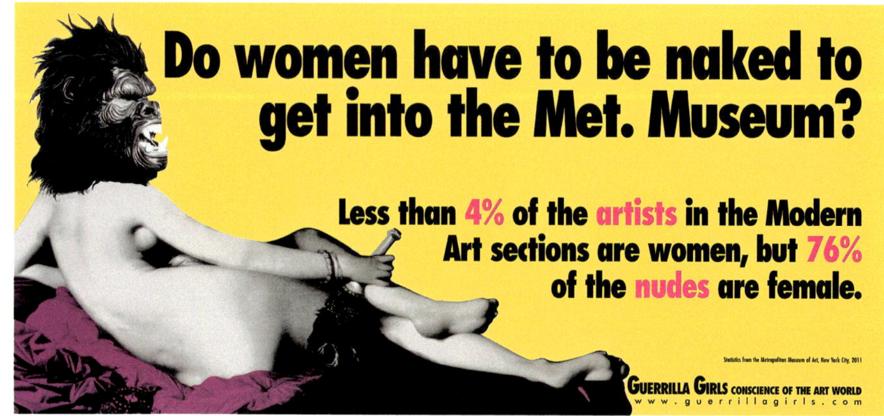

Anonymous
Maestrani / Choco-Boy, 1937
Chocolat Maestrani, St. Gallen, CH

Hennes & Mauritz Advertising Department
Top 14.90 / H&M, 2001
Hennes & Mauritz, H&M AB, Stockholm, SE

Anonymous
Migros-Kaffee / Ein Begriff!
(A Household Name!), ca. 1930
Migros AG, Zurich, CH

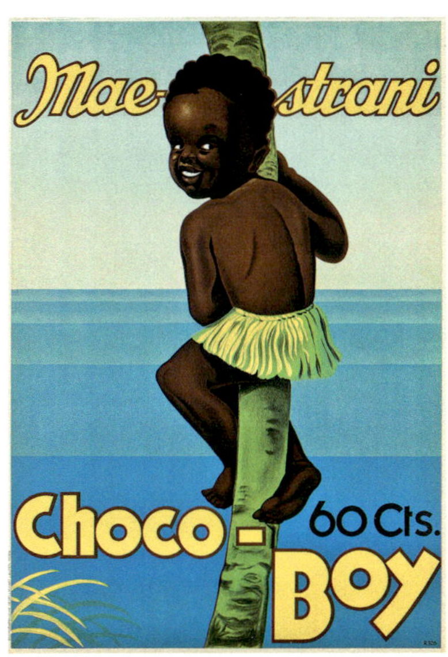

p. 70

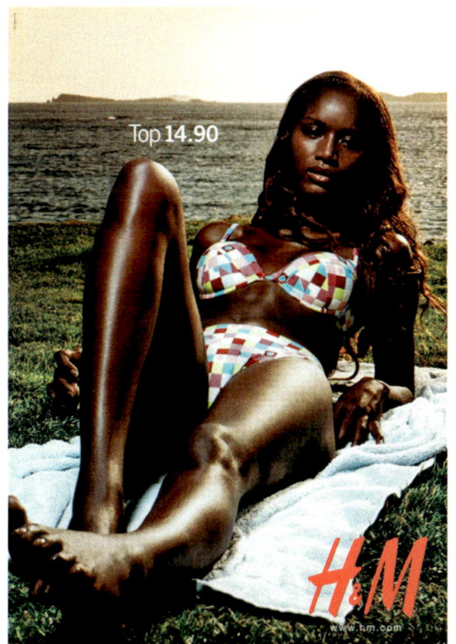

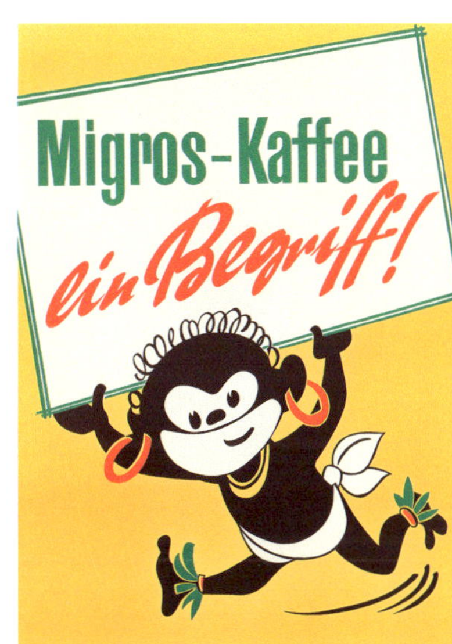

Gino Boccasile
AOI / Lloyd Triestino, 1936
Lloyd Triestino, Triest, IT

Anonymous
Jardin zoologique d'acclimatation
cinghalais (Sinhalese "Zoological Garden"
for Acclimatization), 1883
Unknown assignment

Charles Lévy
Folies-Bergère / Tous les soirs (Every Night) /
Les Raynors, ca. 1882
Folies-Bergère, Paris, FR

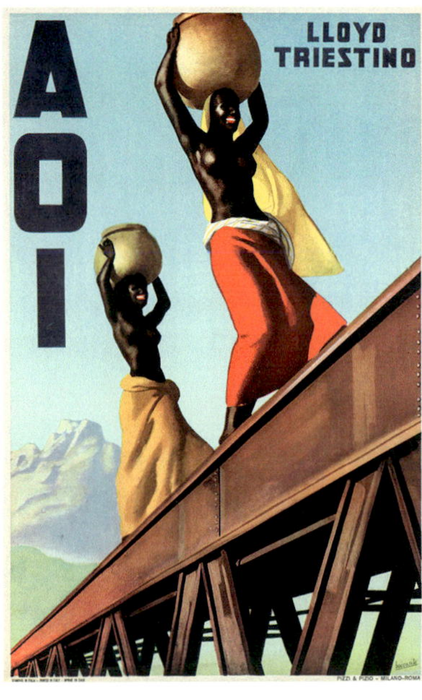

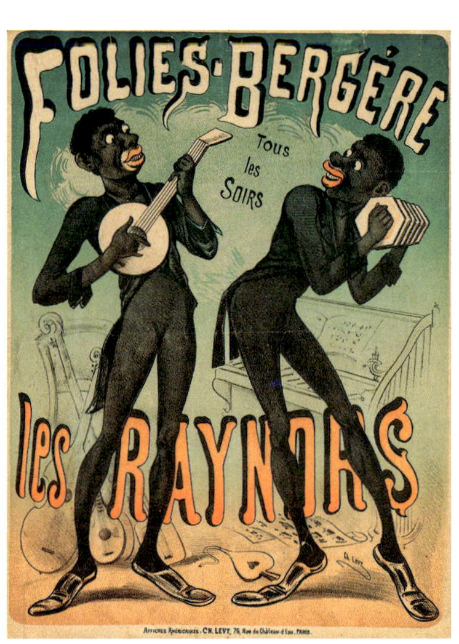

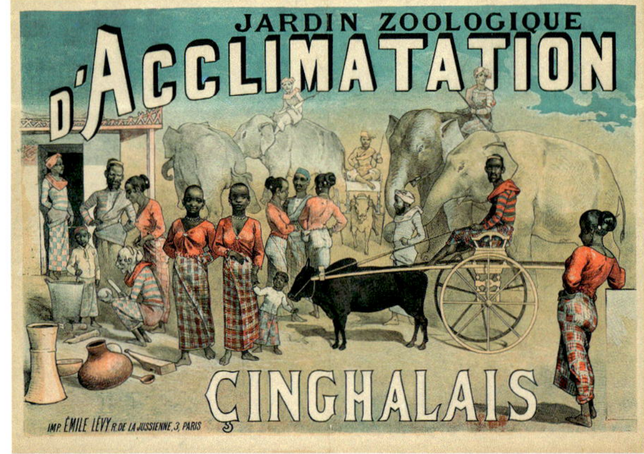

Emil Schraner
Schöne und gesunde Zähne mit Amantin /
Die grüne Zahnpasta mit Chlorophyll, Fluor
und Ammonium (Beautiful and Healthy Teeth
with Amantin / The Green Toothpaste with
Chlorophyll, Fluorine and Ammonium), 1952
Hamol AG, Zurich, CH

This Amantin poster is a prime example of the
anti-Black racism found in images from the
1920s to the 1960s. The depiction of Black bodies for the promotion of colonial goods was
commonly justified by the geographical origin
of the products. However, Black people were
also featured as popular protagonists for black
or white colored products, quite often ones
from the realms of cosmetics and cleaning. In
this poster, the bright white smile contrasts
with the Black skin color. It brings together several classic stereotypes of Black advertising
figures: Infantilization, servile submissiveness
and naive savagery. In an ostensibly innocu-
ous manner, the product posters of that era per-
petuate the colonial gaze.

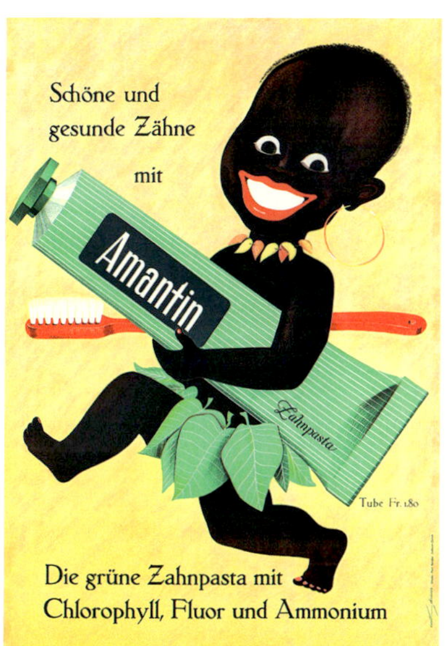

Semen Borisovič Raev
Jazva rasizma / JUAR (The Scars of Racism /
 South Africa), 1985
Izdatel'stvo "Plakat," Moscow, SU

Privat Livemont
Absinthe Robette, 1896
Unknown assignment

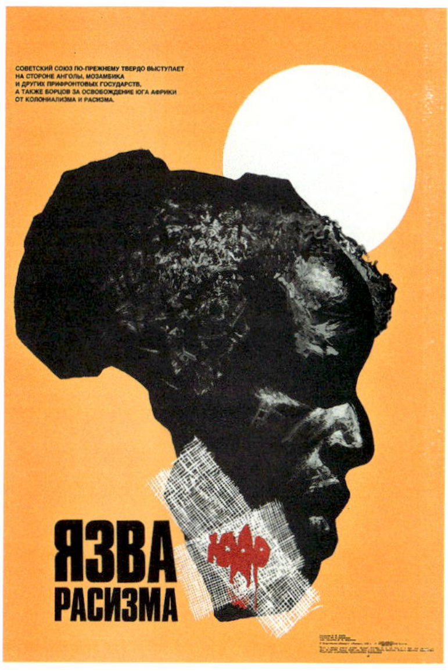

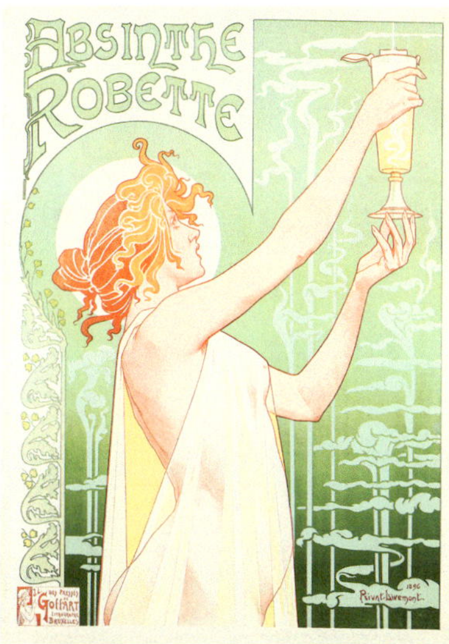

Chezel
Zoologischer Garten Basel / N****dorf
aus dem Senegal (Basel Zoological Garden /
Black Village from Senegal), 1928
Zoologischer Garten Basel, CH

Until the 1960s, so-called "human zoos" presented people from faraway countries to a wide audience. They served as a key interface between scientific and popular racism and were perceived as evidence of hierarchical differences between ethnic groups. The dancing Senegalese in his oriental-style costume caters, above all, to European fantasies and yearnings. His depiction continues the tradition of nineteenth-century paintings where Black people made appearances as "exotic" entertainment at the gallant parties of a fashionable white society. Such figures typically oscillate between the poles of threatening and adorable. When Josephine Baker performed her banana dance in the late 1920s, she very deliberately played with the stereotypes of her white audiences and held up a mirror to them.

Paul Krawutschke
Automobil-Ausstellung Genf
(Geneva Motor Show), 1906
Automobil-Ausstellung Genf, Geneva, CH

Anonymous
Herta 15 Jahre alt wiegt 500 ℔ / Eine Prämie
v. 50000 G.Mark demjenigen, der ein zweites
Kind im gleichen Gewicht und gleichen
Alter nachweisen kann (Herta, 15 Years Old,
Weighs 500 ℔ / Reward Money of 50000 G.Marks
to Whoever Can Provide Evidence of a Second
Child of the Same Weight and Age), 1923
Unknown assignment

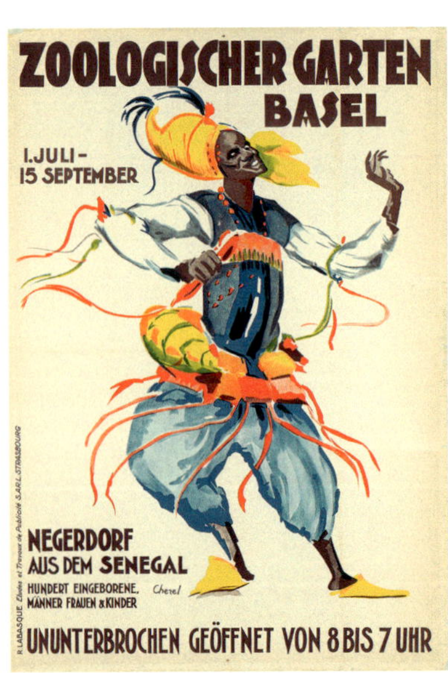

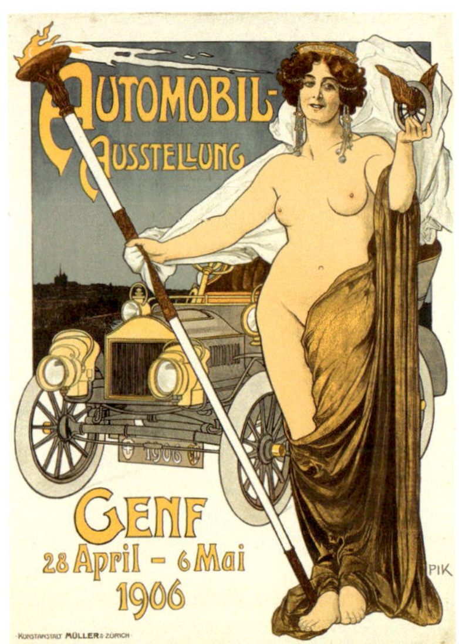

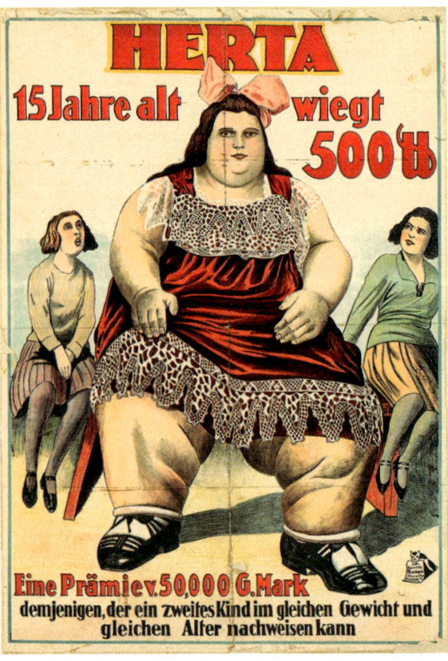

By examining how extra-
ordinary bodies are perceived,
represented, and evaluated,
we can discern what matters
in our society, which values prevail, what people fear,
the criteria by which be-
longing and non-belonging
are organized, and also
which lives are considered
worth living and which
are not.

When discourses materialize in bodies and attributions are thereby normalized and naturalized, they always result in a shift in power.

Marilyn Umurungi

Anonymous
Vivi-Kola / Kolahaltiges Tafelgetränk
mit Eglisauer Mineralwasser
(Soft Drink Containing Cola, with
Eglisau Mineral Water), ca. 1940
Mineralquelle Eglisau AG, CH

Karl Bickel
Ja / Alter / Invalidität (Yes / Age / Disability), 1925
Schweizerischer Verband des Personals
öffentlicher Dienste, VPOD, Zurich, CH

Publicis Werbeagentur AG
Schnelle medizinische Hilfe
(Quick Medical Help), 2006
Médecins Sans Frontières, Geneva, CH

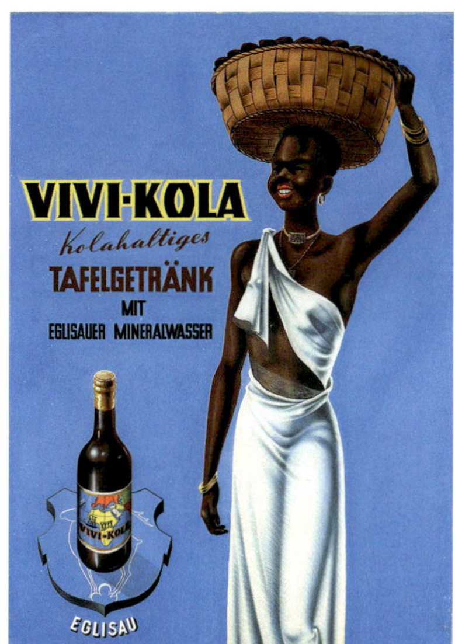

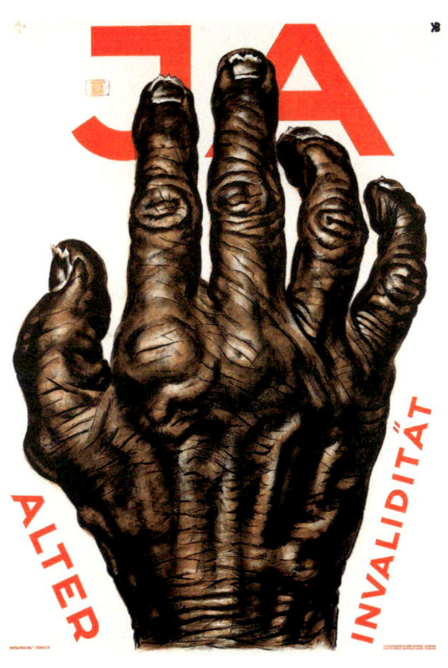

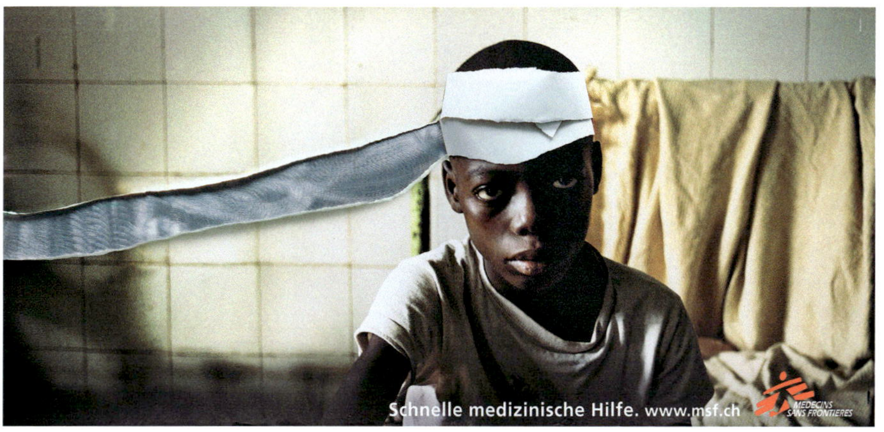

Oliviero Toscani
Oliviero Toscani (photo)
United Colors of Benetton, 1989
Benetton Group S.p.A., Ponzano Veneto, IT

Anonymous
It's Fun in South Africa, 1953
Union-Castle Line, London, GB

In the late 1980s, Oliviero Toscani designed the first Benetton campaigns that broke with the run-of the-mill imagery of fashion advertising. They featured uncommented photographs, often highlighted simple contrasts to great effect and addressed social and political conflicts through the manner of their staging. This is exemplified by Toscani's poster from 1989, the year in which the process towards the abolition of apartheid commenced in South Africa. The image is a reference to the Black wet nurses common during the colonization of the Americas from the sixteenth to the eighteenth century, thus carrying forward the history of enslavement and racism. Women were forced to withhold their breast from their own child so that they could feed the child of their slave owners. We have not yet reached the end of this story. Even though the forms of enslavement have changed, the exploitation of Black and of female bodies is ongoing.

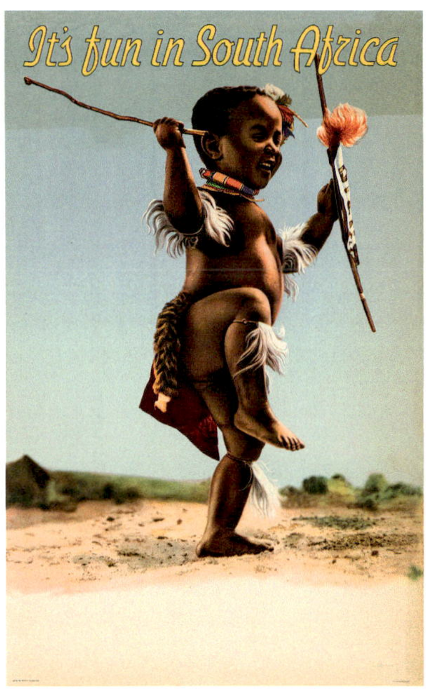

p.17

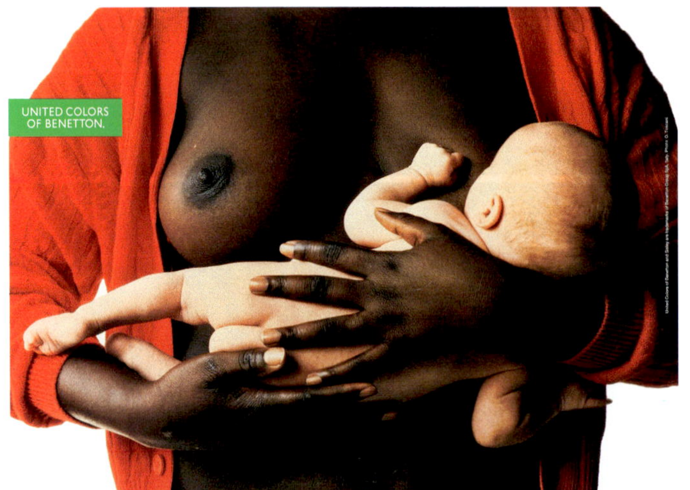

Roman Cieślewicz
CD / Corps diplomatique, 1994 (design 1974)
Private project

Roman Cieślewicz's rendering of the Corps Diplomatique, the diplomatic representatives of one state in another state, presents us with a cynical combination of word and image that depicts it as a starved, curled-up Black child. His poster denounces the exploitation and visual instrumentalization of African countries by the Global North—both based on sweeping preconceptions and undifferentiated representations of an entire continent. Cieślewicz conceived of the poster as an ideal mass medium when it comes to critical intervention in sociopolitical processes. One can, of course, also draw a direct connection to current aid campaign imagery, social posters or media coverage, which in large part still portray Black people as pitiful victims and follow default image strategies.

Lang Gysi Knoll, Werbeagentur AG
Richard Avedon (photo)
Besuchen Sie die Mutter aller Messen
(Visit the Mother of All Trade Shows), 2000
Mustermesse Basel, Muba, CH

Anonymous
Just Feel Magic. Calida Bodywear, 2006
Calida AG, Sursee, CH

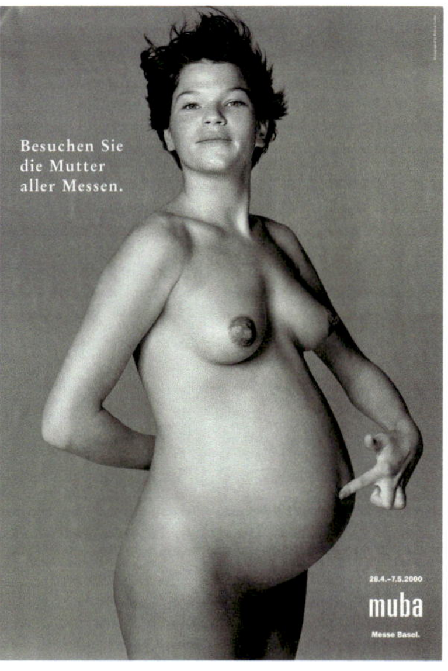

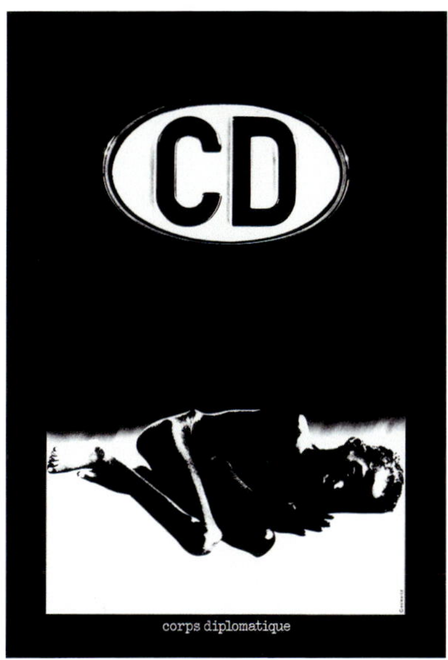

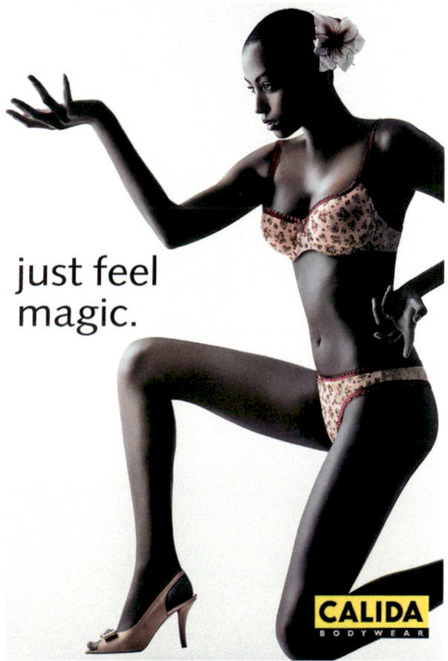

Ludwig Hohlwein
Riquet Pralinen (Riquet Chocolates), 1920
Riquet und Co. AG, Gautzsch-Leipzig, DE

Publicis Werbeagentur AG
Rocco Rorandelli (photo)
Es gibt einen Weg aus jedem Unrecht.
Wir kämpfen gegen Kinderarbeit.
(There Is a Way Out of Every Injustice.
We Are Fighting Against Child Labor.), 2007
Terre des hommes, Tdh, Lausanne, CH

Advico Young & Rubicam AG
2 Monate Karibik Fr. 1534.– / Helvetic Tours / Mehr
erleben für weniger Franken (2 Months Caribbean
Fr. 1534.– / Helvetic Tours / Experience More for
Less Francs), 2000
Helvetic Tours, Zurich, CH

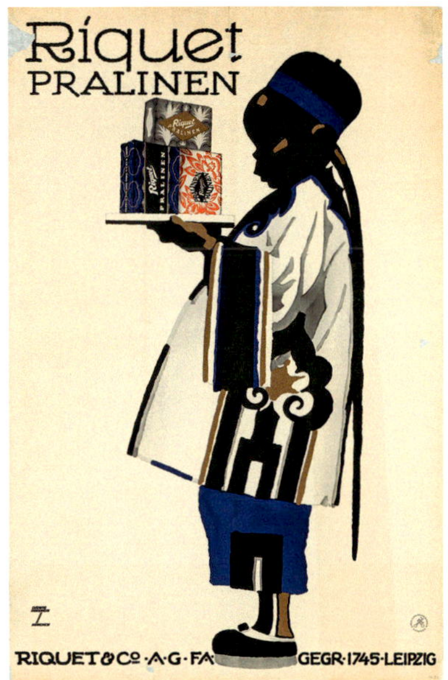

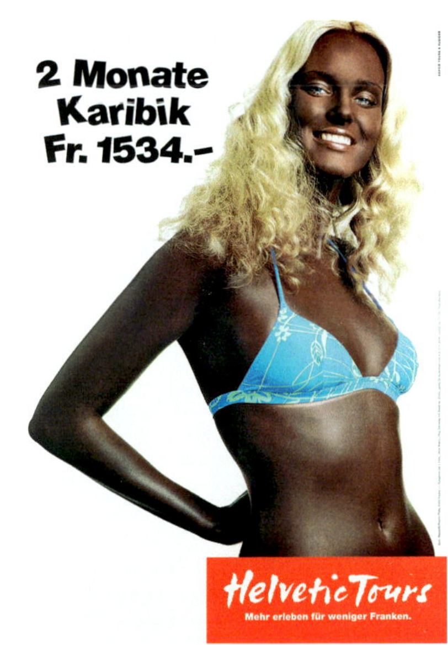

p.74

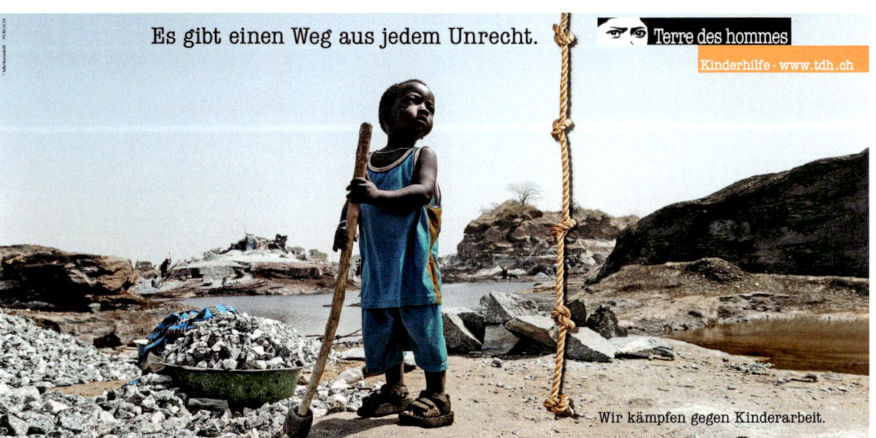

Ina Hattenhauer
Menschen in Entwicklungsländern brauchen
Massnahmen, die nicht nur heute helfen,
sondern auch übermorgen wirken (People
in Developing Countries Need Measures That
Not Only Help Today, but Also Have an Impact
the Day After Tomorrow), 2005
Stiftung Nord-Süd-Brücken, Berlin, DE

Oliviero Toscani
Oliviero Toscani (photo)
United Colors of Benetton, 1991
Benetton Group S.p.A., Ponzano Veneto, IT

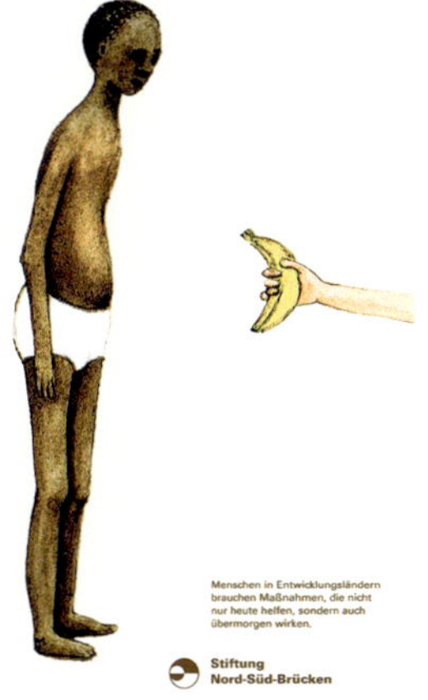

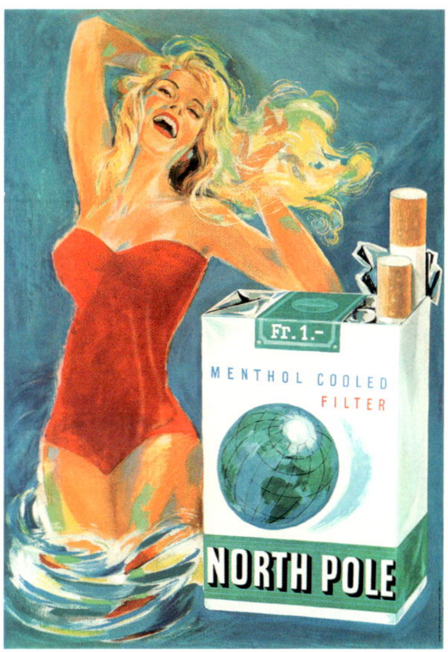

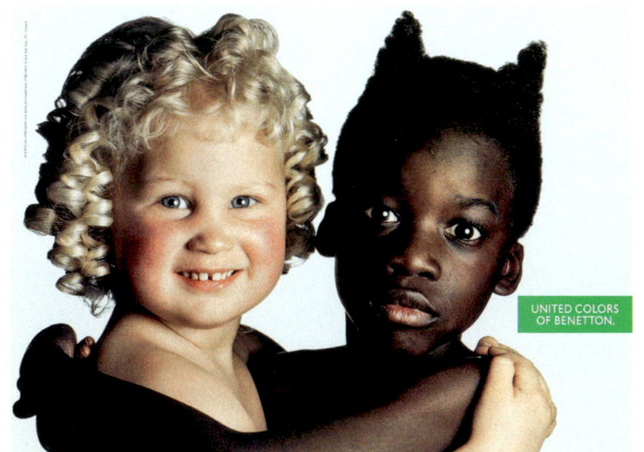

Grafisches Atelier Stankowski + Duschek /
Karl Duschek, Anton Stankowski
Helmut Newton (photo)
Die Eisenbahn in der zeitgenössischen Kunst
(The Railroad in Contemporary Art), 1994
Amt für Touristik, Göppingen, DE

Anonymous
… to the Stars. Joop! Nightflight, 1997
Joop! GmbH, Hamburg, DE

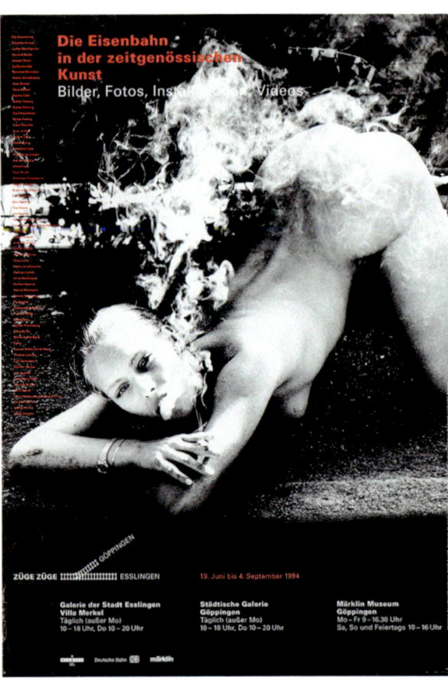

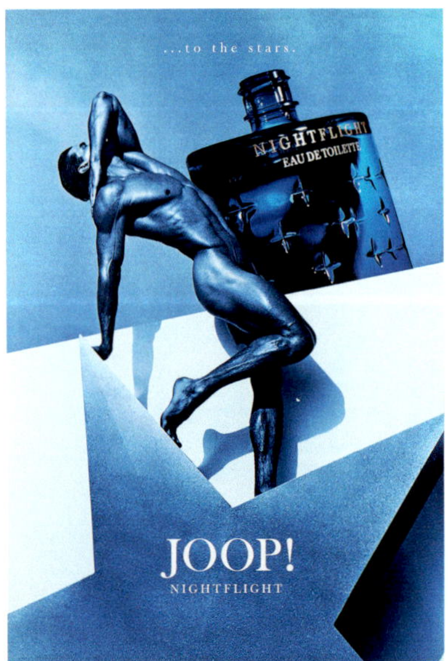

Ikko Tanaka
Irving Penn (photo)
Issey Miyake 1999, 1999
Issey Miyake Inc., Tokyo, JP

Like his fashion designs, Issey Miyake's billboard
advertising is striking for its intricate silhouettes and textures. The rich use of colors that distinguishes this fashion designer is translated
graphically through the juxtaposition of a red font,
the blue, semi-transparent textile, and the
model's Black skin that is set against a white background. The choice of the Black model thus
seems to be primarily motivated by aesthetic considerations. Around 2000, Black women were
still not welcome in the industry, with only a few
exceptions. Here, graphic designer Ikko Tanaka
and photographer Irving Penn constructed an
image of the Black female body that blends the
patriarchal play of veiling and unveiling with a
sense of mystification, which is further amplified
by the accentuation of one eye.

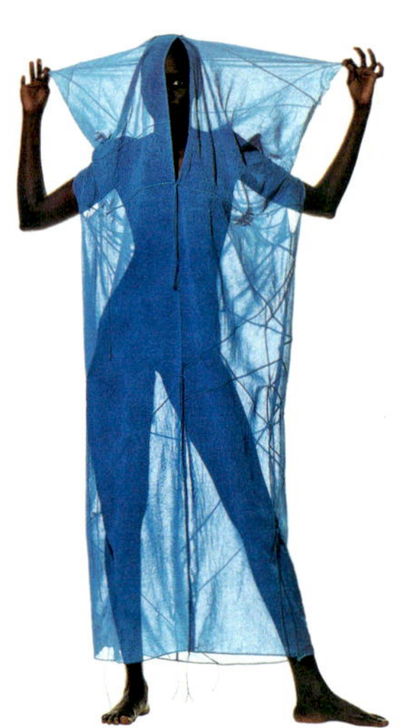

GGK Wien
Elfie Semotan (photo)
Palmers for Men, ca. 1993
Palmers Textil AG, Wiener Neudorf, AT

Frieder Grindler
Bekenntnis einer Prostituierten
(Confession of a Prostitute), 1972
Renitenztheater, Stuttgart, DE

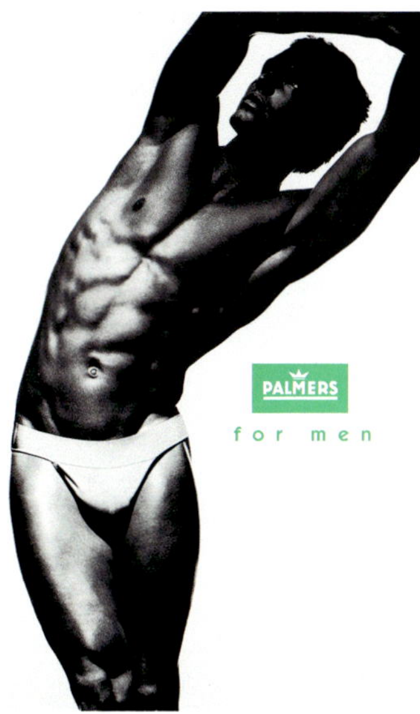

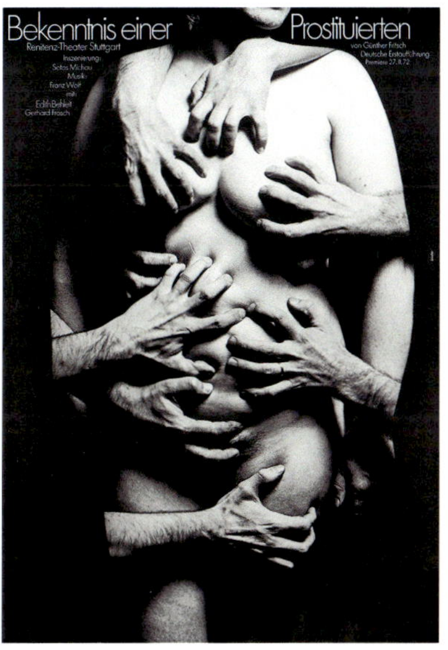

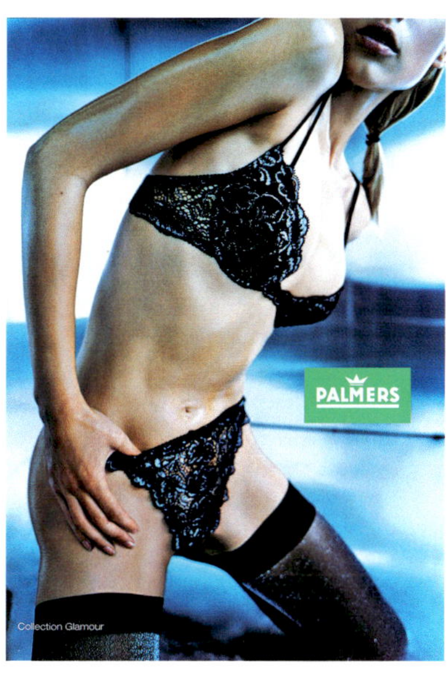

Hans Falk
Einheitsliste / Sozialdemokraten und
Gewerkschafter (Unity List / Social
Democrats and Trade Unionists), 1946
Social Democratic Party of the Canton
of Zurich, SP, CH

Wyler Werbung
Édouard Manet (pictorial reference)
Glatt / ABM / Jelmoli / Globus / Pick Pay.
Die grosse Wein-Auswahl Zürichs
(Zurich's Great Wine Selection), 1992
Einkaufszentrum Glatt, Wallisellen, CH

Otto Baumberger
Wollt Ihr solche Frauen? Frauenstimmrecht Nein
(Do You Want Women Like That? No to Women's
Suffrage), 1920
Unknown assignment

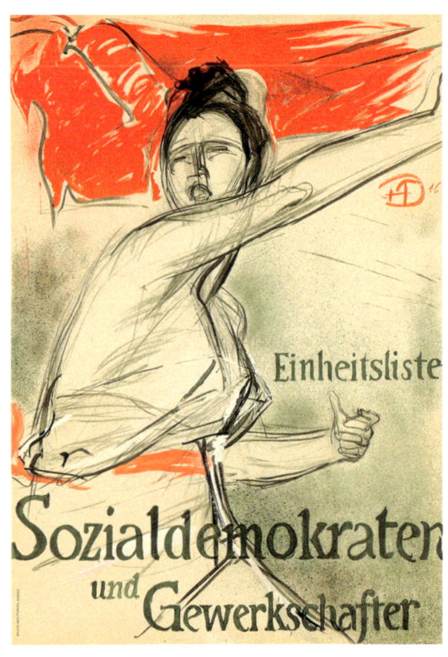

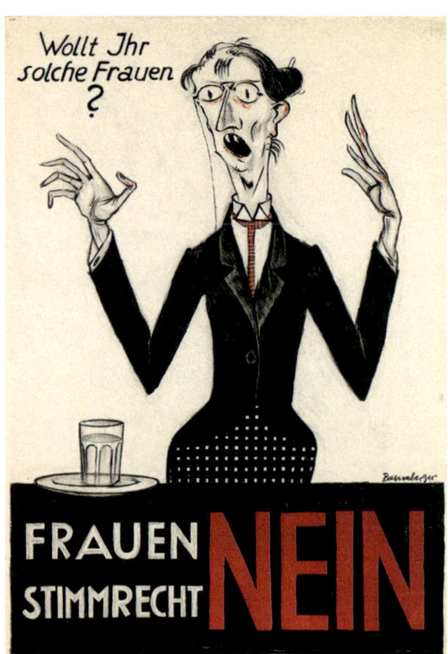

p. 33

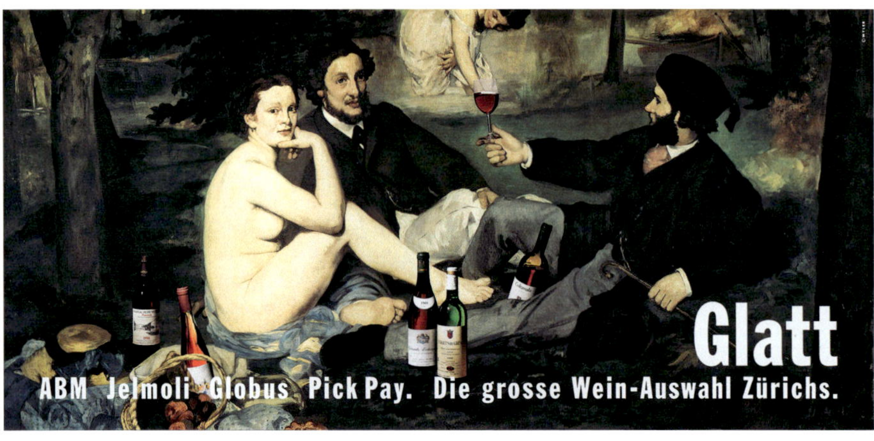

Thus, in the early nineteenth century, a patriarchally dominated scientific discourse laid the foundation for clearly defined gender roles that were organized in a decidedly binary fashion and would become further entrenched in the course of industrialization. In this context, the feminine became a special case, a pathological one that needed to be explained, while the masculine, as a normative concept, "merged into the general category of human nature and vanished."

Thus, in the seventeenth century, attributions were already established with which European people encountered those who looked "different:" from "exceptionally beautiful" to "ugly," along with the devaluation of character through terms like "wild" and "little reason" … This underscores the connection between perception and devaluation, which led to racism, exclusion, discrimination, and exploitation from the sixteenth century onwards, and in the twentieth century, to genocide and annihilation.

Advico Young & Rubicam AG
Arbeitssklave / Menschen sind keine Ware
(Work Slave / People Are Not Commodities), 2007
Brot für alle, BFA, Bern, CH

Michal Batory
Michal Batory (photo)
Cantieri / Chai-llot, 2002
Théâtre national de Chaillot, Paris, FR

Oliviero Toscani
Patrick Robert (photo)
United Colors of Benetton, 1992
Benetton Group S.p.A., Ponzano Veneto, IT

Oliviero Toscani's play with provocation and the controversies triggered by the Benetton campaigns reached a climax in 1992. He introduced horrific images, which had been widely disseminated in the news media, into the idyllic, standardized, retouched world of advertising. This shift in context imbued these images with a new and explosive power that sparked a fierce backlash. The emotionally unsettling news agency photo illustrated the despair of refugees who could not all fit into the truck, which they wrongly thought would be their rescue. Here, human beings are not depicted as possessing bodily integrity, but as part of an anonymous, politically manipulatable and extremely vulnerable "mass of bodies." The poster thus stands in stark contrast with mainstream consumer posters that celebrate the individual in terms of self-optimization and the cult of the body.

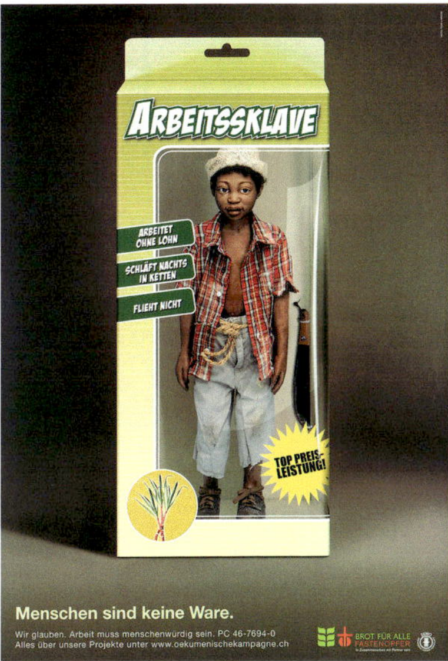

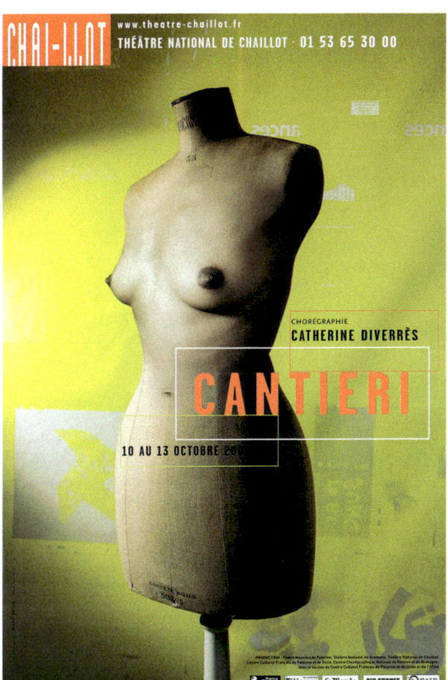

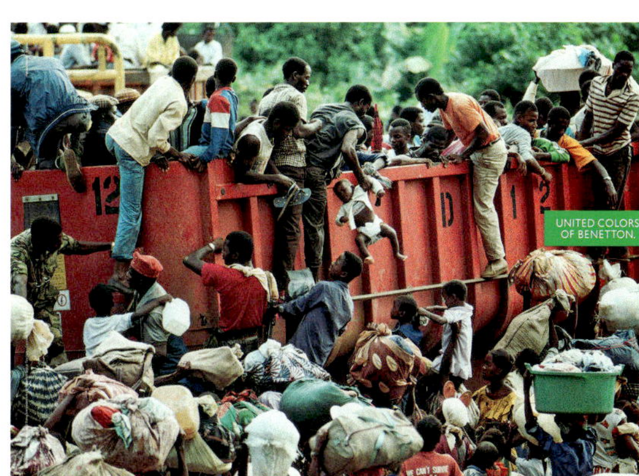

Werner Jeker
Donigan Cumming (photo)
Donigan Cumming, 1996
Musée de l'Elysée Lausanne, CH

Society largely considers depictions of elderly bodies and their intimacy taboo. Photographer Donigan Cumming devoted himself to this subject matter and created a series of pictures that portray journalist and actress Nettie Harris and her body, which is marked by a long life. The photograph of this exhibition poster shows the massive back of an old man, which covers nearly the entire surface of the image. Harris leans against his shoulder, her exhausted face and closed eyes are visible in minute detail and stand out against the black background. Notwithstanding its great formal reduction, the scene radiates emotional intensity and restrained eroticism. The poster probes the acceptance of a different perspective on the human body. The painful realism of this photograph is unsettling and thereby highlights the extent to which our perception of bodies in public spaces is normalized and conditioned.

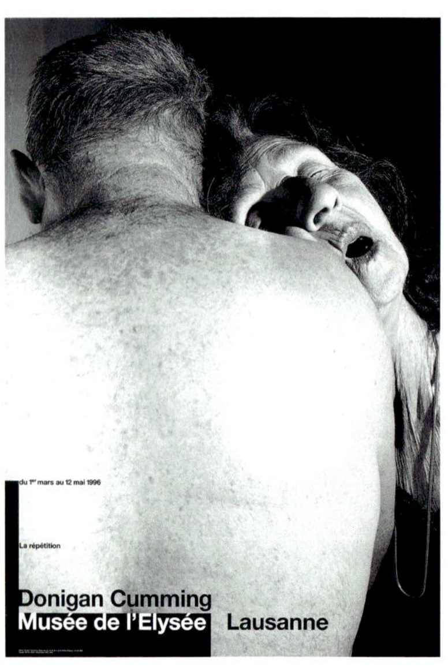

Anonymous
Terry Richardson (photo)
Sisley, 2000
Benetton Group S.p.A., Ponzano Veneto, IT

Gruppo Creativo LBG
Serge Libiszewski (photo)
Prénatal / Tutto per la futura mamma
e per il suo bambino (Everything for
the Future Mother and Her Child), 1964
Prénatal S.p.A., Agrate Brianza, IT

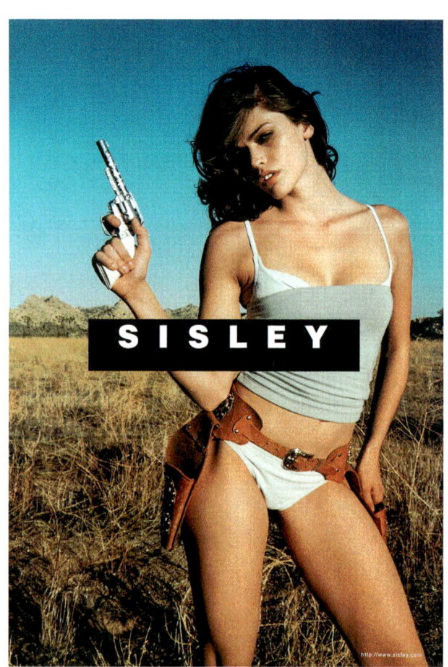

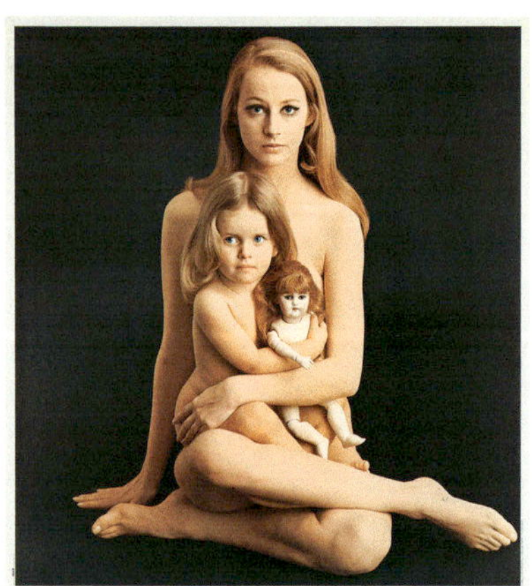

Devilstudio
Eram / Aucun corps de femme n'a été
exploité dans cette publicité (No Female Body
Was Exploited in This Ad) / 399F Alexandre
Matthieu pour Eram, 2001 (reprint 2022)
Eram, Saint-Pierre-Montlimart, FR

Anonymous
Diesel Denim Division / Antique Dirty Denim, 1998
Diesel Concept S.A., Balerna, CH

Oliviero Toscani
Oliviero Toscani (photo)
United Colors of Benetton, 1990
Benetton Group S.p.A., Ponzano Veneto, IT

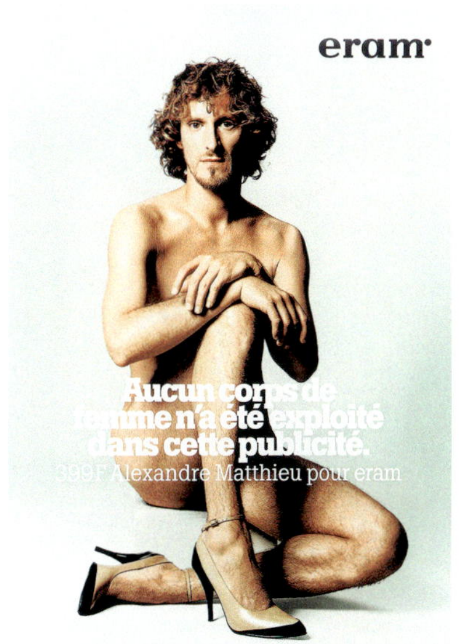

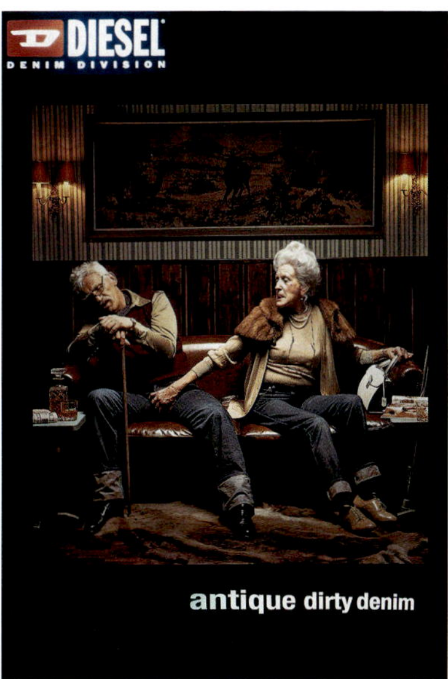

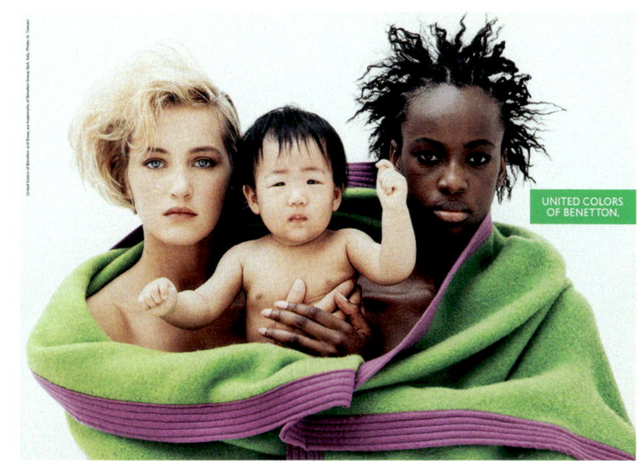

Gino Boccasile
Lugano, 1939
Verkehrsverein Lugano, CH

Anonymous
P.S.U. / Homes forts, al front!
(Strong Men to the Front!), 1936
Partido Socialista Unificat, P.S.U., ES

Pal (Jean de Paléologue)
Rayon d'or / Dernier mot de l'éclairage
(The Last Word in Lighting), 1895
Salle d'Expériences, Paris, FR

Pal pioneered a concept that still dominates
advertising today. He inserted the female nude
as an erotic eye-catcher in product posters
whose content did not justify the use of such
imagery. Advertising modern kerosene lamps,
this poster shows a lamp and a star, which
form a symbolic celestial body. A nude woman
embraces the light, and her feminine curves
are accentuated by her posture. Her body is
wrapped in a see-through veil and rendered
realistically, while her elf wings whisk her away
to a fairy tale world, which somewhat softens
her sensual charisma. The simultaneous exaltation and objectification of the female body
is a topos that runs through all of art history
and has also influenced advertising.

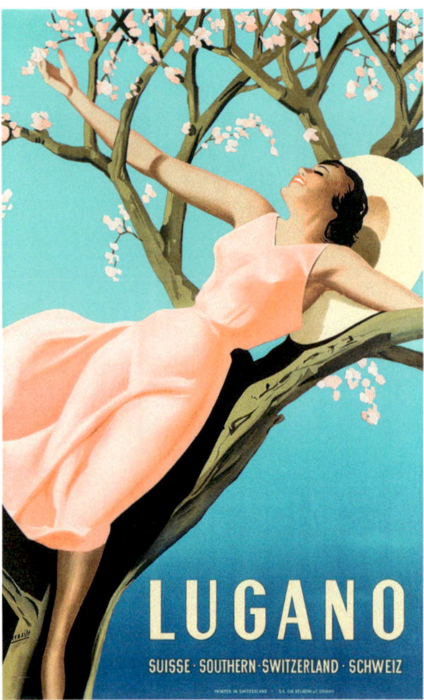

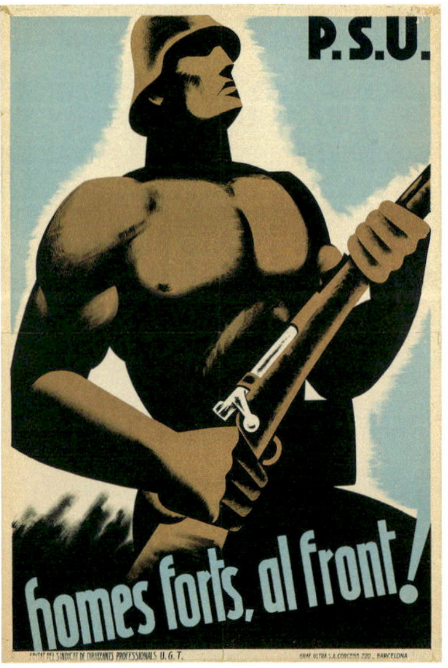

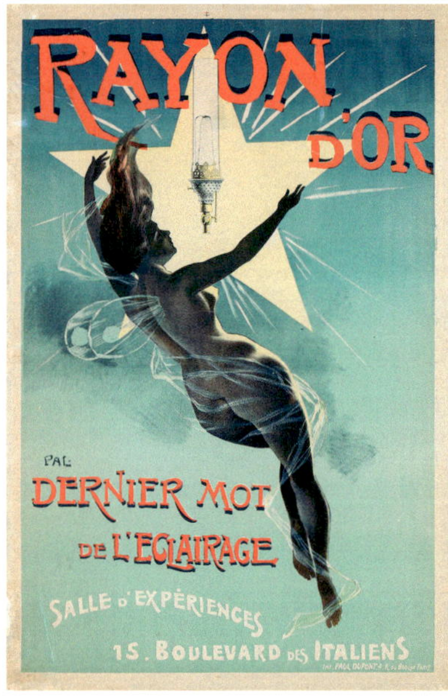

Hans Rippstein
Aarg. Arbeiter Turn u. Sporttag /
Der Satus für die Jugend / Der Jugend
die Zukunft (Workers' Gymnastics and
Sports Day / Seeds Planted for the Young /
The Future Belongs to the Young), 1933
Schweizerischer Arbeiter-Turn- und
Sportverband, SATUS, Bern, CH

Anonymous
Mustang / On the Wild Side, 1995
Mustang Holding GmbH, Schwäbisch Hall, DE

Urs Lüthi
Autonomes Jugendzentrum / 6 Tage Zürcher
Manifest (Autonomous Youth Center / 6 Days
Zurich Manfesto), 1968
Komitee Autonomes Jugendzentrum, Zurich, CH

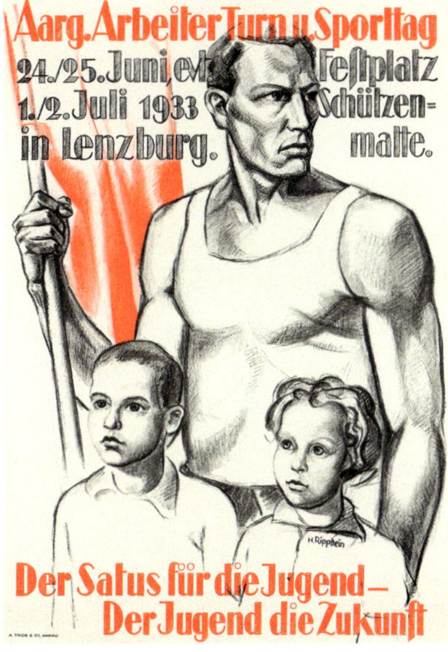

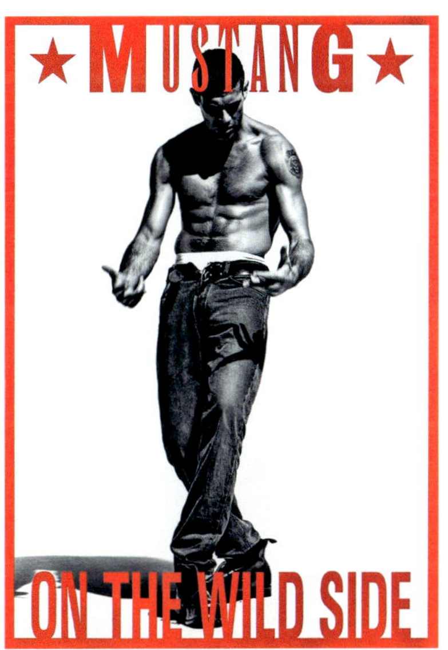

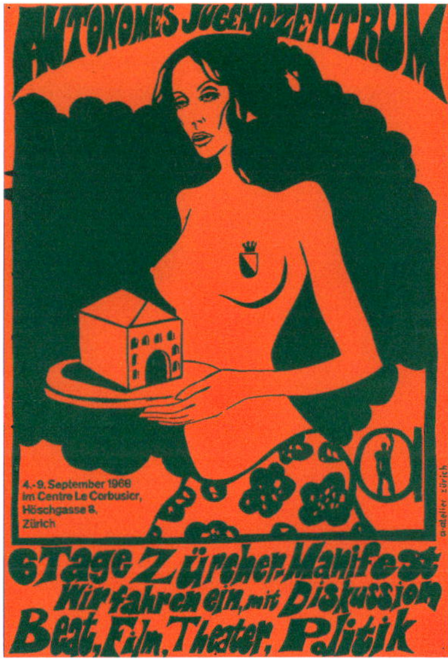

Anonymous
Thomas von Ubrizsy (photo)
16-jährig und tabu? Nein … Ta-Bou
(Sixteen and Taboo? No … Ta-Bou), 1994
Ta-Bou Beachwear, Zurich, CH

Adidas AG, Global Marketing
I'm Possible / Impossible Is Nothing /
Adidas, 2022
Adidas AG, Herzogenaurach, DE

Karl Bickel
Elektrische Licht- Stark- & Schwachstrom
Anlagen (Electric Luminous Flux Installations,
High & Low Voltage Systems) / S. Mazzanti, 1915
S. Mazzanti, Zurich, CH

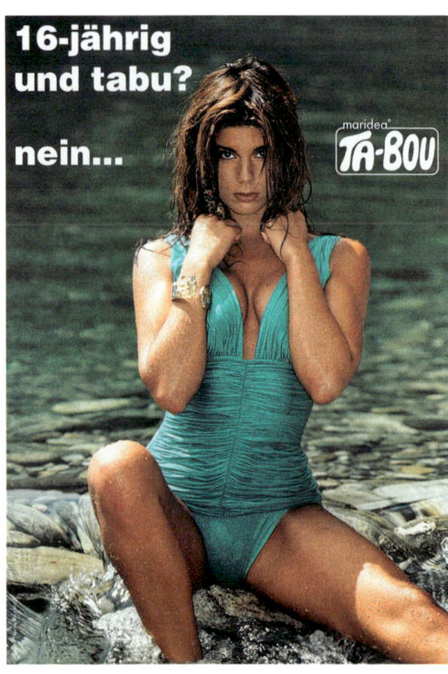

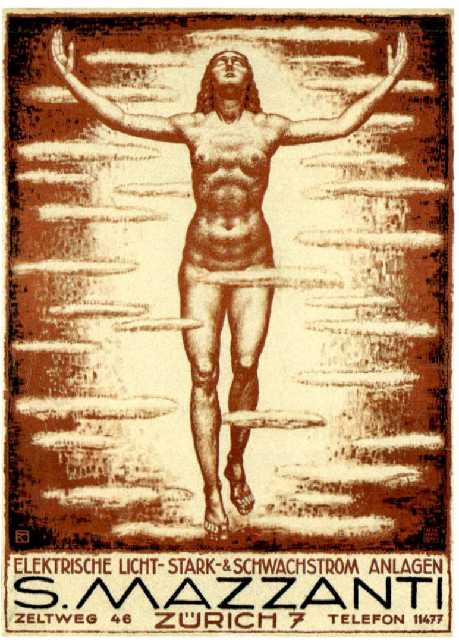

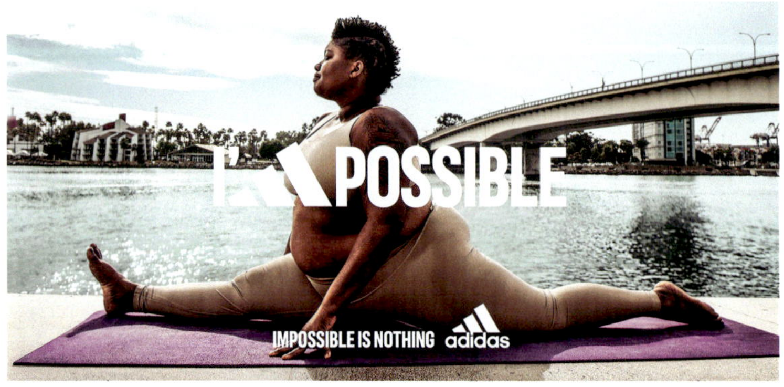

p.105

Atelier Bundi / Stephan Bundi
Stephan Bundi (photo)
Wolfgang Amadeus Mozart / Don Giovanni, 2011
Theater Biel Solothurn, CH

Peter Marti
Rifle / Jeans and Jackets, 1986
Rifle Schweiz, Denges, CH

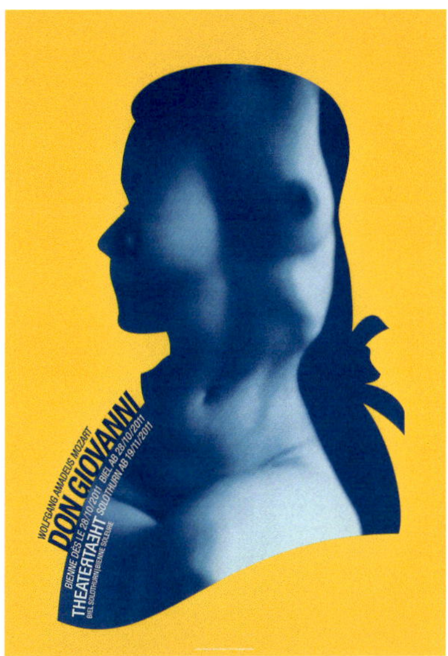

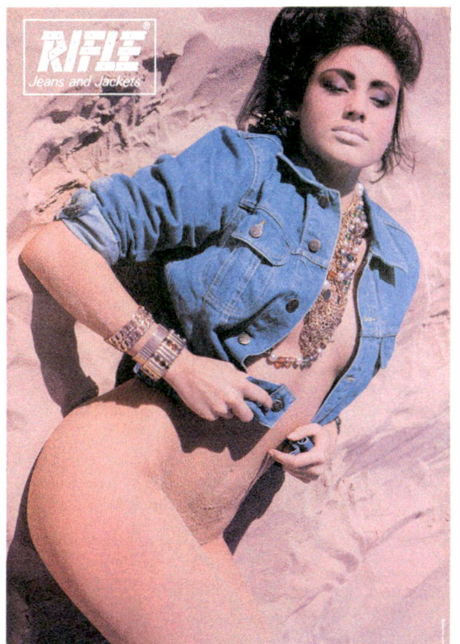

Viktor Rutz
Vevey, 1948
Office du Tourisme, Vevey, CH

Viktor Rutz's bathing woman presents herself to the viewer fully aware of her physical attractiveness. She is thus a testimony to the epochal cultural change that manifested itself, among other things, in the images of women and men appearing in advertising after World War II. Her posture quotes Botticelli's famous painting of Venus, the goddess of love, which somewhat softens the provocative display of her erotic body. Furthermore, the female figure is embedded in the iconography of the four seasons. The demurely dressed women in the background personify spring and autumn, while the protagonist is the embodiment of summer, which simultaneously works to legitimize the revealing depiction of her feminine charms.

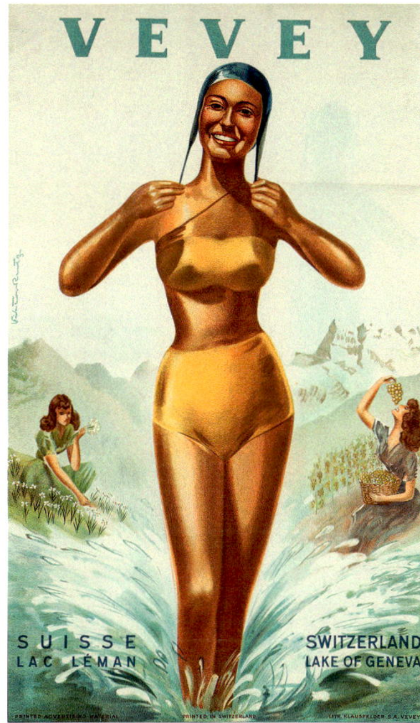

p. 13

A. U. Steinmann
N*******-Schimpansi / Mit Wilhelm
Eggert quer durch Afrika (Across Africa
with Wilhelm Eggert), 1939
Resta-Film, Zurich, CH

Nike Design / Alan Colvin, Kar Wu
Fred Ingram (illustration)
Michael Jordan / Nike, 1991
Nike Inc., Beaverton, US

Vittorio Brodmann, AA Bronson,
Richard Hawkins
Lionel Bovier (concept)
[B]ronson / Horror Monsters /
The Little Monsters, 2015
JRP Ringier Kunstverlag AG,
Zurich, CH

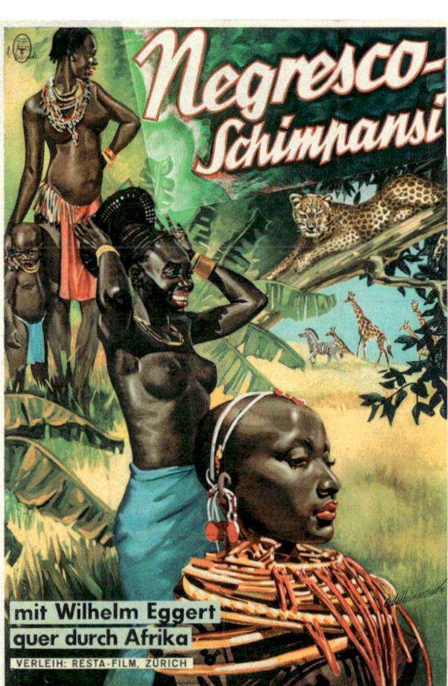

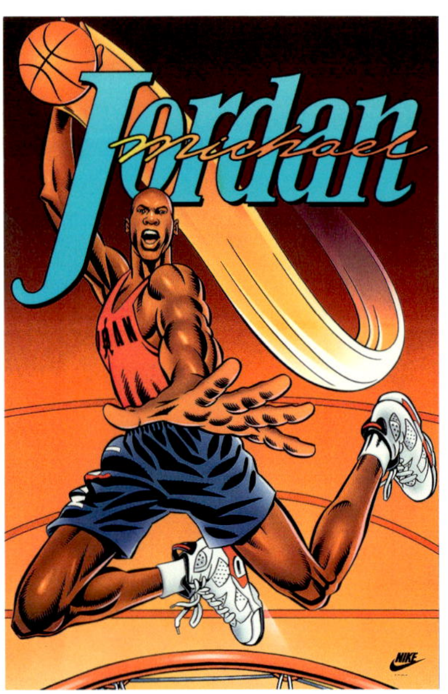

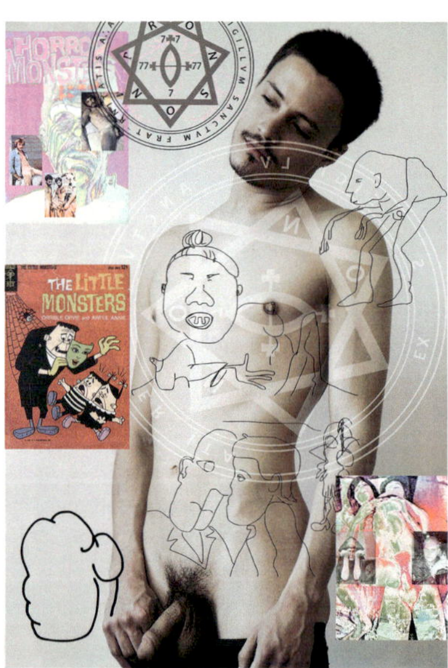

Nevertheless, social media platforms, due to their openness and accessibility, offer the potential for resistance by marginalized bodies … Disabled or trans bodies, which are more or less absent in mainstream media contexts, gain new visibility, even though it may not always be free from beauty ideals.

Identification and Illusion. Bodies on Social Media

Maria Schreiber

People with disabilities undermine the modern understanding of intact and self-determined subjectivity. At least in the modern West, growing up means gradually overcoming the feeling of dependence, imperfection, and vulnerability through awareness of one's own sovereignty.

Markus Dederich

ZHdK, Visual Communication / Andrea Koch
René Burri (photo)
René Burri, 2005
Museum für Gestaltung Zürich, CH

Oliviero Toscani
Therese Frare (photo)
United Colors of Benetton, 1992
Benetton Group S.p.A., Ponzano Veneto, IT

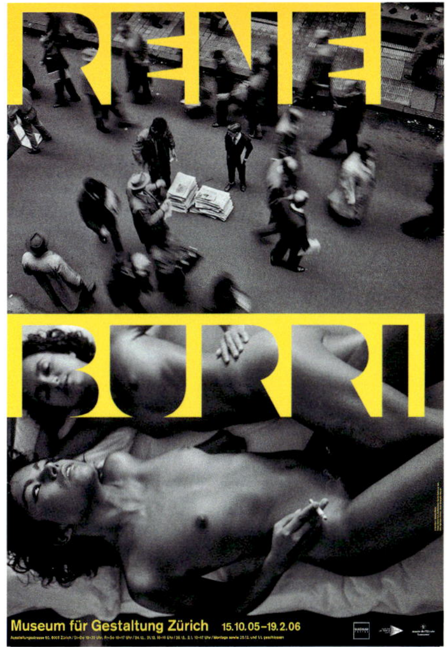

p. 104

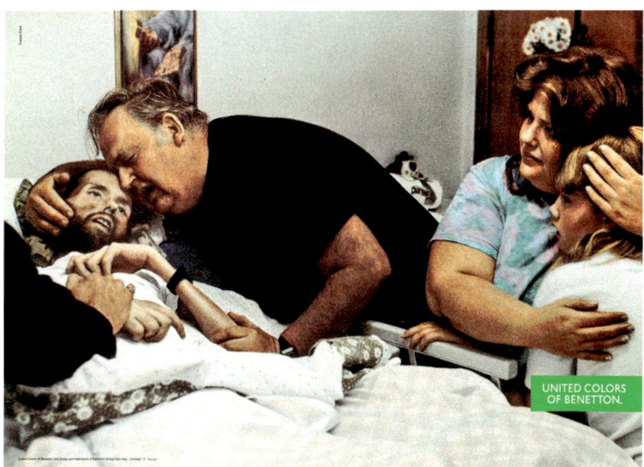

Büro X Design GmbH
Gottfried Helnwein (illustration)
Jeanmaire. Ein Stück Schweiz / von Urs Widmer
(A Piece of Switzerland / by Urs Widmer), 1992
Lukas Leuenberger

In 1977, Swiss general Jean-Louis Jeanmaire was sentenced to eighteen years in prison for alleged Soviet espionage and treason. While Jeanmaire was ostracized as a public enemy, he steadfastly maintained his claims of innocence. In his play, which premiered in 1992, Urs Widmer portrayed Jeanmaire as a symbol of contemporary national history, of discourses on power and myths. The theater poster features an illustration by Austrian artist and provocateur Gottfried Helnwein. It shows Jeanmaire having dropped his pants—a literal depiction of a German phrase that translates as "confessing an often-unpleasant truth." A realistic portrayal of a man's nude body at an advanced age was a first in Swiss poster history. Even though the Jeanmaire family had officially given their permission for the poster, its public display was deemed a violation of moral and ethical norms and was therefore banned; the military hat and the genitals were painted over.

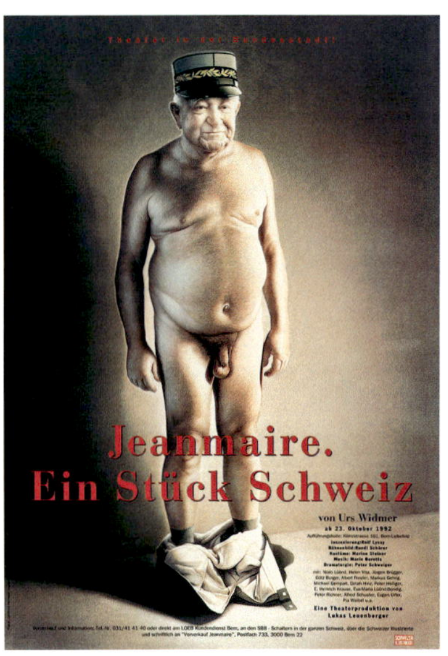

Ikko Tanaka
Irving Penn (photo)
Issey Miyake 1998, 1998
Issey Miyake Inc., Tokyo, JP

Celestino Piatti
Unsere Hilfe / Hoffnung für Afrika
(Our Aid / Hope for Africa), 1985
Deutscher Caritasverband e. V., Freiburg, DE

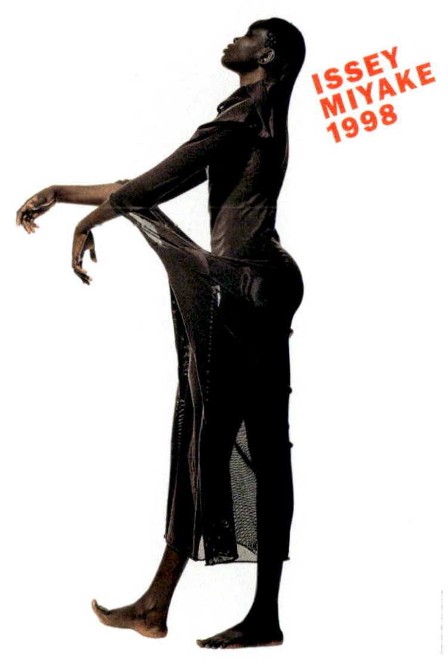

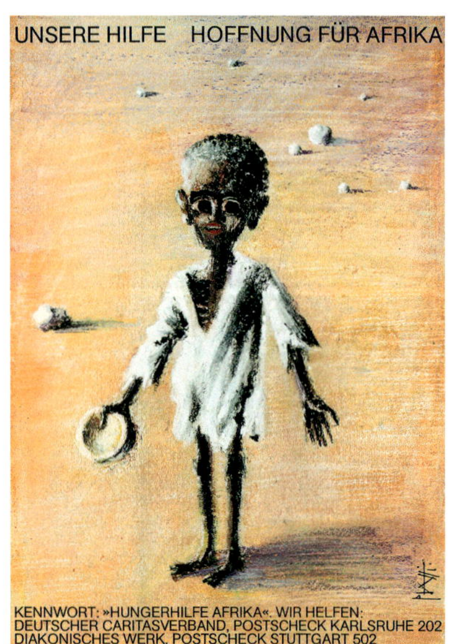

Donigan Cumming (photo)
Le Corps / The Body, 1994
Kunsthalle Bielefeld, DE

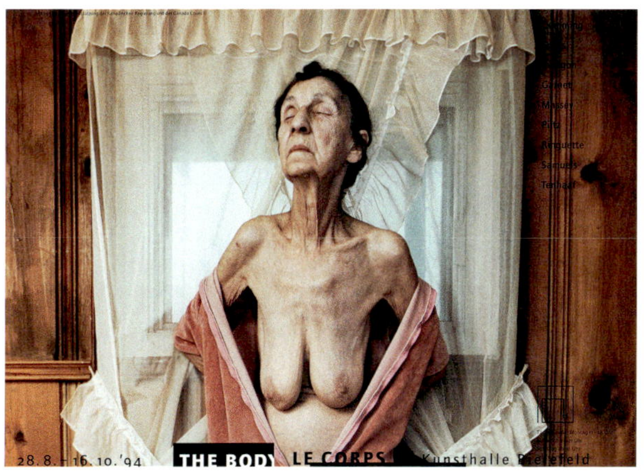

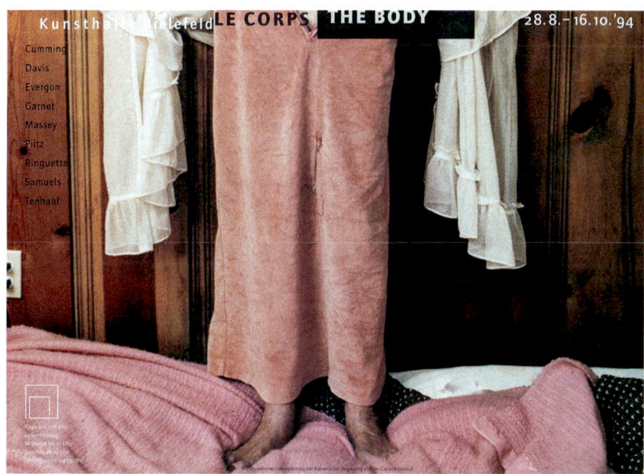

TBWA\Neboko
Sophie Ebrard (photo)
The Reason We Didn't Make Just One New Sports
Bra. Impossible Is Nothing / Adidas, 2022
Adidas AG, Herzogenaurach, DE

Oliviero Toscani
Yves Gellie (photo)
United Colors of Benetton, 1992
Benetton Group S.p.A., Ponzano Veneto, IT

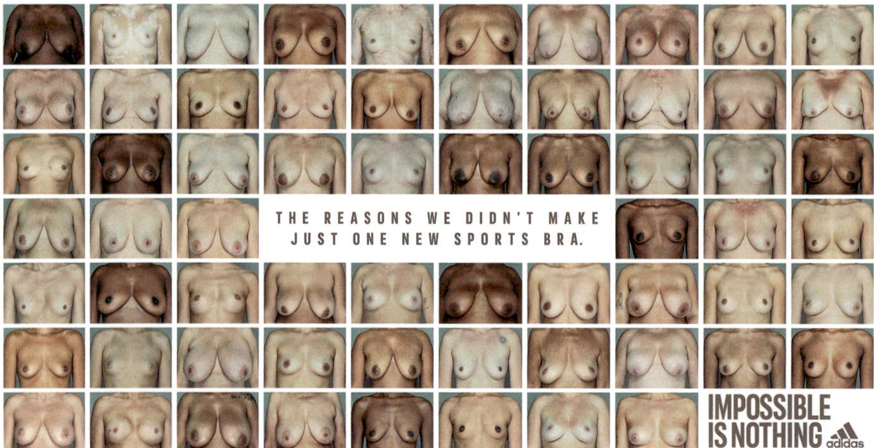

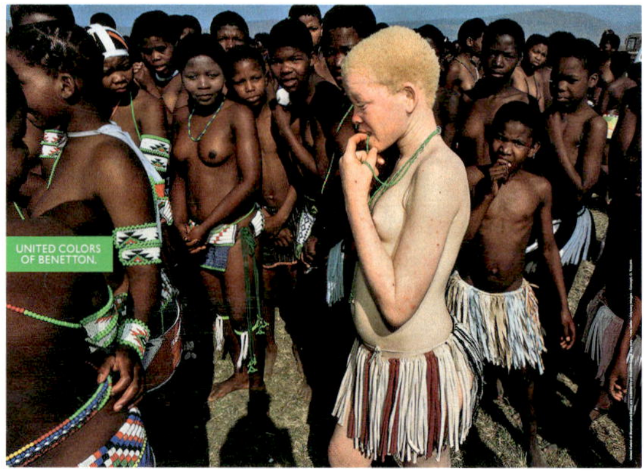

Oliviero Toscani
Oliviero Toscani (photo)
United Colors of Benetton, ca. 1992
Benetton Group S.p.A., Ponzano Veneto, IT

Bartle Bogle Hegarty / Mike Wells
Bill Brandt (photo)
Levi's 517 / Regular Fit, 1995
Levi Strauss & Co., GB

Daniele Buetti
[no text], 1999
Private project

Swiss artist Daniele Buetti first showed works
from his poster series at an exhibition in Biel
in 1997. Buetti had adapted details of classic fashion advertising imagery in an analog manner
and used it to explore ideals of beauty and the cult
of youth. Using a ballpoint pen, he had imprint-
ed ornamental drawings onto the perfect surface
of the models' smoothly retouched skin. The
texture thus added to the body is irritating and
suggestive of injuries. This both shines a light on
the flawlessness touted in the fashion world
and, at the same time, raises critical questions
about it. Buetti's quiet and poetic work inter-
venes in debates around individuality and the
normative beauty craze prevalent in our society,
without claiming to offer conclusive answers.

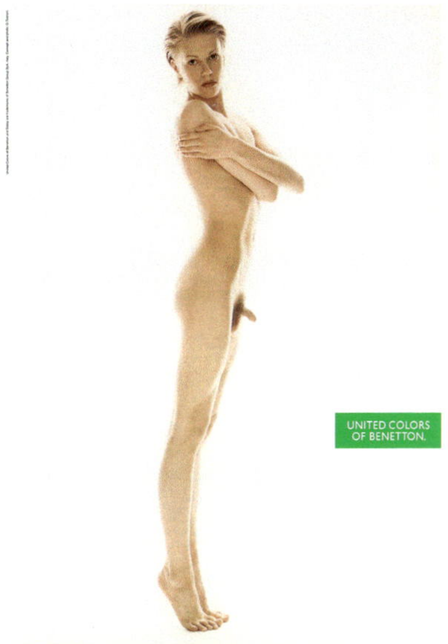

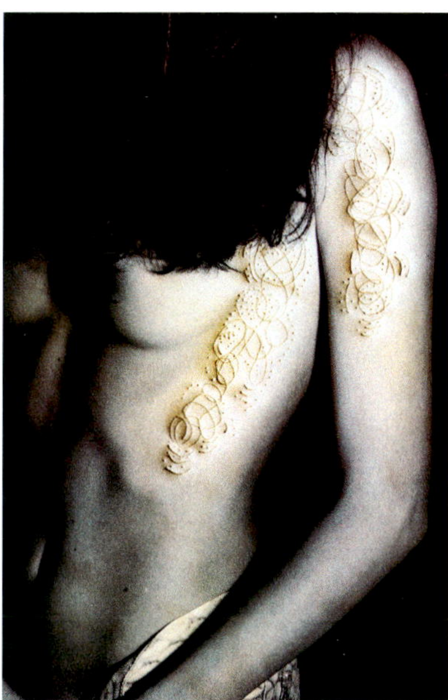

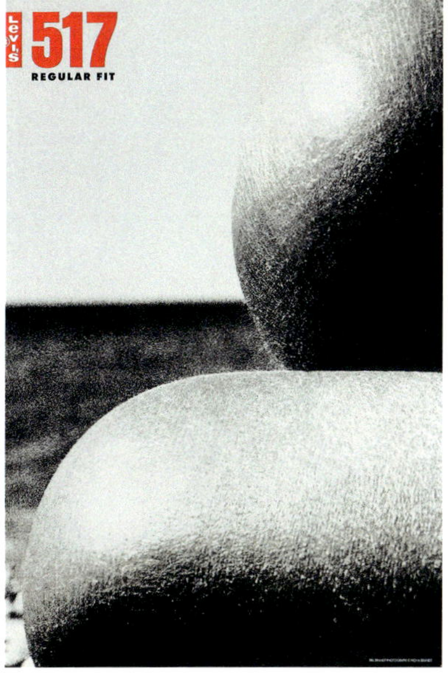

Salvatore Gregorietti / Oliviero Toscani
United Colors of Benetton, 1998
Benetton Group S.p.A., Ponzano Veneto, IT

Cyan / Daniela Haufe, Detlef Fiedler
Daniela Haufe, Detlef Fiedler (photo)
Cie. Toula Limnaios, 2002
Cie. Toula Limnaios, DE

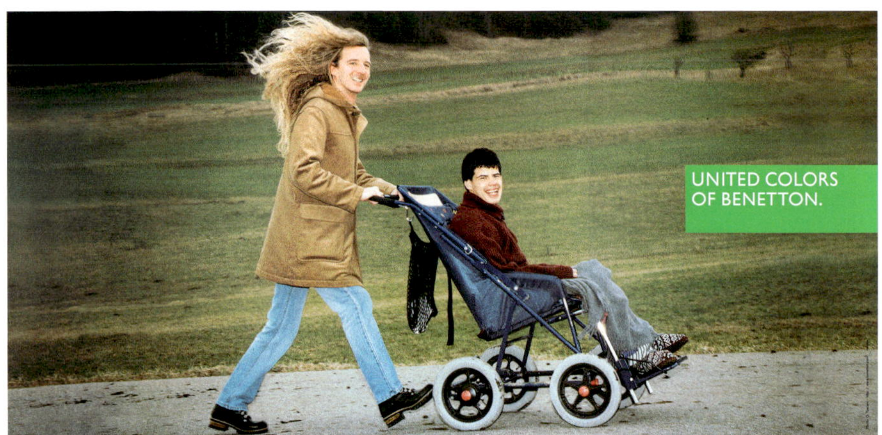

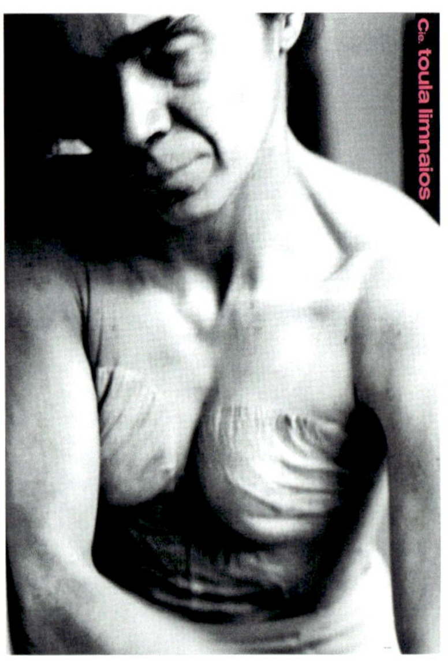

M/M/Michael Amzalag, Mathias Augustyniak
Inez van Lamsweerde, Vinoodh Matadin (photo)
G/The Alphabet/Griet, 2001
Private project

Jung von Matt LIMMAT AG
Wer ist schon perfekt? Kommen Sie näher
(Who's Perfect? Come Closer), 2013
Pro Infirmis, Zurich, CH

Ernst Emil Schlatter
Für das Alter (For Old Age), 1939
Pro Senectute, Zurich, CH

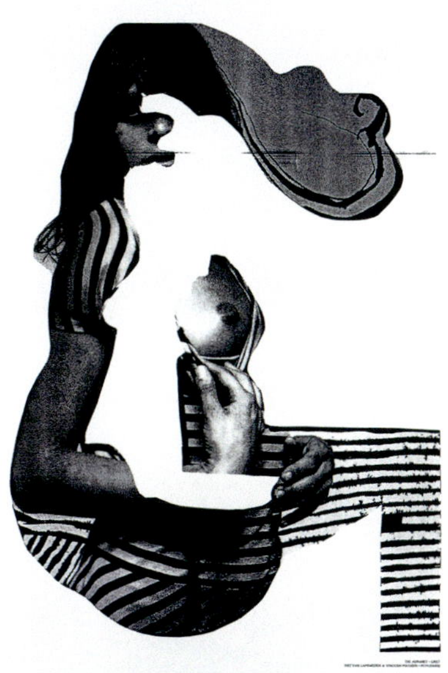

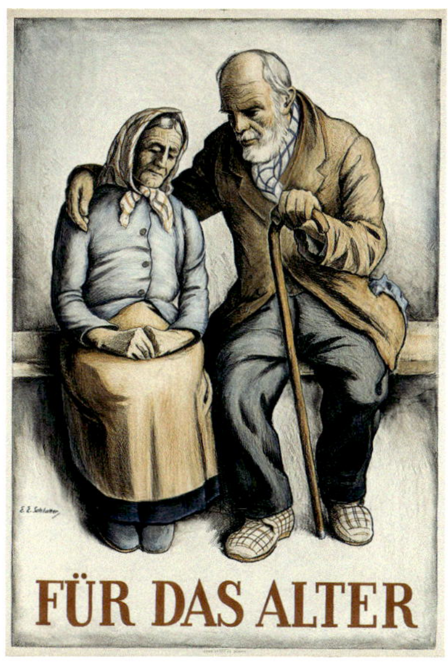

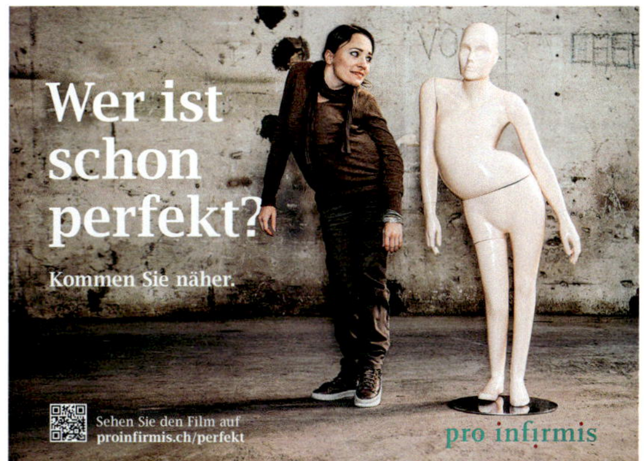

Cornel Windlin
Isabel Truniger (photo)
«Die Klasse» / Fotos ("The Class" / Photos), 1996
Museum für Gestaltung Zürich, CH

Victore Design Works / James Victore
Tom Schierlitz (photo)
Nouveau Salon des Cent /
Exposition internationale d'affiches
(International Poster Exhibition) /
Hommage à Toulouse-Lautrec, 2001
Musée Toulouse-Lautrec, Albi, FR

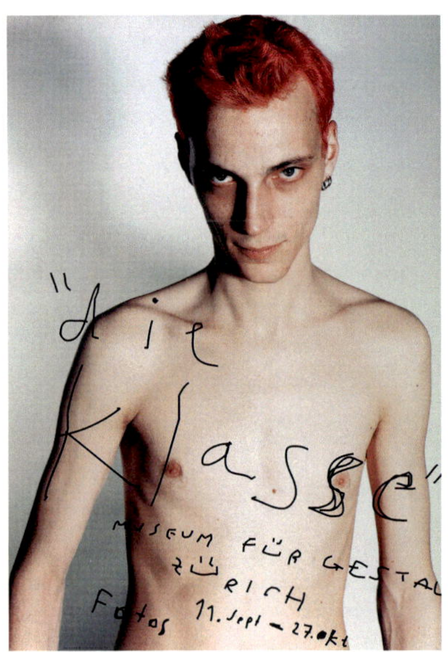

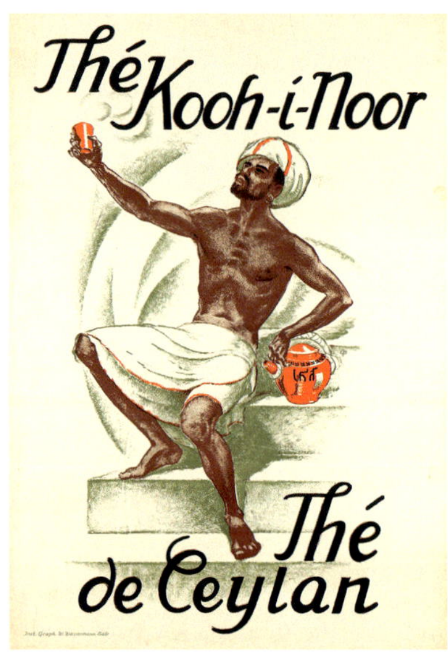

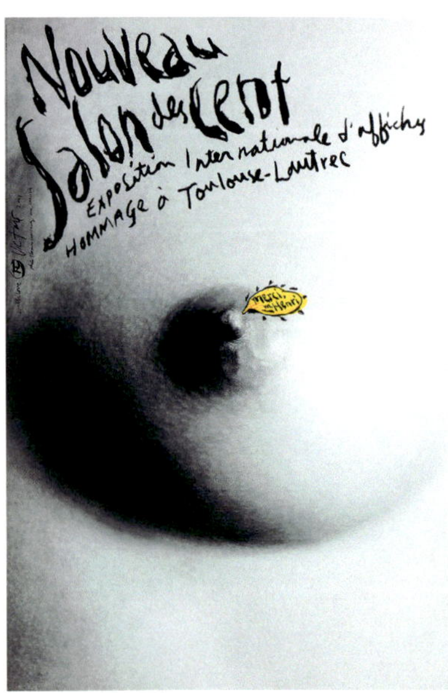

Of course, the media play
a dual role here: On the one
hand, they serve as a resonance chamber for societal
notions of gender; on the
other hand, they actively
contribute to the discursive
production of "bodies,
gender identities and sexualities," as well.

Florian Diener

A multilateral understanding of research that deconstructs ethnocentric, androcentric and Eurocentric gaze regimes has led to a new awareness of race and gender, and ultimately to greater courage in dissolving dichotomous constructs in the visual representation of racialized and gendered bodies.

Black Body Entanglement between Essentialism and Constructivism

Marilyn Umurungi

Anonymous
Sabena / Belgien / Kongo / Südafrika
(Sabena / Belgium / Congo / South Africa), 1956
Sabena, Brussels, BE

The colonial regime of Belgian Congo, now the
Democratic Republic of Congo, was marked
by the most extreme forms of brutality. Congo-
lese natives were enslaved in large numbers
and the country's mineral resources were ruth-
lessly exploited. In the 1950s, resistance formed
against the foreign rulers, and in the 1960s,
the country gained independence. Against this
backdrop, the 1956 poster of Belgian airline
Sabena reads like a visual justification of colonization: Colonial powers projected their white
fantasies onto the image of a Black female
dancer which did not in any way reflect the reality of the country. While the plane symbolizes
progress and civilization, the sexualized female
body is rendered a symbol of backwardness,
an embodiment of colonial territories.

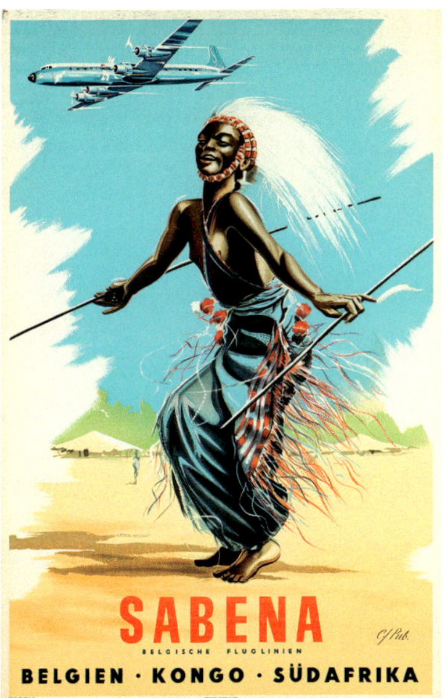

p.72

Guido Brouwers
Pete Stone (photo)
The Future Is Here. Anfernee Hardaway, 1994
Nike Inc., Beaverton, US

Otto Baumberger
Sammelt Steinfels-Bilder
(Collect Steinfels Pictures), 1934
Friedrich Steinfels AG, Zurich, CH

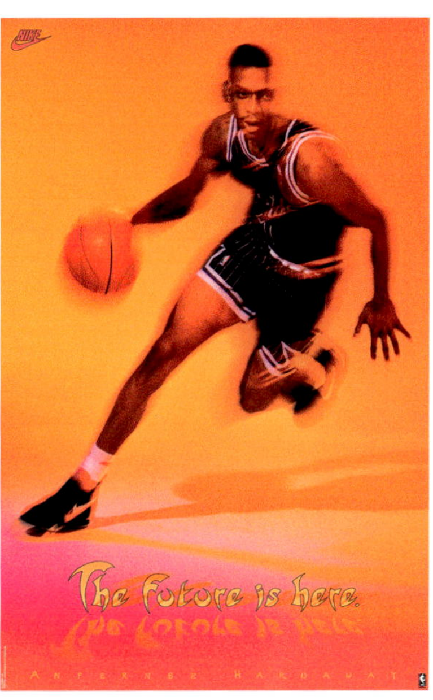

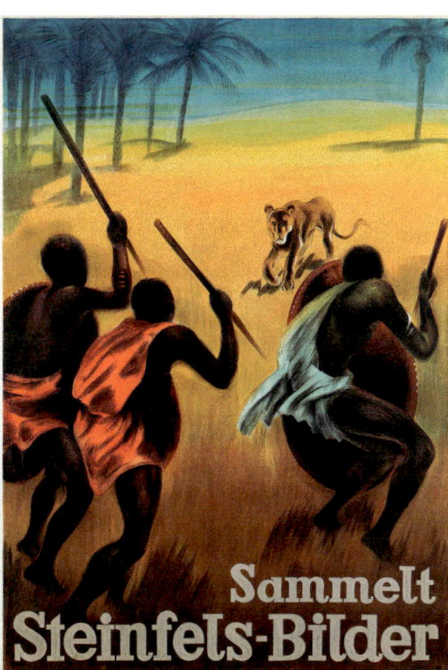

Anonymous
Calvin Klein Jeans / CK, 1993
Calvin Klein Inc., New York, US

Anonymous
Gewinnen Sie! ... Mettler Herrenmoden
(Win! ... Mettler Men's Fashion), 1974
Mettler Herrenmoden, Zurich, CH

George Noordanus
Hendrik-Jan Koldeweij (photo)
PSP / Ontwapenend (Disarming), 1971
Pacifistisch Socialistische Partij, PSP, NL

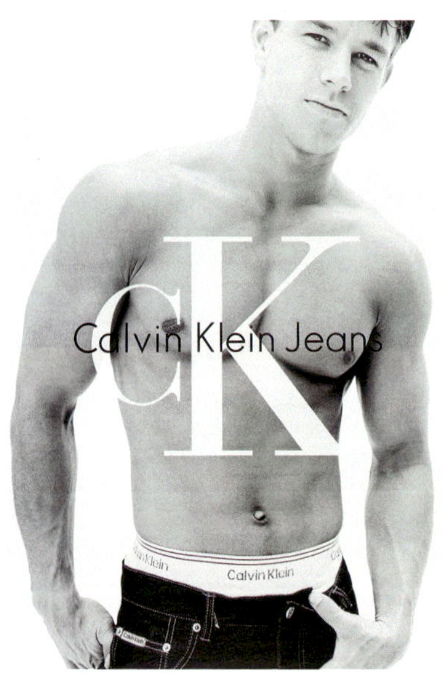

p. 14

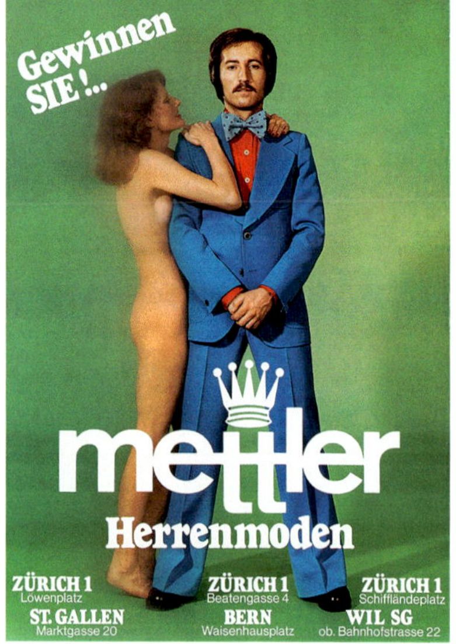

p. 15

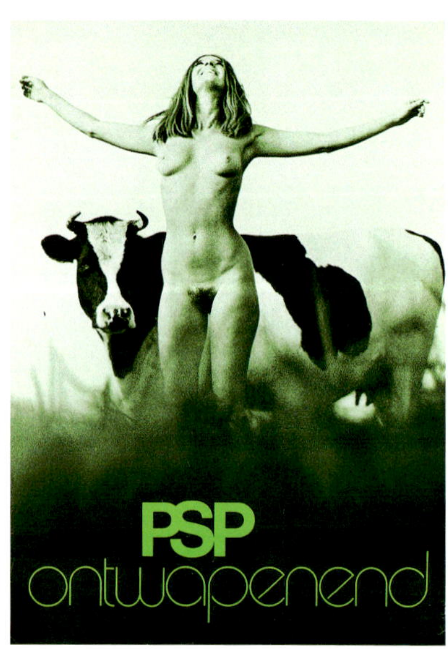

Jonathan Ellery
Bruce Gilden (photo)
Coney Island 1969–1986 / Bruce Gilden, 2001
Trebruk Publishing, US

Pro Infirmis / Handicap sì. Limiti no. / Il segreto
più saporito della Svizzera. Appenzeller
(Disabilities Yes. Limits None. / The Tastiest
Secret in Switzerland. Appenzeller), 2019
Pro Infirmis, Zurich, CH

Committed to a more inclusive Switzerland, the
Pro Infirmis association harnesses innovative
approaches that conceive of advertising as a direct reflection of our society. Its "Ungehindert
behindert" (Unhindered Disability) campaign
deftly exposes how individuals with disabilities
are persistently marginalized through their
invisibility in mainstream media. Well-established advertising visuals of Swiss companies
were recast with people with disabilities, which
illustrates the visual taboo they had been subjected to. The campaign raises questions concern-
ing representation and identification facilitated
by advertising. At the same time, it appeals to
clients to bring more realism and diversity to the
images they communicate.

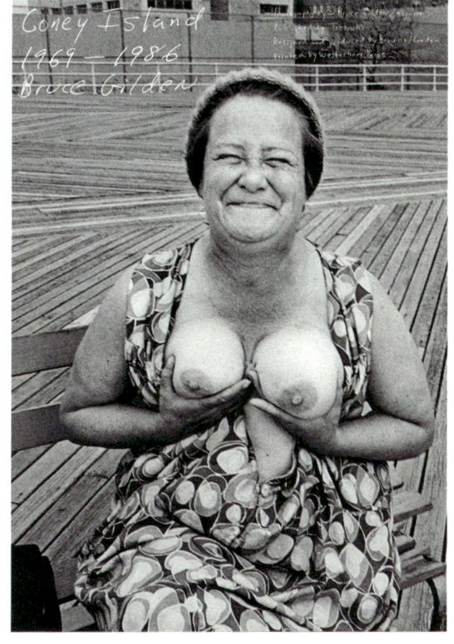

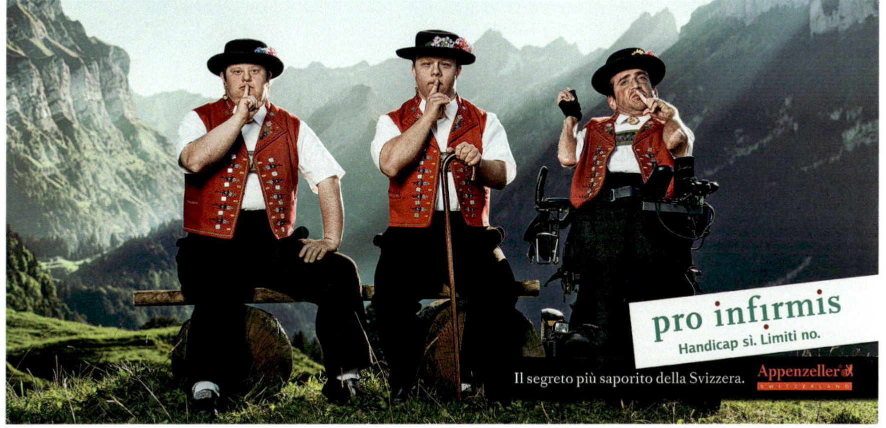

Wieden & Kennedy / Dan Wieden
"I Got so Many Moves, Last Game I Shook
Myself" / NYC, 1996
Nike Inc., Beaverton, US

Klaus Staeck
Leonardo da Vinci (pictorial reference)
Niemand ist vollkommen (Nobody's Perfect), 1981
Private project

Ikko Tanaka
Irving Penn (photo)
Ten Sen Men / The 1st Hiroshima Art Prize /
Issey Miyake, 1990
Hiroshima City Museum of Contemporary Art,
Hiroshima MOCA, JP

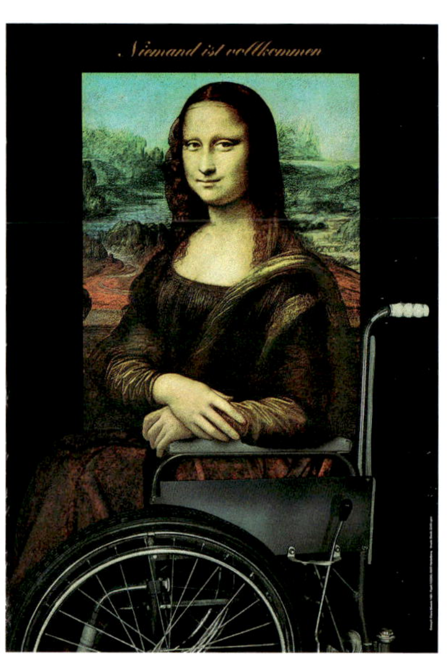

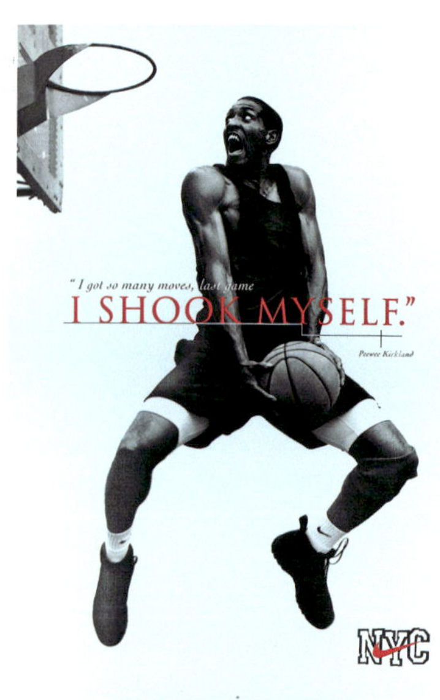

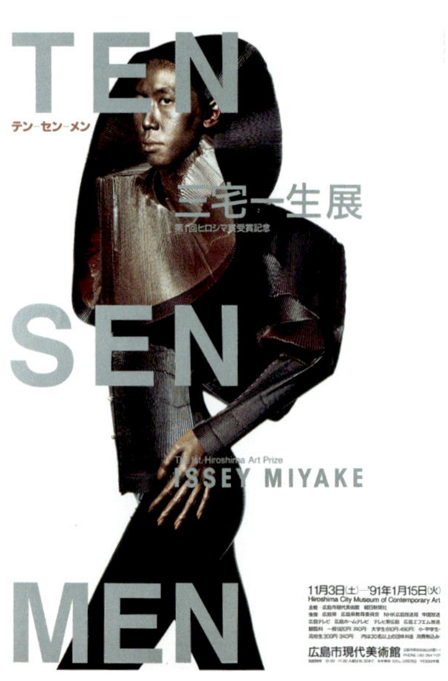

Metzger Lehner Briccola AG
Hannes Schmid (photo)
Olivier Bösch / Tontechniker / Wir lassen uns nicht behindern (Sound Technician / We Will Not Let Ourselves Be Handicapped), 2001
Pro Infirmis, Zurich, CH

In 2001, Pro Infirmis launched its campaign "Wir lassen uns nicht behindern" (We Will Not Let Ourselves Be Handicapped). Its protagonists self-confidently posed in front of the camera of re-nowned photographer Hannes Schmid, openly and defiantly returning the gaze of the public. The individual body portraits marked a paradigm shift, as earlier campaigns had focused on emo-tionally charged images that invariably painted disability as a story that was all about suffer-ing. In 2014, disability rights activist Stella Young sharply criticized this type of appropriation in advertising and coined the term "inspiration porn" to make her point. It describes, in a nutshell, media strategies and modes of negotiation that instrumentalize disabilities as inspiration, mo-tivation, and a way of boosting appreciation of a life free of impairments.

Advico-Delpire AG
Michelangelo Buonarroti (pictorial reference)
Levi's, 1973
Levi Strauss & Co., San Francisco, US

Images3 S.A.
Sylvain Bruschweiler (photo)
http://www.avacah.ch, 2001
Association vaudoise pour la construction adaptée aux personnes handicapées, AVACAH, La Sarraz, CH

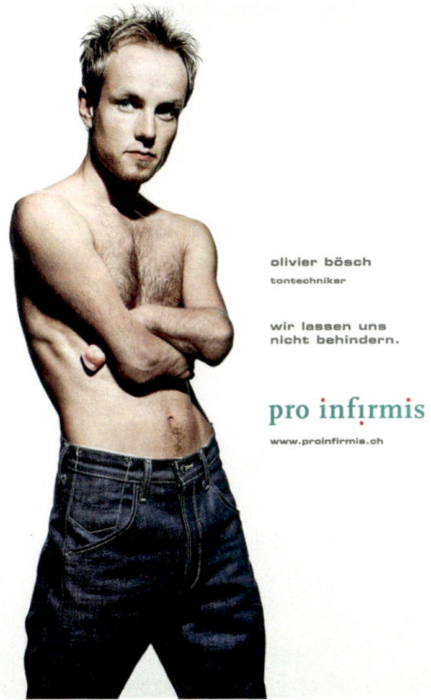

p. 76

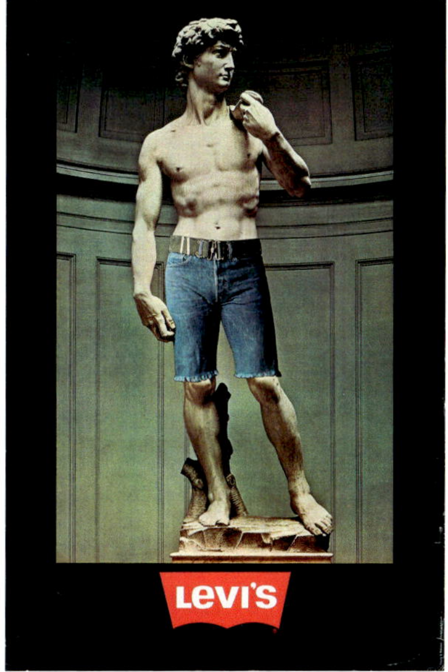

p. 14

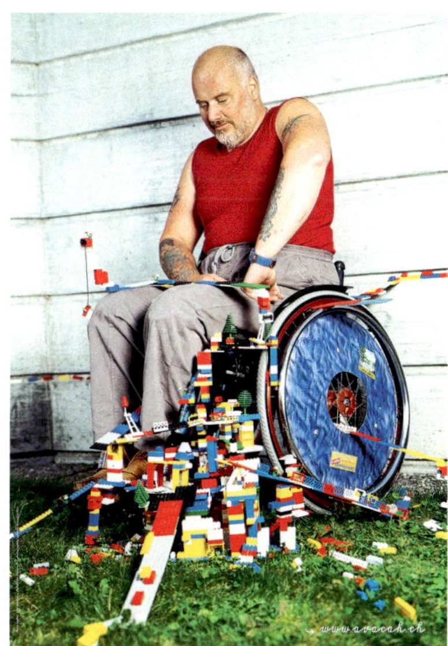

Spinas Gemperle GmbH
Hngr. / Alle 5 Sekunden reisst der Hunger
ein Kind aus dem Leben (Every 5 Seconds
Hunger Takes the Life of a Child), 2008
Caritas Schweiz, Lucerne, CH

Anonymous
Diesel / Nature / Love It While It Lasts, 2004
Diesel, Breganze, IT

Albert Brenet
Imperial Airways / Through Africa
in Days Instead of Weeks, 1935
Imperial Airways Ltd., London, GB

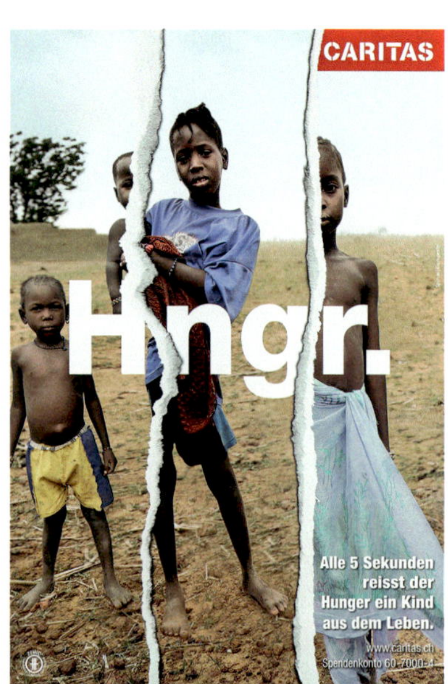

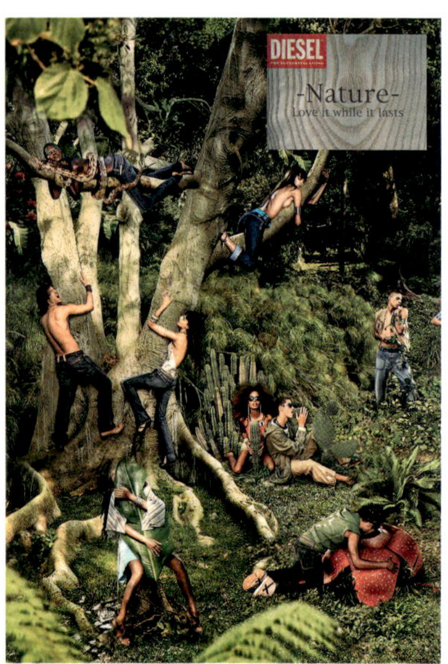

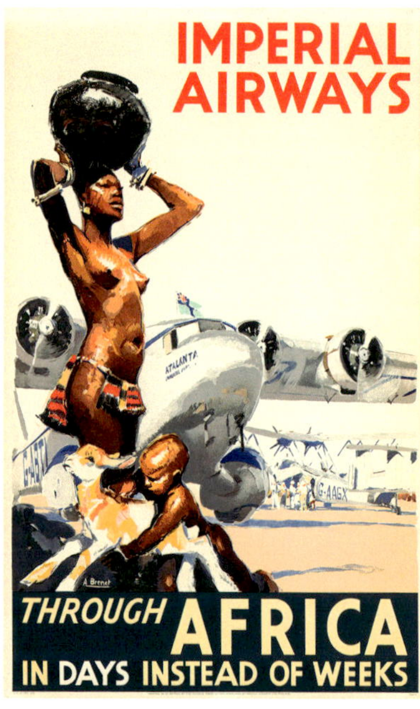

Anonymous
Chantelle / Paris habille les femmes du monde
(Paris Dresses the Woman of the World), 2003
Groupe Chantelle, Cachan, FR

Spinas Civil Voices GmbH
Simon B. Opladen (photo)
A toujours connu la faim. A parfois connu la faim.
Ne connaîtra jamais la faim. Changer, vraiment
(Knew Only Hunger. Sometimes Knew Hunger.
Will Never Know Hunger. For Real Change), 2016
Helvetas Swiss Incooperation, Zurich, CH

Viktor Hasslauer
En Afrique du Sud par la Swissair de Genève
à Johannesburg (Fly Swissair to South
Africa, from Geneva to Johannesburg), 1948
Swissair, Schweizerische Luftverkehr-
Aktiengesellschaft, Kloten, CH

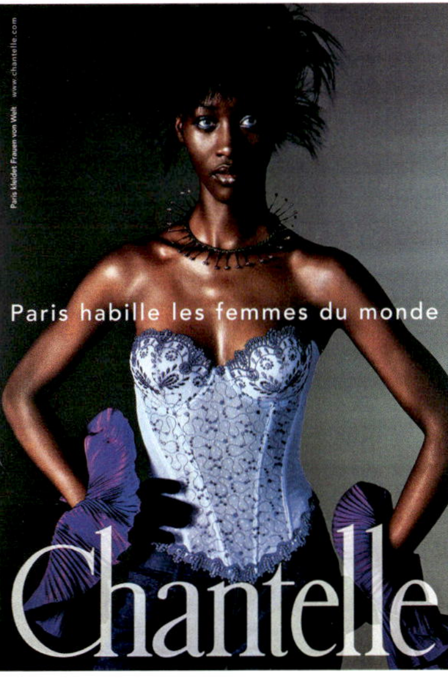

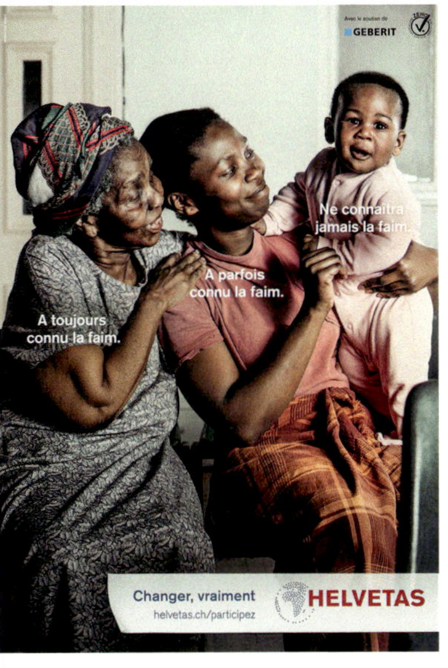

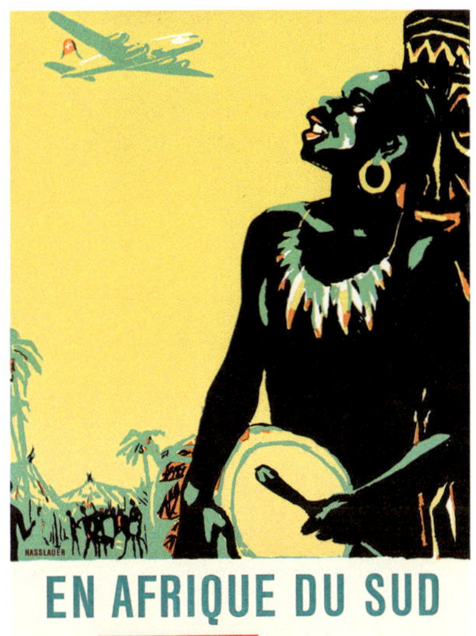

p.73

Metzger Lehner Briccola AG
Hannes Schmid (photo)
Erwin Aljukic / Schauspieler / Wir lassen
uns nicht behindern. (Actor / We Will Not
Let Ourselves Be Handicapped.), 2001
Pro Infirmis, Zurich, CH

Anonymous
Nyhed sloggi / Be Some Body / Not Just
Anybody …, 1997
Triumph International, Spiesshofer und Braun,
Bad Zurzach, CH

Ruf Lanz Werbeagentur AG /
Danielle Knecht-Lanz, Markus Ruf
Big / Und plötzlich machen die Jungs gerne
Hausarbeit. (And Suddenly the Boys Like
Doing Household Chores.), 2016
BIG AG, Zurich, CH

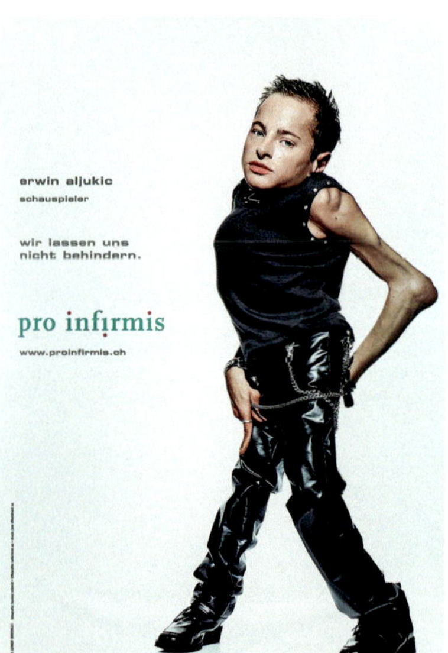

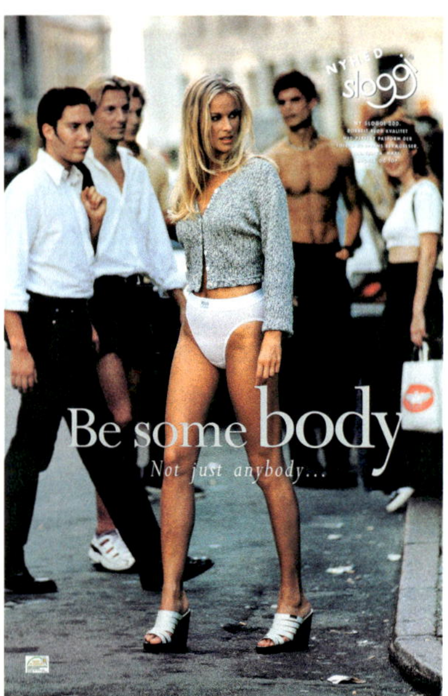

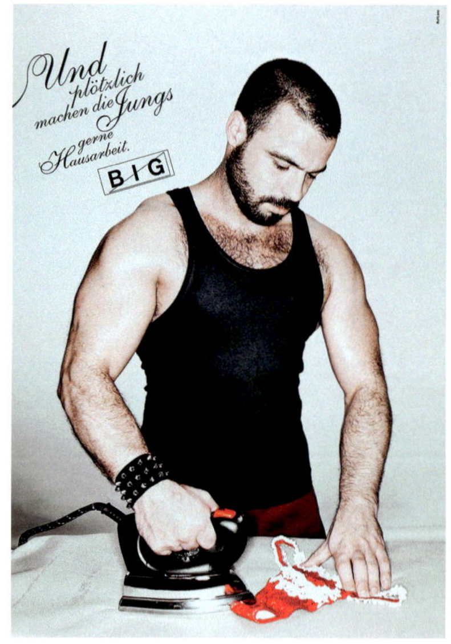